DeVoto's
West

DeVoto's West

History, Conservation, and the Public Good

Bernard DeVoto

Edited by Edward K. Muller

Swallow Press / Ohio University Press
Athens

Swallow Press / Ohio University Press, Athens, Ohio 45701
www.ohio.edu/oupress

Published in association with the Center for American Places,
Santa Fe, New Mexico, and Staunton, Virginia
www.americanplaces.org

12 11 10 09 08 07 06 05   5 4 3 2 1

This book has been brought to publication with the generous assistance of Furthermore,
a program of the J. M. Kaplan Fund.

Library of Congress Cataloging-in-Publication Data

De Voto, Bernard Augustine, 1897–1955.
    DeVoto's West : history, conservation, and the public good / by Bernard DeVoto ;
edited by Edward K. Muller.
        p. cm.
    "Published in association with the Center for American Places Santa Fe, New Mexico,
and Staunton, Virginia."
    "DeVoto's West collects twenty-two of DeVoto's essays on the American West and con-
vervation issues"—Introd.
    Includes bibliographical references (p.   ) and index.
    ISBN 0-8040-1072-2 (cloth : acid-free paper)—ISBN 0-8040-1073-0 (pbk. : acid-free
paper)
    1. West (U.S.)—Environmental conditions. 2. Environmental protection—West (U.S.)
3. Conservation of natural resources—West (U.S.) 4. Public lands—West (U.S.) 5. Common good. 6. Environmental degradation—West (U.S.) 7. West (U.S.)—History. 8. West
(U.S.)—Description and travel. I. Muller, Edward K. II. Title.
    GE155.W47D4 2005
    333.72'0978—dc22

                                                            2004028391

For
Wilbur Zelinsky

Contents

Preface

Nearly twenty-five years ago, I spent an enjoyable weekend driving with Wilbur Zelinsky to and from a conference in Louisville, Kentucky. Amid hours of conversation about various aspects of Americana and the passing landscape, we also discussed our favorite authors of both fiction and nonfiction. Here was an eminent geographer who shared my enjoyment of reading broadly for personal and professional enrichment. Although newly tenured and feeling a bit more secure about my place in academia, I still found Wilbur's enthusiasm for my delight in the writings of, for example, John O'Hara or H. L. Mencken warmly supportive and encouraging.

In the years following graduate school, and once my family was securely tucked in at night, I had developed the habit of reading for pleasure the work of North American writers, most of whom incorporated a strong sense of place in their work. I did this at first without professional calculation. I especially enjoyed reading Wallace Stegner, whose novels and essays stirred my imagination about the relationships between the land and the people of the American West. I always kept my eyes open for Stegner writings. Browsing in a San Francisco used bookstore late one April evening in 1996, I ran across Stegner's biography of Bernard DeVoto. To me, DeVoto was the author of a "dated" historical trilogy of the exploration of the American West. In *The Uneasy Chair,* Stegner presented a man of much broader talents than I had imagined. DeVoto's lifespan, 1897–1955, overlapped the lives of many of my favorite writers, and yet I knew of him only as a historian. He was, among other things, an essayist of the first rank, including, and perhaps especially, of the American West. To my surprise, he was also a well-known conservationist at midcentury, a leader of the opposition to privatization and despoilment of the public lands that are concentrated in the West. And, more astonishing to me, his defense of the public lands between 1946 and 1954 sounded quite familiar, for he could well have been describing and attacking the efforts of western senators and representatives of the 1994 Republican-led Congress to develop and even privatize the public lands. The issues and language of the two periods are strikingly similar, the actors practically interchangeable. Further research into DeVoto's essays revealed an informed, coherent, and lively body of writings on the American West and the public lands. Forgotten with the passage of time, these essays needed to be collected after the half century that had elapsed and made available to the general reading public, in order that more people would have a better perspective on the issues raised by this most recent attack on the public lands. DeVoto's arguments on behalf of maintaining the integrity of the public lands and national parks are as compelling today as they were in post–World War II America. This collection of essays is my effort to add DeVoto's voice to the debate at the turn of the twentieth century.

I am grateful to Wilbur Zelinsky, a friend and mentor, for encouraging me many years ago to keep reading widely in American literature and letters. He understands the excitement in discovering the work of a writer who opens up new vistas and fills in, through the story of his or her career and personal life, some of the gaps in our understanding of the web of relationships that comprise the intellectual milieu of a particular time. I extend my thanks to Mark DeVoto for his support of this book and generous permission to reprint his father's essays and photograph. I am indebted to George Thompson, President of the Center for American Places, for his immediate support of this project and helpful assistance at several points in the enterprise. I am appreciative for the help of Randall B. Jones at the Center for American Places, who assisted in important ways, and Nancy Basmajian of Ohio University Press, who provided careful editing. Also, my thanks to Rain Worthington for her good work in typing into a digital format DeVoto's original essays. I wish to express my gratitude for the financial assistance of the Richard D. and Mary Jane Edwards Endowed Publication Fund in the School of Arts and Sciences at the University of Pittsburgh.

Finally, I thank the Department of History of the University of Pittsburgh for underwriting bibliographical assistance. Original spellings
of words were retained when it was not possible to determine with
confidence whether idiosyncracies resulted from typographical errors or
Devoto's stylistic creativity. Of course, I am solely responsible for factual errors, omissions, and misinterpretations.

EDWARD K. MULLER
Pittsburgh, Pennsylvania

Introduction

During the summer of 1946, Bernard DeVoto toured the American West by automobile. He had grown up in the West; and after two decades of writing, he had established himself as an expert on the region. Having just completed two book-length manuscripts on the West, one a novel and the other an award-winning history of the mountain fur trade, DeVoto set out to see both the national parks and the northwest passage of Lewis and Clark in preparation for a book on that storied expedition.[1] He planned to support the more-than-thirteen-thousand-mile journey by writing articles on his venture for popular magazines, but by the end of the second month he had determined to enlist his writing against those westerners desirous of ruinously exploiting the region's extensive public lands. In the words of writer Wallace Stegner, his friend and a fellow westerner, "DeVoto went West in 1946 a historian and tourist. He came back an embattled conservationist."[2]

He began his crusade against western efforts to privatize the public domain with a pair of long essays in the December 1946 and January 1947 issues of *Harper's Magazine*. During the nine years until his death in November 1955, he published nearly three dozen essays advocating the importance of federal control over, as well as the conservation of, the nation's public lands. Most of these essays appeared in his monthly *Harper's* column, The Easy Chair; the others were longer articles in *Harper's* and in a variety of popular magazines such as the *Saturday Evening Post* and *Collier's*. Together, they represented a sustained, impassioned, and complex argument for the conservation of public lands, which speaks eloquently today to the same issues that cause heated debates in Congress and around the West.

DeVoto began by describing the westerner's penchant for cooperating with nonwestern capitalists in liquidating the region's resources.

He then charged western stockmen, especially cattle ranchers, with overgrazing fragile river watersheds, much of them national forest lands, and thereby causing serious environmental degradation and flooding. He reported on the stockmen's and their Republican congressional allies' proposed legislation for "returning" the public lands to the people. With the election of Democrat Harry Truman as president in 1948, the challenge to the public lands temporarily subsided, and DeVoto turned his attention to the national parks and monuments, which were suffering the effects of a declining budget and threatened by development proposals of the Bureau of Reclamation and the Army Corps of Engineers. However, in 1951 the pending return of a Republican administration advocating less government and greater local control stirred him to resume his defense of the public domain.

DeVoto's West collects twenty-two of DeVoto's essays on the American West and conservation issues. They offer a sampling of his western sensibilities and provide a coherent, lively, and timely argument for the conservation of the nation's public lands. The essays are grouped into five parts. The first part contains five essays, written between 1927 and 1952, in which DeVoto introduces the reader to his West and lays out his concern for exploitation of its resources. Part II presents five essays from 1947 and 1948, in which he exposes the western "land grab" and develops his argument for keeping the public lands under federal control. In the third part, comprising four essays written between 1947 and 1954, he explores the importance of water and watersheds for erosion and flooding in the West and critiques federal efforts to dam western rivers without proper evaluation of alternatives and consequences. In the four essays in part IV, DeVoto laments Congress's inadequate support of the national parks and the attempts to develop resources in these preserved areas. Part V contains four essays dating from 1951 to 1955, which decry the Eisenhower administration's collaboration with western interests to once again privatize and develop the public lands.

DeVoto earned his living as a professional writer. He worked as a novelist, short story writer, literary critic, historian, essayist, editor, and teacher. His novels did not sell well. His short stories and serialized novels earned him money, but they are not memorable. He gained some recognition for literary criticism, especially a book-length study of Mark Twain.[3] He also derived income from essays, editing, and, later, historical writing. As an essayist, DeVoto wrote with a vigorous, icono-clastic, and at times vituperative style. He commented on the Ameri-can scene and the development of American civilization. Toward the end of his career, he energetically defended Americans' civil rights against McCarthyism and fought for the conservation of our national resources. While maintaining this career as an essayist, DeVoto turned to writing the history of American western exploration. He produced a successful trilogy on the topic and edited *The Journals of Lewis and Clark*.[4] His historical work displays an astonishing breadth of reading, attention to fact, and a passion for his subject. He wrote history in a narrative style as a deliberate contrast to what he considered to be the boring, pedantic character of most academic history writing.

DeVoto's histories focus on the American West. Although he lived most of his adult life in the East, he considered himself a westerner. He was born in Ogden, Utah, in 1897. His mother was Mormon, his fa-ther a Catholic of Italian descent. Some of DeVoto's friends believed that his skepticism of conventional thought came from this parental combination. He wrote in 1940: "I came to conclude that absolutes were a mirage. And in my desert country, mirages are also common-place."[5] He enjoyed time spent on his maternal grandfather's nearby farm, hiking in the Wasatch Mountains, and shooting. These experi-ences remained important to him all of his life. At the same time, he never felt at home in the provincial, post-frontier Mormon society of Utah. Small in stature, brilliant, bookish, brash, and educated in a Catholic school, he felt free of Ogden's social and intellectual con-straints only in the nearby mountains or on the farm. Stegner saw DeVoto's love of hiking and especially shooting as the outgrowth of a lonely childhood.[6] DeVoto remained in Utah through his freshman year at the University of Utah, after which he transferred to Harvard University.

Arriving at Harvard in 1915, DeVoto exuberantly breathed in the air of what he took for intellectual freedom and sophistication. With the exception of brief stints in the army during World War I, back in Ogden after the war, as an English instructor at Northwestern University, and in New York City, he spent his adult years in and around Cambridge,

Massachusetts, making his way as a writer. In 1927, at the age of thirty, DeVoto decided once and for all to make his living with his pen. He aspired to be a novelist, and during the course of his long writing life he published six novels under his own name and four under the pen name of John August.[7] While working on his novels, none of which received critical acclaim or financial success, he turned out magazine articles, short stories for popular magazines, essays of literary criticism, and book reviews. Although many of these short pieces of social criticism were serious efforts and helped him build a literary reputation, many others, like those for *Collier's* and the *Saturday Evening Post,* were mainly produced for income.[8] Nonetheless, his sights were set higher than this hackwork. DeVoto enjoyed his first book publishing success in 1932 with *Mark Twain's America,* in which, through a combination of literary criticism, history, and biography, he challenged Van Wyck Brooks's explanation for the sorrowful state of American letters and art.[9] DeVoto taught writing and literature courses at Harvard in the 1930s, but was eventually rebuffed in his bid for a permanent position. He eagerly taught many summers at the Bread Loaf Writers' Conferences in Vermont, where he jousted and drank with the likes of Wallace Stegner, Robert Frost, and Katherine Anne Porter. He worked in various editorial capacities as well, including editorship of the *Saturday Review of Literature.* In 1935 he accepted the offer to write the monthly column The Easy Chair for *Harper's Magazine.* The Easy Chair was the longest-running editorial feature in American journalism. Only five men occupied the chair before DeVoto, most notably George William Curtis from 1853 to 1892 and William Dean Howells from 1900 to 1920. As a commentator on the American scene, DeVoto had the opportunity in this column to reach a broad audience of American leaders, opinionmakers, and the reading public.[10]

Both as a student at Harvard and as a professional writer, DeVoto recognized the distinctiveness and utility of his western roots and sensibilities. In the East, as in Ogden, he was cast as an outsider, but he thrived on the East's intellectual climate and successfully aspired to be part of the intellectual community. Although he addressed a great variety of subjects in his essays, he frequently turned to western topics and themes. At first he scorned the West, and especially Mormon Utah. In an article published in H. L. Mencken's *American Mercury* in 1926 and written in an appropriately Menckenian style, he lambasted Utah for its anti-intellectualism and lack of distinction in letters and the arts.[11] Over the years he often charged the West with provincialism for being unable to accept criticism and for giving unqualified praise to anything produced by a westerner.[12] Despite this early alienation, DeVoto slowly developed serious and enduring interest in western history, the influence of the West on American life, and the condition of the contemporary West. He staked out a position as an authority on the West in some early book reviews, articles, and novels. His view of the West deepened, grew more complex, and eventually led to his best work, the historical trilogy published in the 1940s and early 1950s. From his vantage in the East, he could look with some detachment on the West, romanticize its bold landscapes, and yet analyze its failings as well.[13]

Reading John Wesley Powell and Walter Prescott Webb, as well as his childhood in Utah, led DeVoto to believe that the land and climate were the defining features of the region.[14] In this view, the West began where total annual rainfall dipped below twenty inches. Aridity, therefore, was at the heart of his West. The wide-open vistas free of dense vegetation, the striking blue skies, and the ever-present mountain backdrops framed a beautiful landscape, which attracted DeVoto in a way that the environment of the East did not. He favored the high country most of all, that place where he sought personal renewal. At the same time, however, he recognized that the rugged topography and climatic extremes of the West created a harsh environment. "Western geography," he wrote, "is violent. . . . It is a country of blizzards, cloudbursts, northers, chinooks, every kind of sudden storm, of floods, landslides, mudflows, even earthquakes, and the U.S. volcano is Western. . . . You could love such a country but you were bound to hate it, too—and the splits in the Western soul begin here."[15] This understanding of the environment, especially of the importance of aridity and the need for water, informed both his belief in conservation and his analysis of western economics, politics, and social relations.[16]

DeVoto grew up in the West as the frontier was passing.[17] He described the period in a 1935 *Harper's* article, "Fossil Remnants of the Frontier," as a "pause between frontier society and industrialism. . . . We were really *fin de siècle*, we were the frontier's afterglow."[18] From the vantage of that childhood experience and of being an expatriate, he recognized the western myths that writers and westerners themselves believed about the frontier. Ever the skeptic and iconoclast, he set about demythologizing the West. He dismissed both the noble Indian image and the romance of violence as myths. At a time when academics, notably Frederick Jackson Turner, and popular writers celebrated American individualism as born and continually refurbished on the frontier, DeVoto scoffed at the notion, particularly for the arid West, where the hardships of the climate demanded cooperation for survival, let alone success. Frontiersmen were community builders, not rugged individualists, he noted more than once. "How indeed did the frontier community exist at all except by means of a close-knit cooperation? Especially, how did a frontier community in the desert exist?"[19]

His physical and intellectual distance from the West freed him to expose western contradictions in a 1934 *Harper's* essay. Like others before him, he described the West as a colony of eastern capital interests, which exercised absentee control and siphoned off large portions of the profits. Despite the heroic pioneering saga of western settlement, westerners became indebted to eastern corporations that exploited the region's great natural resources. Adopting Walter P. Webb's popular thesis, he argued that the markedly different western environment forced this last frontiersman to "ally himself with . . . the Industrial Revolution. . . . The West, then, was born of industrialism. When the age of machinery crossed the hundredth meridian the frontier . . . promptly came under the plow. But industrialism [also] has other products than machines. . . . [T]he pioneer found prepared and waiting there for him the worst of all, financial organization."[20] Absentee owners and outside speculators—such as mining companies, railroad corporations, and banks—enriched themselves, despoiled western lands, and left many westerners in debt. He went further, however, with this analysis than westerners liked and charged that regional timbermen, miners, and stockmen, by also favoring speculative development and the exploitation of natural resources, aligned themselves with eastern interests in the "liquidation" of the regional economy in a manner that benefitted a few, while most were hurt. Westerners did so even as they railed against absentee control.

This "split" personality carried over into western politics. Seeing the federal government as part of the eastern establishment and buying into the frontier myth of western individualism, westerners implored "government to get out of business, to stop impeding initiative, to break the shackles of regulation . . . [while at the same time] demanding as Western right, as compensation for the West, and as assistance toward Western liberation, the expenditure of more federal funds. . . . It shakes down to a platform: get out and give us more money." In 1946, DeVoto believed that the New Deal and the prosperity of World War II offered the opportunity for the West to achieve at last economic independence. But, he worried, will the West's traditional habits cause it to sell out to the East? "The West [is] its own worst enemy."[21]

While DeVoto was developing his critique of the West between 1926 and 1946, he also embarked on a project to write the history of the westward movement. He wanted to tell the story of exploring and settling the western frontier, using his literary skills but keeping close to the factual record. Academic history was too dry, analytical, and devoid of the common folk engaged in the process. Although his novels of the West failed as literature, writing them taught him literary strategies that he brought to his historical narrative. He wrote his history through the exploration of specific stories, often biographical ones, which stood for larger historical processes and themes, a technique called synecdoche.[22] He used drama to great effect, and frequently followed several events and stories simultaneously. The trilogy that resulted from his project brought him acclaim and cemented his reputation as a western expert. When his first volume on the western movement, *The Year of Decision: 1846,* came out in 1943, it was selected by the Book of the Month Club and serialized by the *Atlantic.*[23] Many academic historians, however, did not appreciate this book. Even friends in academia such as historian Arthur Schlesinger Sr., whose son traveled west with DeVoto in 1940 for several months, objected that it was not history. On a kinder note, Frederick L. Paxson described DeVoto's approach as "a brilliant job on the borderland common to the historian, the essayist, and the analyst." Richard Hofstadter captured the distinction between DeVoto's literary approach and that of the scholar, declaring: "Had he set out to prove it [the book's thesis], he would have written analytical history of an epoch, not the narrative history of the year."[24]

DeVoto followed *The Year of Decision,* which described the Mexican War, the Oregon and Sante Fe trails, and the eviction of the Mormons, among other events, with *Across the Wide Missouri* in 1947, winning both the Bancroft and the Pulitzer prizes. Generally viewed as the best of the trilogy, this second book focused on several decades before 1846 to recount the hardships and heroics of the fur trappers, known as mountain men, and to convey the drama and importance of the fur trade in exploring and opening up the West. It ends, appropriately, with the initial encounter of the mountain men with the first wagon train crossing the Oregon Trail in 1839. Five years after his triumph with *Across the Wide Missouri*, DeVoto published *The Course of Empire*, for which he received the National Book Award.[25] Intending originally to write a narrative about the Lewis and Clark expedition, he instead placed the epic American crossing of the continent between 1804 and 1806 within the larger story of European exploration of North America. These three histories, along with his writing in a variety of forms over the course of more than two decades, gained him election to the National Institute of Arts and Letters and the American Academy of Arts and Sciences, as well as an honorary degree from the University of Colorado—high recognition from a western institution at a time when many westerners still reviled this native son.[26]

Despite the fact that he spent little time in the West until 1940, and then only to travel for extended periods a few times, he was able to bring the people and landscape of the frontier West to life in his historical writing.[27] Wallace Stegner believed that DeVoto was too judgmental to write good novels of the West. In fiction he had to speak through other people and create an imaginary world. Instead, Stegner declared, "He wanted to judge, he wanted to denounce, he wanted to express his own ideas and his own feelings. He wasn't willing to suppress himself quite enough—or he didn't know how."[28] Stegner concluded, "when he wrote history, when he brought together the whole story of the West as frontier, as dream and discovery, exploration and confrontation, he would be magnificent."[29] He could do this while living in the East because he devoured historical knowledge. "He was," in Stegner's words, "loaded, he was a learned man."[30] He relied on the perceptions of the participants when the record permitted; and as his friend and fellow writer Catherine Drinker Bowen observed, "maps lined his study walls."[31] The West of his childhood remained with him forever; his friends believed that this experience gave him special in-

sight and passion for the region.[32] DeVoto may have renounced his
western roots early in his career and become an exile, but through his
writing about the West he reconciled his differences and "came
home."[33]

DeVoto's ambiguous relationship with the West and his expatria-
tion in the East may have been, as some friends believed, partially responsible for his adopting a national or continental perspective of the
westward movement and of the West, instead of a regional or provincial one. In his foreword to Stegner's book on John Wesley Powell,
DeVoto argued that historians misunderstood "the meaning of the
West in American history" because they persisted in seeing its history
as "merely sectional," outside the mainstream of national history. This
is nonsense, he averred, for "the experience of the West is just as in-
separable from the central energies of American history [as other regions' experiences are]."[34] The grand theme of his trilogy was not simply the West, but instead "the development of the continental nation."[35]
Bowen quoted DeVoto as writing, "As a historian . . . I have interested
myself in the growth among the American people of the feeling that
they were properly a single nation between two oceans; in the development of what I have called the continental mind."[36] It was this ability to see the West as part of the national whole, despite the region's
relatively recent settlement, its "colonial" economic and political status, its particularistic myths, and its distinctive environment, that allowed DeVoto to see the vast public lands of the West as a national resource, not simply a regional one. This insight, along with his passion
for the landscape, lay at the root of his defense of the public lands in
1946.

⟫◆⟪

Having completed by spring 1946 the manuscript for *Across the Wide
Missouri* and also a novel set in the West, *Mountain Time,* DeVoto
turned his attention to the long-anticipated journey around the West.
Already planning a book on the Lewis and Clark expedition, he felt the
need to see the explorers' route—the topography, rivers, mountains,
and forts—for himself. His last trip to the West in 1940 with Arthur
Schlesinger Jr. had inspired him to return, but the war intervened,
making such travel impossible. With the war over, he piled his family

into the car and set out on a three-month tour of the northern half of the West. In addition to the Lewis and Clark sites, DeVoto spent time meeting with friends and officials of the National Park Service and the National Forest Service. They informed him of the problems afflicting the public lands, ranging from neglected maintenance to overgrazing of mountainous watersheds, erosion, and flooding. He also learned of resolutions passed by the American Livestock Association and the National Woolgrowers Association to cede public lands to the states. Given the critique of the West he had been developing over the years, he understood the significance of this issue for the region's future, and inserted himself into the brewing controversy.[37]

Federal management of the public lands held the best hope, in DeVoto's view, for wise use rather than rampant exploitation of the land's finite natural resources, as well as for protection of critical mountain watersheds, which would diminish erosion and ruinous downstream flooding. Because the public lands, although concentrated in western states, constituted a national resource, he believed it to be not only necessary, but also appropriate, for the lands to remain under the control of the federal government. Accordingly, he wished to bring the plot to remove the public lands from national control, the land grab as he called it, to the attention of the American public, so that political pressure would be put on Congress not to pass such legislation.

DeVoto opened his attack on the westerners' land grab with three essays in back-to-back issues of *Harper's*. In the first essay, "The Anxious West," he introduced westerners to his readers. He described their accent, dress, food preferences, and predilection for drinking and gambling. He sketched out some western myths, especially the romance of cattle ranching, and extolled the wide-open spaces and westerners' love of outdoor life. But as the essay progressed, a darker tone emerged. Intellectuals and the wealthy of the West, he wrote, are unhappy because of its economic and cultural colonialism, while at the same time westerners cooperate with eastern interests in exploiting the region's resources. This conclusion set the stage for the sequel in the next issue.[38]

In "The West Against Itself," DeVoto reviewed the region's long history of natural resource exploitation.[39] He then reported how New Deal policies of forest restoration, land reclamation, rural electrification, and subsidies for industrial development had given the West the opportunity to end resource liquidation and break the colonial cycle. However, he lamented, the West's tradition of ruinous exploitation threatened this chance for a more sustainable future. Using the popular western themes of individualism, local control, and the cattle ranching myth to rally political support, a small group of western stockmen, businessmen, and politicians was determined to open all unreserved public domain and the national forests to the cattle and sheep industries for grazing. In the same January 1947 *Harper's* issue, DeVoto focused his Easy Chair column on the destructive flooding caused by clear-cut logging and the overgrazing of cattle in fragile western watersheds.[40]

These three essays began a series, published during 1947 and 1948, in which DeVoto exposed the goals and methods of the western land grab and warned of its dire consequences for the environment and the future of the West. He described the bills placed before Congress, named the senators and congressmen proposing the legislation, and attacked the sheep- and cattle-grazing associations and the U.S. Chamber of Commerce, which put their considerable political and financial muscle behind the proposals. He ridiculed the proponents' orchestrated and biased Congressional hearings on the issue and deemed the strategy of returning public lands to the states only a first step toward ultimate privatization. He particularly enjoyed his opponents' outrage at the essays and mocked their characterization of him and his fellow conservationists as communist New Dealers. Finally, in 1948 he became partisan, charging that Republicans were leading this assault on the public lands and ironically turning their back on the great Republican conservationist heritage of Theodore Roosevelt and Gifford Pinchot. The *Harper's* publishers worried that DeVoto was becoming too controversial.

The western plan in the 1940s to divest the federal government of control over the public lands was only the latest in a series of such efforts over the years. DeVoto was well aware of this fact.[41] Throughout the nineteenth century, federal policy was to dispose of the public domain as rapidly as possible in support of unrestricted settlement and development. In the second half of the century, however, a few people, such as George Perkins Marsh, John Muir, John Wesley Powell, and Carl Schurz, recognized the exhaustibility of our natural resources, urged more responsible use of them, and even advocated the preservation of specific places. In the final three decades of the century, Congress erected the legislative foundation to set aside areas of the public domain for parks, dam sites, and forest reserves. By World War I, more than 150 million acres had been reserved as national forests, especially under the leadership of President Theodore Roosevelt and Chief of the Bureau of Forestry Gifford Pinchot. Moreover, the Supreme Court had decided in *U.S. v. Light* that "all public lands are held in trust for the people of the whole country."[42] From the outset, reservation of public lands under federal control engendered strong opposition from ranchers, land speculators, irrigation companies, timbermen, miners, and those sympathetic with states rights issues. The West's traditional resentment of the East and the federal government and a growing sense of western regional identity exacerbated the strong feelings. Although they failed in their efforts to have forest reserves ceded to the states, western opponents did score some victories. But, the progressive era conservation philosophy—best captured in the phrase "the greatest good to the greatest number for the longest time"— prevailed.[43]

Between the world wars, more utilitarian goals steered land policy. Although recreational uses of parks and forest lands increased and preservation of wilderness refuges gained some credence from the advocacy of Aldo Leopold and Robert Marshall, the building of large dams for irrigation and urban water supplies and the Army Corps of Engineers' river projects for flood control, power generation, and improved navigation typified the period. The western graziers also pushed for the opening of unreserved public lands, and the subsequent struggle with conservationists culminated in the Taylor Grazing Act of 1934, which established federal control over grazing. The new Grazing Service's efforts to set fees for use of these lands continued the long fight over public lands. Opponents of federal control gained a victory in 1946, when the Grazing Service was combined with the General Land Office to form a weak Bureau of Land Management. This success in weakening federal control over grazing emboldened the stockmen to push once again for the transfer of public lands to the states or even to private ownership. Senator E. V. Robertson of Wyoming proposed a bill giving unreserved lands to the states and appointing a commission

to evaluate all federal lands, thereby creating the potential for disman-
tling the national parks, forests, and wildlife areas.[44]

DeVoto's crusade against the land grab came at a time when conservation groups were weak and elitist in approach. Using The Easy Chair
as bully pulpit and developing a personal network of like-minded
conservationists, he gleaned information from friends in Washington
and around the West, urged colleagues like Wallace Stegner to write articles, and orchestrated the placing of articles in popular magazines.[45]
The proposed legislation of Wyoming Congressman Frank Barrett and
Senator Robertson failed, and the election of Democrat Harry S. Truman as president temporarily ended this phase of what recent writers
have called the Sagebrush Rebellion.

DeVoto kept alive the issue of conservation of public lands. He favorably reviewed and publicized new conservation books and wrote
several articles on the national forests, watershed protection, and the
national parks for magazines other than *Harper's*. In January 1948,
after receiving acclaim for *Across the Wide Missouri* and spearheading
the attack on the land grab, he was appointed by Secretary of the Interior Julius Krug to the National Park System Advisory Board. This position expanded DeVoto's conservation network, provided inspection
tours of the national parks, and aligned him with the National Park
Service.[46]

Aridity had been at the heart of DeVoto's conception of what
shaped the West, and as he looked to the future he still saw water as
the defining issue. In the late 1940s, he described the unusual floods
and mudflows occurring as a result of timber clear-cutting and overgrazing in mountain watersheds. Restoration projects by the National
Forest Service and the Soil Conservation Service underscored both the
causes and the solution. By the 1950s, DeVoto drew his readers' attention to the increasing demand for water by continued agricultural and
industrial development of the West. He worried that the Bureau of
Reclamation was preparing dam projects of enormous expense and
consequence without proper oversight, particularly as to interstate implications and national priorities. The public needed to be informed,
DeVoto believed, about the bureau's plans, to understand the consequences of these plans, and to let Congress know its sentiments on the
issue.[47]

Even as he developed the themes of watershed protection and enormous dam projects, DeVoto returned to his earlier defense of federal control over public lands. In 1951 DeVoto launched a new series of essays in *Harper's* against what he saw as a renewed western Republican assault on public lands. Republican legislative policies, he wrote, constituted another land grab by the "boys in the backroom." Moreover, he charged that the western position was part of the traditional anti-governmental attitude of "get out and give us more money."[48] The federal government's control over public lands and hence its regulation of grazing, logging, mining, and oil drilling on these lands, as imperfect as such regulation was, provided the only protection of resources and watersheds. Local control and private ownership of the West's natural resources and the reduction of governmental interference, which Republican policy proposed, would, in DeVoto's opinion, not only reverse years of conservation but also destroy the West in the long run. Unlike his crusade of the 1940s, this campaign became more politically partisan as DeVoto urged Democrats to contest aggressively the Eisenhower administration. Conservation, he predicted, would be a winning issue. For the first time in his career, he even hitched his interests to electoral politics, first advising Adlai Stevenson in the 1952 presidential campaign and later, during the last few years of his life, maintaining a relationship with the Illinois senator over conservation issues.[49] He argued that water for western cities and recreation were becoming higher public priorities for the use of the public lands than traditional resource activities. Although written in the 1950s, this insight into the changing priorities of the West has largely come true and captures one of the key political divisions between the "old" and the "new" West today.[50]

While DeVoto vigorously attacked Republican land policies in the 1950s, he also revealed the deteriorating conditions of the national parks and development threats to their protected status. In 1949 he outlined the National Park Service's budgetary dilemma. Inattention during the war, rising postwar attendance, and congressional demands for new parks overwhelmed the Park Service's already inadequate funding. Consequently, the Park Service could not properly address vandalism, deteriorating public facilities, and planned improvements.[51] Four years later, DeVoto rehearsed similar concerns and added to them the declining morale of park rangers living in shabby park housing, facing rent increases, and depending more and more on their wives' working for private businesses. He proposed closing the most popular national parks in order that the anticipated public outcry would pressure Congress for increased funding.[52]

Perhaps a more serious threat to the parks was the pressure on Congress, often from within government, to legislate exceptions to the principle of no resource exploitation in the parks, which was established with the creation of the National Park Service in 1916. DeVoto first described the threat to the parks in a 1950 *Saturday Evening Post* article, and then returned to the issue in 1954 and 1955 in The Easy Chair, when the new secretary of the interior, Douglas McKay, recommended allowing dam projects in a national monument.[53] Whereas some western interests, supported by congressional allies, had often coveted the parks' mineral and timber resources, this time they joined forces with the Bureau of Reclamation and the Army Corps of Engineers to develop the parks' water resources. DeVoto specifically denounced Bureau and Corps plans to construct dams and holding reservoirs or lakes in Dinosaur National Monument in Colorado's Green River valley. He also noted projects planned for other parks and monuments, including Glacier National Park and Kentucky's Mammoth Cave National Park. He believed that the estimated benefits of flood control, irrigation, and recreation not only could be produced by dam projects at alternative sites outside the parks, but also did not outweigh the principle of the inviolate protection of the national parks. If the public knew what legislators, governmental agencies, and a few western interests were plotting in smoke-filled backrooms, it would vociferously demand, DeVoto claimed, the parks' complete protection. He intended to let the public know. Once Congress breached the principle, he wrote in 1954, "the national park as we know it, as it was intended to be, will be open to destruction."[54] Although he recognized that the Colorado River's water would be necessary for western cities, he advocated a full and unbiased review of all developmental possibilities, especially those not in parks.

Many historians and environmentalists believe that the modern environmental movement emerged with the successful fight to stop the construction of the Echo Park Dam in Dinosaur National Monument.

What had been prior to World War II largely a conservation movement interested in the wise and efficient development of natural resources broadened in the two decades after the war into more of a
middle-class movement concerned with the amenities and quality of
life provided by the natural environment. While fundamental social
changes in American society lay at the heart of this transformation, the
Bureau of Reclamation's plan to erect a dam and submerge a scenic
canyon of the Green River in northwest Colorado and northeast Utah
as part of the Colorado River Storage Project (CRSP) politicized the
Wilderness Society, led by Howard Zahniser, and the Sierra Club,
under David Brower. They made the Echo Park Dam proposal a national issue through direct mail campaigns, a book edited by Wallace
Stegner, articles in newspapers and magazines, and even a movie. The
battle highlighted the conflict between development and wilderness
amenity values; it not only challenged the prevailing ethos of development but also pitted national priorities against regional and local
ones. These newly energized environmental organizations had found a
means and constituency to pursue their preservationist objectives in
the future.[55]

DeVoto called the American public's attention to the threat posed
by governmental development plans to the national parks in his 1950
Saturday Evening Post article, "Shall We Let Them Ruin the National
Parks?" which the *Reader's Digest* reprinted for an even broader audience. The clamor following his 1953 proposal in The Easy Chair to
close the parks is credited as a critical step in garnering public support
for the parks in the face of congressional neglect and even direct threat
to their integrity.[56] In his biography of DeVoto, Wallace Stegner underscored DeVoto's role not only in publicizing the fight against Echo
Park Dam but also in building the new environmental movement.[57]

DeVoto's defense of the public lands embraced both traditional and
new environmental positions. In a conservationist manner, he advocated federal control of the public lands as the best means to protect and restore important western watersheds and timber resources.
Moreover, since the public lands were national resources—not regional ones, as western opponents argued—he appealed to a national
audience to express its opinion and pressure Congress. As DeVoto
became more involved in public lands issues, he expressed the impor-

tance of preserving scenic places for public enjoyment and personal renewal.[58] DeVoto believed development was necessary and inevitable, but not at the expense of specifically reserved areas. The principle of preservation embodied in the 1916 act creating the national parks was sacrosanct.

DeVoto wrote feverishly for his conservation agenda once the Eisenhower administration was in place, but he did not live to see the successes (and failures) of his fight. He died on November 13, 1955, five months before Congress passed the CRSP bill without the Echo Park Dam component. He had been recognized as a champion of conservation before his death. People and organizations throughout the movement trusted and depended on him. The Sierra Club had made him an honorary member.[59] After his death more acclaim came his way. His friend Arthur Schlesinger Jr. observed in 1963: "He was the first conservationist in nearly half a century . . . to command a national audience. . . . No man did more to arouse public interest against this reversal [of conservation policy] than DeVoto."[60] In a similar assessment, Stegner wrote, "In the years before conservation and environmental concern became a mass movement and a shibboleth, *The Easy Chair* was its stoutest champion."[61] Indeed, DeVoto was instrumental in building a conservation lobby. Senator Richard Neuberger of Oregon, an ally in the long fight, exclaimed that DeVoto was "the most illustrious conservationist who has lived in modern times."[62] Stegner believed DeVoto should be ranked with conservationist heroes like George Perkins Marsh, George Wesley Powell, Karl Schurz, Gifford Pinchot, and Theodore Roosevelt.[63] Stegner had been prompted to enter the conservation foray in the mid-1940s by DeVoto, and many saw Stegner as carrying on his role. Stegner never believed he could do that with the style or energy of his friend. Stegner recalled, in reflecting on the aftermath of DeVoto's death, that "editorial writers and politicians and conservationists memorialized him and regretted his passing and wondered who would do his work. They were agreed it would take three men. They called him hardheaded and softhearted, the nation's environmental conscience and liberty's watchdog, the West's most comprehensive historian and most affectionate spokesman and most acid critic."[64] Forest Service friends and others scattered his ashes over a favorite spot of his near the Lochsa River in Idaho, dedicated a grove of

western red cedar to him in the surrounding Clearwater National Forest, and erected a plaque in his memory.[65]

⇒◦◦⇐

The passage of the Wilderness Act in 1964, which authorized the setting aside of large areas as wilderness free of commercial development,
represented a victory for the Wilderness Society, the Sierra Club, and
other preservationists, who had been fighting for the concept for more
than a decade. It was the culmination of the forces unleashed in the
Echo Park Dam controversy. But, the Wilderness Act and others that
followed it also rekindled the anti–public lands movement that had
struggled periodically against federal control since the 1880s. By 1980 a
full-fledged, western sagebrush rebellion was once again underway, demanding the "return" of federal lands to the states, where local interests could manage the lands better than absentee eastern, governmental bureaucrats. Buoyed in 1980 by the vocal support of the newly
elected, western president, Ronald Reagan, and his sympathetic and
combative secretary of the interior, James Watt, as well as by the out-
spoken backing of key politicians such as Utah's Senator Orrin Hatch,
western "rebels" passed state legislation asserting state control of public lands and staged a conference in Salt Lake City akin to events in the
1940s, which had whipped up support for transferring the lands. Although this recent "land grab" seemed on the verge of success by 1982,
it, like others before it, failed to effect the desired result. Law did not
support the concept of "return." Alarmed by threats to wilderness
areas, preservationists rallied their national constituency behind federal
control. High-profile political supporters of the "rebels" did not follow
through in Washington, and Watt's verbal excesses discredited the
movement. Moreover, as DeVoto had understood in the 1950s, the
West itself was changing so that rapidly growing western urban areas
concerned with the public lands' amenity values were gaining political
clout at the expense of the traditional, rural resource interests. As it had
in DeVoto's time, the public lands issue raised national versus local
concerns, the West against the East, urban versus rural views, and long-
standing anti–federal government feelings. The rebellion did result in
the establishment of a process of negotiated settlements about management policies for the public lands. But, DeVoto would have been

pleased by the continuation of public lands under federal control for the use of the nation as a whole.[66]

Because the public lands issue involves contradictions in fundamental American values, it never is completely resolved after each period of debate. The Republican electoral victory of 1994, which resulted in that party's control of Congress for the first time since the middle of the century, unleashed again those westerners who wished to obtain private control of public lands. That impetus has carried on under George W. Bush's concern to increase energy production by tapping the resources of public lands. For example, Don Young, representative from Alaska, and the two senators from his state, Ted Stevens and Frank Murkowski, vigorously advocated widespread development of resources on public lands. They attacked the conservationists who wish to preserve Alaskan natural areas from private development under the protection of national parks and wilderness areas, tighter Forest Service regulations, and enforcement of the Endangered Species Act. Similarly, efforts in the 1990s by Secretary of the Interior Bruce Babbitt to raise grazing fees on public lands encountered arguments by western stockmen and politicians resembling those propounded in the 1940s and 1950s. DeVoto would have found the issues and language familiar and exasperating. "They [environmentalists] are Communists," Congressman Young said in September 1998. "They believe in the communal ownership of all natural resources, including the land."[67] Headlines of newspaper and magazine articles are also familiar: "The Endangered West," "Open for Business," "Range Reform," "The Rancher Subsidy," or "The Wild West's Not-So-Natural Disasters." Except for the fact that he had been dead for forty years, DeVoto himself could have been suspected of writing the title of a 1995 *New York Times* editorial: "The Congressional Land Grab."[68]

Bernard DeVoto is no longer a commonly recognized name of American letters. Yet, his western history trilogy still reads well today. Nor is he commonly recognized in the pantheon of conservation heroes. Yet, his essays on American conservation should be considered American land classics. Despite their being a half century old, DeVoto's essays have surprising currency today. Readers of his ten-year crusade to protect public lands will be struck by the similarity of goals, language, and issues with this latest reincarnation of the exploitation versus conservation debate. Although in 1955 DeVoto republished five of the *Harper's* pieces in the collection of essays entitled *The Easy Chair*, they and the others of this new collection deserve, perhaps demand, republication a half century later when their style, passion, and insight "retain an astonishing vitality" and provide an important perspective on current land policy debates. Writing in 1985, Stegner doubted "that any body of like essays from the twenties, thirties, and forties would prove, on examination, to have dated so little." Moreover, he concluded that DeVoto's essays, including those on western lands and conservation, will be "found as near as such things come to being permanent, a part of the tradition, a part of the literature."[69]

NOTES

1. *Across the Wide Missouri* (Boston: Houghton Mifflin, 1947), and *Mountain Time* (Boston: Little, Brown, 1947).

2. Wallace Stegner, *The Uneasy Chair: A Biography of Bernard DeVoto* (Salt Lake City, UT: Gibbs Smith, 1988), 297.

3. *Mark Twain's America* (Boston: Little, Brown, 1932).

4. *The Journals of Lewis and Clark* (Boston: Houghton Mifflin, 1953).

5. As quoted in Catherine Drinker Bowen, "The Historian," in *Four Portraits and One Subject: Bernard DeVoto* (Boston: Houghton Mifflin, 1963), 21.

6. Wallace Stegner, *The Sound of Mountain Water* (Lincoln: University of Nebraska Press, 1985; originally written in 1960), 259; and Stegner, "The Personality," in *Four Portraits,* 91.

7. Stegner, *Sound of Mountain Water,* 267. Stegner noted that DeVoto wrote a seventh novel and part of an eighth, neither of which was published. The four novels published under a pen name, John August, were serialized for magazines.

8. Wallace Stegner and Richard W. Etulain, *Conversations with Wallace Stegner on Western History and Literature* (Salt Lake City: University of Utah Press, rev. ed., 1990), 171.

9. Stegner, *Sound of Mountain Water,* 271; and Stegner, *Uneasy Chair,* 106–15.

10. Bernard DeVoto, *The Easy Chair* (Boston: Houghton Mifflin, 1955), vii–ix.

11. "Utah," *American Mercury* 7 (March 1926): 317–23.

12. Letter to Robert C. Eliot (editor of the *Salt Lake Telegram*), 1930, in Wallace Stegner, ed., *The Letters of Bernard DeVoto* (Garden City, NY: Doubleday, 1975), 21.

13. Curt Meine, "Wallace Stegner: Geobiographer," in Curt Meine, ed., *Wallace Stegner and the Continental Vision: Essays on Literature, History, and Landscape* (Washington, DC: Island Press, 1997), 132–33.

14. Stegner and Etulain, *Conversations with Wallace Stegner*, 182.

15. Bernard DeVoto, foreword to B. A. Botkin, ed., *A Treasury of Western Folklore* (New York: Crown, 1951), viii–ix.

16. Curt Meine, "Wallace Stegner: Geobiographer," in Meine, *Continental Vision*, 130.

17. Stegner, *Sound of Mountain Water*, 257.

18. "Fossil Remnants of the Frontier: Notes on a Utah Boyhood," *Harper's Magazine* 170 (April 1935): 600.

19. "Fossil Remnants," 599; and Arthur M. Schlesinger Jr., "The Citizen," in *Four Portraits*, 51.

20. "The West: A Plundered Province," *Harper's Magazine* 169 (August 1934): 357–58; and Walter P. Webb, *The Great Plains* (Boston: Ginn and Company, 1931).

21. "The West Against Itself," *Harper's Magazine* 194 (January 1947): 8–9.

22. Stegner and Etulain, *Conversations with Wallace Stegner*, 145 and 158–61.

23. *The Year of Decision: 1846* (Boston: Little, Brown, 1943).

24. Stegner, *Uneasy Chair*, 237–39.

25. *The Course of Empire* (Boston: Houghton Mifflin, 1952).

26. Stegner, *Uneasy Chair*, 306–7.

27. Stegner, *Uneasy Chair*, 287–88.

28. Stegner and Etulain, *Conversations with Wallace Stegner*, 158–59, and quote, 135.

29. Stegner, "The Personality," in *Four Portraits*, 88.

30. Stegner and Etulain, *Conversations with Wallace Stegner*, 159.

31. Bowen, "The Historian," in *Four Portraits*, 23.

32. Bowen, "The Historian," in *Four Portraits*, 22–23; and Schlesinger, "The Citizen," in *Four Portraits*, 41.

33. Stegner, *Sound of Mountain Water*, 274.

34. Bernard DeVoto, introduction to Wallace Stegner, *Beyond the Hundredth Meridian: John Wesley Powell and the Second Opening of the West* (Boston: Houghton Mifflin, 1954), xvii.

35. Stegner as quoted by Meine, "Introduction," in *Continental Vision,* xix.

36. As quoted in Bowen, "The Historian," in *Four Portraits,* 4.

37. Stegner, *Uneasy Chair,* 285–98.

38. "The Anxious West," *Harper's Magazine* 193 (December 1946): 481–91.

39. "The West Against Itself," *Harper's Magazine* 194 (January 1947): 1–13.

40. "The West," *Harper's Magazine* 194 (January 1947), 45–48.

41. Bernard DeVoto letter to Harold Stassen, June 10, 1948, in Stegner, *Letters,* 351–57.

42. William L. Graf, *Wilderness Preservation and the Sagebrush Rebellions* (Savage, MD: Rowman & Littlefield, 1990), .3–137, quote from 134.

43. Roderick Nash, *The American Conservation Movement* (St. Charles, MO: Forum Press, 1974), 7–10; and Samuel P. Hays, *Conservation and the Gospel of Efficiency: The Progressive Conservation Movement, 1890–1920* (New York: Atheneum, 1979; originally published by Harvard University Press, 1959), chapters 4, 5, and 12.

44. Hal K. Rothman, *Saving the Planet: The American Response to the Environment in the Twentieth Century* (Chicago: Ivan R. Dee, 2000), 69–84; and Graf, *Sagebrush Rebellions,* 166–67.

45. Stegner and Etulain, *Conversations with Wallace Stegner,* 170–71.

46. Stegner, *Uneasy Chair,* 306–7.

47. In addition to the articles in part III, DeVoto wrote several articles on the water issue, including "The Desert Threat," *University of Colorado Bulletin* 48 (July 1948; this was the address he gave at commencement exercises June 14, 1947); "Water Runs Downhill," *Woman's Day,* January 1949; and "Our Great West, Boom or Bust?" *Collier's,* December 25, 1953.

48. "The West Against Itself," *Harper's Magazine* 194 (January 1947): 8.

49. DeVoto letters to Adlai Stevenson, May 19, 1954; June 11, 1954; August 24, 1954; and August 29, 1954, in Stegner, *Letters,* 370–74; and Stegner, *Uneasy Chair,* 317–19.

50. DeVoto; and Samuel P. Hays, "The New Environmental West," *Journal of Policy History* 3, no. 3 (1991): 223–48.

51. "National Park Service," *Harper's Magazine* 198 (March 1949).

52. "Let's Close the National Parks," *Harper's Magazine* 207 (October 1953).

53. "Shall We Let Them Ruin Our National Parks?" *Saturday Evening Post,* July 22, 1950; "Parks and Pictures," *Harper's Magazine* 208 (February 1954); and "Current Comic Strips," *Harper's Magazine* 210 (May 1955).

54. "Intramural Giveaway," *Harper's Magazine* 208 (March 1954): 10.

55. Rothman, *Saving the Planet,* 100–107; and Samuel P. Hays, "The Structure of Environmental Politics Since World War II," in Samuel P. Hays, ed., *Explorations in Environmental History* (Pittsburgh: University of Pittsburgh Press, 1998), 315–33.

56. Rothman, *Saving the Planet,* 135–36. Also, see notes 50 and 51 above.

57. Stegner, *Uneasy Chair,* 313–14 and 321.

58. "The High Country," *Woman's Day,* December 1952.

59. Stegner, *Uneasy Chair,* 322.

60. Schlesinger, "The Citizen," in *Four Portraits,* 74–75.

61. Stegner, *Letters,* 347.

62. As quoted in Schlesinger, "The Citizen," in *Four Portraits,* 75.

63. Stegner, *Uneasy Chair,* 297.

64. Stegner, *Uneasy Chair,* 380; and Stegner and Etulain, *Conversations,* 183.

65. Stegner, *Uneasy Chair,* 381–82 and photographic insert.

66. Graf, *Sagebrush Rebellions,* 197–263; Rothman, *Saving the Planet,* 162–83; and C. Brant Short, *Ronald Reagan and the Public Lands: America's Conservation Debate, 1979–1984* (College Station: Texas A & M University Press, 1989), 11–12.

67. John H. Cushman Jr., "Alaska Delegation Pushes Agenda of Development," *New York Times,* September 13, 1998.

68. "The Congressional Land Grab," *New York Times,* November 15, 1995.

69. Stegner, *Sound of Mountain Water,* 270–71.

ONE
DeVoto's West

*The point of all this is that in the
West we are, far more than any
other part of the country, in touch
with the earth and subject to it. . . .
Our awareness is very deep, and this
awareness is a fundamental characteristic of us and our land.*

"Footnote on the West," *1927*

Footnote on the West

(*Harper's Monthly Magazine*, November 1927)

Anyone can tell a New Englander from a Southerner by his speech. An expert phonetician can name the State from which a man comes, and usually the county, frequently the city, and sometimes the very street as well. There is, however, an enormous geographical division of this country which has few dialectical peculiarities and none that the layman can distinguish. An expert, hearing a native of these parts, must listen attentively in order to classify the subject. The native will eventually betray himself by a few inconspicuous signs. He will say "laig" for "leg," though he will not say "aig" for "egg." He will say "jest" instead of "just," though he will not say "jestice." There is one sound which he will invariably butcher, the sound of *au* in such words as "haughty," "naughty," "daughter," and "August." And, whatever his words, he will speak them in a tune that is just a little different, too little for untrained ears to identify, from that sung by any other group of Americans. It is a sort of *rubato* rhythm that retards the utterance of certain key-words in any sentence and, without stressing them, gives them the emphasis of prolonged time-intervals. This is the drawl, made notorious by one kind of fiction. The Southern drawl is a chant,

but this drawl is a hesitation. And that, apart from differences of vo-
cabulary, is about the sum of speech peculiarities in this vast portion of
the country. It is a much smaller sum than that of the Middle West,
New England, or the South.

Now there may be significance in this fact. It may indicate something
about the natives of these parts—may be an outward and visible sign
of an inward and spiritual identity. There are two ways of looking at it.
One may remark that a people so barren of speech idiosyncrasies must
be a dull and un-individual race. Or one may observe that theirs is probably the purest English spoken on the continent. As a native of this section, one who faithfully flattens the *au* to this day, I have never decided
which point of view comes nearer to suggesting the truth about the
Intermountain West.

We are undoubtedly a race, we Westerners, though mostly we fail
to understand the implications of our unity. If you are a Bostonian to
whom Cincinnati seems so far west that it must be a Pacific port, or to
whom Omaha is a State, you can offend us by lumping us as Westerners with Chicagoans, with the electorate who keep Senator LaFollette
in office, and with the Ku Kluxers of Indiana. It is a graver offense to
speak of us as Westerners along with Kansans, Nebraskans, and Iowans.
But the outrage we will not permit is your bland impulse to call us
Westerners and then, without a filter, to apply the same term of the people of Los Angeles. If Californians are Westerners, then, be assured, we
live in the State of Maine.

Not the least hope that inspires this essay is the hope that I may help
to attach to the word West the geographical implications it has in the
part of the country to which it properly applies. Briefly, then, the West
is the Intermountain West, the land that is dominated by the Rocky
Mountains. The fact that there are no ranges called the Rocky Mountains is only a minor paradox in this wholly paradoxical land, and need
disturb no one. Montana, Idaho, Wyoming, Colorado, and Utah are
West. Nevada is West by attraction. The eastern fringe of Washington
and Oregon is West, but the rest of them is something else—littoral,
or Pacific, or what you will, anything to indicate that the life lived there
differs in fundamental ways from that lived within the shadow of the
Rockies. California is not West, oh, decidedly and emphatically and

with all the insistence of our nature, California is not West. To our sorrow, Arizona and New Mexico are not West, for they are Southwest, and Spanish and Indian civilization separates them from us. We should like to claim them; we regret them more than any other part of the country, and much more (I cannot courteously point out how much more) than we regret California. The lines of this demarcation are sharp and the land that it sets off is an entity; it once had a separate civilization, and remnants of that civilization are part of us to-day. Actually, Cheyenne is not much farther west than North Platte, but spiritually, in thought and civilization, they are unmistakably distinct. Cheyenne is West, whereas North Platte is Middle West. And, we must patiently insist, there is a difference.

What is that difference? Perhaps I am no fit person to explain, for the necessities of the two professions I practice have forced me, the West being what it is, to spend a large part of my life elsewhere. Of the last twelve years, I have not spent a total of three in the West, and those three are the aggregate of temporary stays. And, it is only fair to confess, a number of newspapers in the West have accused me of intolerably misrepresenting my native land; and a number of organizations, of the kind that adopt Resolutions, have whereas-ed me half deaf with condemnation on the same grounds. But that is a custom of the country and must not be thought of as heartfelt. And anyway, it is time that the Easterners who understand us, good folk like Mr. Struthers Burt, Mrs. Gerould, and Mrs. Rinehart, had some native annotations, and mine will do as well as any, pending the appearance of someone more acceptable to the luncheon-clubs.

II

It happens that, while I write this, I am at the easternmost corner of Cape Cod, where the fog has not lifted for a total of twelve hours in four weeks. The last five years I have spent in Chicago, where, by local admission, there are two seasons, August and winter, the former occurring every fifth or sixth year, and where sunlight is as much a matter of rumor as the Southern Cross. The four years preceding the Chicago ordeal I spent in Boston, and the climate of Boston need not be more than alluded to. When I think back over these years of exile from the sun, I invariably conclude that such punishments are visited on Westerners who were tourists in previous existences, and Kim's Lama would understand them.

The glory of the eagle, you will remember, was looking at the sun. The West is the land of the eagle, for the sun shines there. Our sun is not an occasional visitor, for the unpoetic fact is that it shines on us thirty days (and from May to December, one more) out of thirty-one. Still less is it a reluctant luminescence veiled with mists. It is instead a vital, penetrating influence, a physical and a metaphysical immanence. It is a living element. As the elder god, it has been everywhere worshiped far oftener than any other, save in purely Nordic climates where as an absent god it has had an anonymous altar, and this vital principle moulds us Westerners from the moment we are conceived. Sunlight is bred in us. There is little chiaroscuro in our lives. We perhaps lose something in subtlety, bearing in mind that crepuscular, mist-born attenuations of mood are well thought of by the more correct intellectuals. But on the other hand, as sun-worshipers, as folk whose lives are swayed by the elder deity, we have moods that are distinctly pagan — and paganism, I understand, is championed by the same people. I have sometimes wondered how a hearty paganism was attainable in Manhattan, where the sun is mostly a mere nimbus in the sky. No doubt the will is accepted as the deed, and a good fearless talk in Somebody's Stables will do as a substitute for such orgies as the Moquis or the Utes or the Blackfeet, or we Westerners, their vicars, indulge in at seasonable times.

In the West, too, we have seasons. In the last twelve years I have seen but one spring, and for that heaven sent me back to the mountains. Here, in the West the four seasons are distinct and they come at the appointed time. Life, literature, and art are all bound up with the seasons, and folklore attests their importance. In the spring, for instance, the earth proverbially makes the sunwise turn, sap runs upward, nature germinates all about one, one's blood leaps with the reawakening, and desire looking toward birth rises with the warming earth. Folk festivals acknowledge the mystery of reawakening, whether as Easter or the Passover or the earthy frankness of the rites that Frazer discusses in *The Golden Bough*. Think now of spring as it comes to the fog-bound coast of New England, or, through sleet and chill, to the

Great Lakes. There is no sun in it, no warmth, no budding of an inner fire, and I wonder that maids are ever married in these climes, or children ever begotten. For how can life make the sunwise turn when a chill wind is blowing black clouds off Lake Michigan to crowd the smoke pall still lower over Chicago? Jazz and hooch and peripheral stimulation, I suppose, must supply the place of the vital principle itself. Well, in the West we are a responsive people, having spring to respond to. So with the other seasons. You will find in our blood vestigial impulses that may mean to puzzled Easterners that we are emotional folk, but are really the promptings of the Beltane Fires and Allhallow Summer.

Above all, the West is a beautiful country, even when it is hideous. It is, one must understand, both mountains and desert: they merge into each other, and you can step from one to its antithesis in three strides. At one hand will be a spruce forest or a field of melons, and at the other the ground will be corrupt with alkali and greasewood. You may choose either element or a blend of both. It takes a certain hardiness to choose the desert, for one who is not habituated to it is oppressed by desolation. But the choice is repaid. No other life is quite so rich in colors or perfumes, and none is so intimately aware of the basic rhythm of the earth, the blueprint plans of creation. In the West we say that when a man has once lived in the desert, he will come back to it again. He will.

But the mountains are more lovely still. It is no part of my purpose to describe them, for I have never been able to deal seriously with those who have not seen them. It is enough that nowhere in the West are you out of sight of them. Men are impelled to love the countryside in which they live. Therefore it has always seemed to me a great pathos that the love of millions of people must be expended on the monotony, the swamps, the abortive hills, the flatness and the sameness of the Middle West. There will yet be a philosopher to explain the Middle West by its unimaginative landscape. That it is a soul-sick region is attested by its literature. Miss Cather, Mr. Sinclair Lewis, Mr. Floyd Dell, Mr. And Mrs. Haldeman-Julius, Miss Suckow, Mr. Frederick, Mr. Muilenberg, and lesser novelists are significantly unanimous in reporting its frustration, dullness, and spiritual insolvency. The horizon of the Middle West is a flat ring, and nowhere that you go in it, save in upper Wisconsin, will you find relief. It is monotonous as a picket fence, and its beauty is only that of flat surfaces, weak colors, and the tamed and cautious order of its farms. As a result, nervous depression is the commonplace mood of the Middle West. But in the West the horizon is a line of peaks, with gigantic perspectives, played over by barbaric colors that are a persistent fire in the mountain sun.

This great beauty of line and color definitely preserves the West from the neurasthenias of the prairies. I do not mean to say that the typical Westerner is a beauty-lover. Far from it. But one does not have to be eloquent about beauty, or even to be aware of it, in order to obey its influence. A very platitude of psychology says that loveliness is a spiritual antiseptic, a tonic. It is an inoculation against melancholy, and its baleful fruits of compulsion and inhibition. And even the worst atrocity inflicted on the West, the fiction of cowboys and stage-robbers, recognizes as a Western characteristic a certain spiritual resiliency backed by an inner serenity. The Westerner has a typical humorous irony, and the word I need to describe it is obviously "hard-boiled." He does not join the bonanza hunts of the mind and spirit. He is the only practicing cynic in America. You will not palm off on him any kind of millennium whatsoever: political, economic, or social. You cannot drum up anywhere in the West a corporal's guard of adherents to any plan for ushering in perfection—whereas the moment you unfold the standard in Indiana or Iowa, New York or California, oh, especially California, the mob rushing to raise it is a stampede. Nor will any swami, bahai, or mystical Hindu gatgoober convert him to concentration, rhythmic belly-breathing, or the music of the spheres. His soul is acidulous and tonic—because he has been reared in the hills.

The West, too, is a dangerous country. Now it seems to me demonstrated that the harder you must labor to support life in a country, the more life will recompense you with an affection for the severities you have labored in. An agonizing dawn-to-midnight battle with glacial bowlders and dismembered granite produced New England. The sweat of that swinking gave us the first autochthonous white civilization in this country, and incidentally created a love of the New England countryside that has become proverbial if not odious. Something of that process is observable in the West to-day, where survival has never been possible except by the utmost extremity of labor. St. Louis or Chicago or Des Moines cost but little in the building: economic necessity called them into life, and they grew as effortlessly as trees. But Denver and Salt Lake City and Pocatello were thrust into the desert a thousand miles from economic support. They were like germs of life blown into a barren planet and their function must always be at its maximum if they were to persist. They and the ranches that are symbiotically joined with them were won from the desert. Not from the woods or the prairies, not from the river bottoms or the canebrakes, not from great alluvial plains where soil was forty feet deep and forty inches of rain fell every year, not from land that rioted with vegetation whether or not it was plowed—but from the desert. I have said that the West is a beautiful country, but I would point out that danger and terror have traditionally a face of beauty.

I am spending this summer in Massachusetts. The press is grave, for this is a drouth year and there has been a forest fire. I must be pardoned a little disdain. I have never lived a summer in the West when there were not forest fires within a day's riding of my home, all summer long, or when the air of three States, each one of them larger than all New England, was not faintly acrid throughout August with the fires of another State five hundred miles away. This Massachusetts drouth has cut down the customary rainfall a full quarter. And that quarter, in inches, is just precisely the total annual rainfall of the State where I was born. Two months ago, when I left Illinois, the press there was clamoring about the corn-borer, which might possibly destroy one-tenth of the crop. Two years ago, in the West, I rode through a valley in which one might have mislaid all of Illinois, and there a wearily familiar story was retold: armies of black beetles had come down out of the peaks, and there was no crop left at all.

The point of all this is that in the West we are, far more than any other part of the country, in touch with the earth and subject to it. Its winds and drouths and plagues are not rumors or spectacles to us, but realities that we must deal with. We sometimes are resentful of the earth, and sometimes we actively hate and fear it, but we are never forgetful or disdainful of it. Our awareness is very deep, and this awareness is a fundamental characteristic of us and our land. I would like to linger on it and emphasize it, for I have an idea that, possessing it, we escape a damnation that is evident in certain other places.

III

The West, like all of America, was once frontier. It was frontier, how-ever, longer and more vividly than any other part, and indeed you may still find portions of it where, alone in America, the frontier persists. Wherever homestead land is still available the old heartbreaking war goes on. You may drive through parts of Idaho, of Wyoming, or Utah where the sagebrush is broken every few miles by a weather-worn shack. To the door of that shack a faded woman will come to gaze at the dust of your automobile till the horizon has risen above it, and somewhere, unseen, her husband is hacking at the sage. But not the presence of the frontier but its memory is powerful in the West to-day.

The frontier has created an extraordinary number of myths, and they have got themselves accepted as realities. So far as they make the rest of the world think of us in preposterous symbols, they do no great harm but rather add to our sum of laughter. But, alas, they have worked into our own thinking, and we see ourselves not as we are but as the myths have made us out to be. The result is only sometimes amusing, but it is always harmful to us and especially to our future. One myth, for instance, exhibits the West as the last great stand of American in-dividualism—the place where a man dares to be himself against the world. Nothing could be more absurdly unrealistic. The West has never been individualistic and is not now. In the nature of things, no horde of individualists could have existed in the desert to which the pioneers came. Only a completely co-operative group, who shared the rigors of the land and banded together to resist them, could have survived. The rapidity with which frontier communities set up local governments is evidence of this anti-individual necessity. Some of these were in fact so outrageously repressive that their memory is perpetuated in grins, but they were always effective. I will be forgiven if I find still stronger evi-dence in those executive bodies that had no shadow of legality, the vigilance committees. No doubt they were required for the security of the common endeavor, and I rejoice in the realistic way in which they met the situation; but invariably, besides suppressing the desperado, they suppressed also quite guiltless citizens who happened to displease the majority. As John Gale almost wrote in a book I once attributed to him, the true individualist in the West was to be found at one end of a rope whose other end was in the hands of the vigilance committee.

Consequently, the West has always lacked one essential of civilization, a nucleus of minority or unorthodox opinion. There has never been any dissent, and no one can name any leader, political or social or philosophical or artistic, of heretical thought. The name of Senator Borah may perhaps occur to you, but alas, he is a Middle Westerner who obeyed the Horace Greeley tradition, and I suspect that his acceptance in the West is due to our realistic understanding that, however horribly he may revolt in oratory, in the end he invariably votes with the rest of us. No, we have never been on the side of change nor have we ever granted the right of a minority to exist. We crushed them at birth on the frontier, and so formed a habit that has come to be a conditioned response. The Brahmin of the Back Bay and the Tory everywhere will jealously preserve the right of an opponent to differ from him, for he understands that he must do so if he is to preserve his own identity. But the West has never mastered this elementary principle, and its frontier tradition of suppression is still supreme. It will permit no eccentricity whatsoever in dress, behavior, or belief—or anything else.

If the folkways dictate the pasting of a bathing-girl on our windshields, we will create a corps of pasters to put them on all windshields found without them. If the Chamber of Commerce ordains a Smile-Damn-You!-week, there will be uniformed sentinels on the street-corners to make you smile. If we elect to hold a fête to commemorate the Pony Express or the coming of the railroad, and resolve to grow whiskers to revive the old days, then every male in town must grow whiskers. If he demurs, a committee waits upon him and forbids him to shave till the celebration is over. If he still asserts his right to wear his hair with a difference, the committee calls again and reminds him of its economic power to enforce its orders. Perhaps he can't grow a beard? Well, there is crêpe-hair on the market. He is a traitor, you see, for he has dared to oppose the community will, and he must be dealt with.

In moments of exasperation I have sometimes thought that this committee was the complete symbol of the West, and though it is not that, it does represent a grave defect in our civilization. It is seconded by our complete inability to stand criticism. The New Yorker, or any other adequately civilized man, is always pleased when fault is found with his civilization, the Westerner is only convinced that the fault-finder is a bigamist, an embezzler, a Bolshevik, and probably an opprobrious kind of pervert as well. The West, he knows, is faultless—and only a corrupt and vicious man could pretend to see a flaw in it. Obviously a corrupt and vicious man is not entitled to the protection of the law; wherefore, to the vigilance committee with him.

Another favorite myth, and one that ties up neatly with this one, has to do with the nature of the pioneers. We will talk for hours about the superior quality of the emigrants who left the East for the rousing adventure of the desert. The Pioneer means to us a heroic compound of all the virtues, and chiefly of courage and intelligence. The fact is that, apart from mining rushes which attracted all the less stable elements of the East indiscriminately, there were just three classes from whom the bulk of the Western migration was made up: restless, unadjusted folk such as old soldiers, rivermen, and roustabouts; people who for one reason or another had occasion to evade the law, whether the criminal code or bankruptcy proceedings; and, by far the largest class, those who were driven West by economic pressure, which is to say those who had found competition in the East too strenuous for them, which is to say further, the unfit. The typical pioneer was a middle-aged chap with a half-grown family. He had been thrown out of work by a shutdown of Eastern mills or by foreclosure on his Middle-Western lands. What he expected in the West was only survival, only solvency, which may be expressed as free land. Though he came to work the land he was probably not a farmer at all and certainly not a good farmer. If he had been the latter he would have stayed on his own acres which, wherever they might be, were incomparably richer and more easily worked than any he could find in the West.

This fact joins up, on the one hand, with our aversion to personal freedom, and on the other hand it creates our democracy. The hand-clasp, you will remember, is a little stronger. Well, we have had our full share of the sumptuary legislation that goes with that hand-clasp, and I need not specify it here but only refer the interested to the reports of our law-making bodies, which have loyally expressed our taboos. Instead, I mention the democracy of our business—which is strangely out of keeping with our native cynicism. We have got so used to the General Confession as a public institution that we endure without a

protest—nay, actually with the pride of democratic men—the Booster
in the most awful purity of the type. And this is our heritage from in-
ferior or defeated men—a great yearning to be as other men. Elsewhere,
the Rotary badge may be laid away at bedtime or when men meet in
secret over a pint of bootleg for the communion of male souls. But the
Western Booster counts it secret treason when he has slept without
dreaming of giving Denver a million by 1930, or waked without invok-
ing the god of Florida real estate over his toothbrush. For other Boosters there may be occasional recess and surcease from function, but not
for him. Tarantulas have stung him to make the West equal to the
Middle West in vulgarity, in sameness, and in false values—and he will
dance his obscene and desirous envy till he dies.

And this great lust to make the West democratically identical with
portions of the country it has the great good fortune not to resemble is our most pathetic and most ridiculous characteristic. In the nature of things the West cannot be the Middle West, no matter how
much we will the identity, and the will is in itself preposterous. It is the
inferiority-yearning, of course, and it means that the Booster portion
of the West does not understand its country or its people. To profane
the sanctuary of the mountains with the barbarities of the prairies is to
soil beauty and to defile purity and, generally, to lay oneself open to the
ribald laughter of the world. Fortunately, I repeat, it cannot be done.

IV

Whatever the date of its beginning, the bulk of Western settlement
occurred during the Sixties and Seventies of the last century, an age
almost incredible to this generation. The Forties we can understand,
the Eighties are familiar ground, but the cynical materialism that followed the Civil War is incomprehensible to-day, even in the procon-
sulate of an Executive who goes to the Middle West and dons rodeo-
pants (not, you must understand, ranch-pants or *chaparajos*). In the
Seventies the national taste reached the lowest level it has ever known.
Look at the styles as they are preserved in Godey's. Recall the society
that was edified by Jim Fisk. Inspect an 1870 room in a museum and
take note of the glassware, the furniture, and the decorations. Think
back to the literature of America after Poe and Melville and Hawthorne
had died and the New England school had spent it force, and before

such people as Mark Twain and Henry James had emerged. It was a nadir.

These tastes and sentiments, these intellectual and artistic impulses, the pioneers brought West with them. They at once took up their death-grapple with the soil, and the West has never thoroughly outgrown their tastes. In its whole extent there are not more than a dozen public buildings that are even decent, and practically all of these are concentrated in Denver. There is no Western architecture—no native architecture developed from the Western soil and appropriate to the Western scene. The Southwest has achieved an architecture, native, beautiful, and appropriate, and southern California was on its way toward one before Iowa and the movies flooded it and put an end to all art. But not even a start has been made in the West. For all public purposes the Seventies are unchanged; for private purposes the Seventies have struck a compromise with the bungalow, and so an atrocity has begotten upon an absurdity a child that can only be called a monster.

Neither is there any other native art in the West. The explanation for this grave lack must be the corrupt taste of our formative period and the actual poverty that has attended our struggle with the desert. Artists enough, certainly, have been born in the West. A surprising number of the best in America—painters, writers, sculptors, and musicians— were born within sight of the peaks. To catalogue them here would be invidious, but I must mention one. Think of the poet, aesthetician, critic, controversialist, and complete boulevardier who is above all others the most utter of advanced folk—the purple-whiskered, fire-breathing, ring-tailed gyascutus to whom anyone's else farthest futurism is day before yesterday, the man who may be said to have invented E .E. Cummings and to have dreamed T. S. Eliot, the man who has created unassisted the gaudiest exoticisms of our most febrile arts. Then think of the Idaho desert, drab with sage, white with alkali, torrid with sun, waterless peaks rising above it, heat-mirage distorting its horizons—a place where, one thinks, only the most nerveless of Mr. Mencken's morons could survive. And then reflect that here, among the cowhands and the rattlesnakes, Ezra Pound was born.

They are born in the West but there is no native culture to hold or nourish them. The art galleries of the West are non-existent; its journalism is mediocre; its libraries are rudimentary; its museums are antique shops; its universities, all but one, are high-schools; its music does not exist outside of the movie houses. Now and then a Chamber of Commerce will get behind a traveling orchestra or opera company and boost it for the glory of Snakeville, or a Legislature will solemnly authorize a fourteen-by-twenty-four panorama of the discovery of antimony in Cactus Gulch. But, as yet, there is no popular toleration of art, and an artist means, to the typical Westerner, a queer chap who is deficient in virility or has something the matter with his lungs. Wherefore our artists naturally stampede eastward, all of them that are worth a damn (I add the reservation to forestall the mail from Salt Lake City). I am not, however, particularly dismayed by this fact, for they go east from everywhere west of the Hudson, and south from New England, and north from Baltimore. And there is one significant difference. I can think of no reason why an artist should go back to Kankakee or Memphis. But our Western artists come home, from time to time. As we say, when a man has once lived in the desert, he will come back.

Finally, the Westerner not only has no desire for intimate beauty but displays an ominous tendency to corrupt his countryside. I know of no city, town, or village in all the West that is beautiful in itself, apart from its setting. New England villages, merely by the use of white paint and the discreet grouping of elms and steeples and roses, are lovely in themselves; and in the South and along the Green Bay shore of Wisconsin one is constantly delighted by the human scene. But in the West, one must keep one's eyes on the mountains or be constantly affronted not only by the unlovely buildings and groupings but also by an altogether unpardonable frowziness in their surroundings. If old abandoned mining shafts have sometimes been covered up, then vast acreages of dumps neighbor with the city hall, and if sometimes the dumps have been suppressed, still no one has thought to paint the fences. And the West seems to have a diabolical determination to contaminate the mountains. You will hardly find a Podunk in all that expanse that has not its name or its initial in whitewashed cobblestones half-way up a commanding peak, illuminated at night and usually accompanied by a slogan as vulgar as the best minds can make it. Vast projects for covering the mountains with gingerbread-work are always on foot: schemes to pipe a new waterfall here, to set a searchlight on a peak there, to build an artificial ice-cavern elsewhere, and so on. My native town, for instance, has thus far been too poor to carry out its cherished dreams, but some day it will be able to afford them and then the long yearning will be satisfied. In that day, from the tip of a peak that rises a mile above the city will swing a sky-sign which will blaze the blessed sylla-bles of "Ogden" to all the world, and at the entrance to our loveliest canyon, between bastions of granite a thousand feet high, there will be a thirty-foot arch of lath and plaster inscribed with some exquisite sen-timent about the vales and hills.

v

The conclusion is prophecy. It is apparent that when I have praised the West, in these pages, I have praised its countryside, and when I have rebuked it I have been talking about its cities. The Westerners, then, who are most in touch with the Western soil are altogether admirable, and it is only the towns that have gone a-whoring after the false gods of Boosterdom.

This strange aberration is all the more surprising because it is un-natural and against God. The Rotary button is an alien badge in a Western lapel. In Omaha, in Dubuque, in Moline its wearers are born to it and their lives are rightfully devoted to the concepts for which it stands. For the true function of the Middle-Western town is to grow into a city, to increase the aggregate of its farm-loans and its bank-clearings, to bring more factory payrolls to its territory, and to aspire always upward till it has approximated as closely to Chicago as heaven will permit. But the West can never approximate Chicago. Our salva-tion is that we are earth-bound. Our enormous distances can never fill up. Hard facts of soil and climate and limited productivity will keep us always very much as we are. Denver can never become St. Louis, and never, never can Greasewood Corners become Peoria.

We are, I have said, a naturally cynical people, and we have never bought stock in any millennium. We did not suffer fools gladly in the old days when our towns were jumping-off places; we do not suffer them gladly now, in places where we are still desperately wrestling with the desert; and I do not think we shall suffer them gladly any-where much longer. This strange delusion that fools can make desert crossroads into metropolises by shouting and handclapping is one kind of millennial dream, and must eventually be recognized as one. In that day the West will arise with a strong laughter and will lovingly slay its Rotaries.

The rest must follow naturally. The *nach-Chicago* ideal, with its luncheon-clubs and its bungalows and its bathing-girl posters, is an unhealthy cosmopolitanism and quite alien to us. The Booster is a man who yearns to make the citizen of one Portland indistinguishable from the citizen of the other, whose heart is set on forcing San Francisco and New Orleans to duplicate each other, who sees perfection as a nation of standardized cities living standardized lives synchronously. This is cosmopolitanism and it is dangerously allied to the dreams of revolutionists. Well, in the West we have been traditionally derisive of strangers, and we have resisted all their blights and vices but this one. In that great day when we laugh our Boosters into paralysis, we will surge back to our native provincialism. We will rear us a great wall, man it with our Tenth Legion, and decree that no stranger shall tarry within it save he be silent, not giving tongue to his aberrant dreams.

A more thorough-going provincialism, a recognition that our ways are not the ways of Grand Rapids, is what the West must some day achieve. The West for Westerners! We are a desert folk, and the moment we acknowledge the ultimate conditions of our estate, that moment we shall be saved. Left to ourselves, we will do very nicely. Once we have got rid of alien ideals and alien ideas, together with alien arts and architectures and institutions, evolution and inbreeding will develop a native civilization. We are healthier and saner and less trusting than our neighbors on either side, and we live in the sun. Our inheritance and the nature of our countryside are beyond the purchasing of others. When we come to admitting them and abiding by them, rather than aping the insanities of the mist-dwellers, well, in those days they shall look upon us, the foreign devils who the tourist agencies bring among us, with a desolate and hopeless envy in their eyes. But, pending such a time, one remembers the bungalow and the plaster arch, and is dumb.

Fossil Remnants of the Frontier

Notes on a Utah Boyhood

(*Harper's Monthly Magazine*, April 1935)

She was going, she said, to summon Bat Masterson. We had been tormenting her with the ingenious deviltries of childhood and, one small blonde girl against a half-dozen boys, she now proposed to stop it. The invocation brought us to an uneasy pause. Thirty-odd years later, I remember the rustle of cottonwoods while triumph glinted in her eyes and a light buggy came up the road. It drew abreast, and manliness restrained us from bolting but was not capable of a jeer. Two booted men in flannel shirts and wide tan Stetsons sat in that buggy, and a shotgun stuck out from under the seat. They were probably no more than a couple of neighbors bound up "the canyon road" for quail, but a dreadful name lent them awe. They passed. The blonde child said, "That's Bat Masterson and I know him," then stuck out her tongue and disdainfully walked away. The killer-sheriff was not within a thousand miles at the moment, probably, but in Ogden, Utah, at about 1904, his name was a sufficient dissuader of boys.

One of my mother's stories dealt with a friend of hers who married and went to some Wyoming town. There, after some years, her husband was murdered, "on the very steps of the courthouse." The misdemeanor may not have been sanctioned but there was no thought of arresting the misdemeanant. The widow was acquainted with the usages: before the corpse was carried away she dipped a token in the thickening blood. She would save it until her son grew up; then, my mother said, she would give it to him and bid him "wash the stain from your mother's handkerchief." The tale sounds a theme from the border ballads of all ages but it is quite true. To a boy growing up in that culture it had solemnity but nothing of the inappropriate.

The last loose confederacies of rustlers and train robbers were not much later than my birth. In interior Utah and Wyoming there was still much gunfire and such galloping below the skyline as the movies were soon to reproduce, but it was done by individuals, not gangs, by remnants of an outmoded lodge, in a tradition now formalized and obsolete. It was as far as the moon from Ogden. We were Butch Cassidy or Tom Horn. We held up the U.P. at Tipton; we rode down fanning our guns at Laramie; at Winnemucca or Castlegate we robbed banks and turned in our saddles to deal with citizens reckless enough to level rifles at us; we rode back to Robbers' Roost or Hole in the Wall for the orgies that convention demanded. But there was no feeling that such romance was related to our time and place: we were as ritualistic as the boys I see to-day in Cambridge, Massachusetts, firing machine guns from automobiles at government agents who had had the effrontery to pursue John Dillinger.

Utah has little history of Indian trouble. This is due in part to Brigham Young's enlightened policy—he believed, soundly, that it was cheaper to feed Indians than to kill them off—but in greater part to the fact that the Indians of Utah were a degenerate race. The bellicose Utes belonged to the eastward, the Bannocks ranged far to the north, the Apaches seldom came up as far as the Grand Canyon, and the Navajos, who reached our border in greater numbers, were not warlike. The resident tribes were mostly Gosh-Utes and Diggers, technological unemployed, victims of the competitive Indian society which had forced them to the badlands, where such culture as they possessed decayed, sometimes below the use of fire. Thus it was that in the stories of the elders the red slayer was commonly just a beggar and a thief. They had been sufficiently sophisticated to trade on the reputation of their race, so that, finding a woman alone in a farmhouse, they might sometimes frighten her into largesse. But they could not often do even that; my grandmother, startled by the apparition of a blanketed and painted buck singing Injun in her dooryard, simply picked up the weapon known to her generation as a horse pistol. At sight of it the brave forsook the dooryard and the warpath in one stride. The air was full of Indian stories, located elsewhere, of course. Neighbors had ridden to Sand Creek or had campaigned with Custer or Connor or Crook; had fought off Oglalla attacks on wagon trains or stage stations; had galloped to distant settlements and found the naked, scalped, and raped bodies of women, and children curiously dismembered and hung up. Distance was on all these tales, however, and the closest we boys came to them was in the distinction of one playmate. An uncle of his had been captured by Apaches, who cut off his eyelids and the soles of his feet and then tied him to a stake in an ant-bed and left him to the desert sun.

But we inherited the frontier's sentiments about Indians. The ones we saw, to be sure, were just grunting, dour, and mostly drunken grotesques, without terror, whom it was desirable not to approach too closely lest your mother be obliged to wash your hair with kerosene. But the Indian as an image of thought was a savage whose extermination was dictated by the necessities of civilization. The attitude survived long enough to immunize me against one sentimentality of my literary generation. As a historian, I have been able to understand the Indian's side of extermination and to master his strategy, but as a literary critic, I have been withheld from mysticism about the Amerind. I have not found him a beauty-lover, the creator of a deeply spiritual religion, or an accomplished metaphysician who plumbed eternal secrets which his brutish conqueror could never understand. Sibylline women and rapt men from megalopolis have been unable to persuade me that his neolithic culture was anything but a neolithic culture. Remembering the scalp-dance, I have found the Amerind on the whole less likely to civilize the American continent than the Nordic; on Amerind art and religion, I hold, the frontier had a sounder criticism than Greenwich Village.

In such ways, remembered violence tinged life in Ogden during that pause between frontier society and industrialism in which I grew up. I cannot say how it affected our libido and personae. Outwardly, combined with the tradition of the migratory hunter, it did no more than give us a familiarity with firearms earlier than boys were getting it to the eastward. I owned several sub-caliber rifles before I was twelve. By fifteen I was a good off-hand shot and had owned not only twenty-twos but a really formidable arsenal as well. By inheritance, appropriation, and the trafficking of boyhood I had acquired at various times a high-powered rifle, a shotgun, an automatic pistol, and at least three revolvers. My friends were similarly armed, and the gulches above Ogden endlessly echoed with our gunfire. Firearms were our cult, as automobiles and radios became the cult of our successors. We were competent. I knew no boy who did not regularly strap a revolver on his belt, balance a rifle on his shoulder, and disappear with his gang into the hills; but I knew only one boy who was injured in all that time. Early as we came to them, we used our guns with skill. It was a formalized skill without survival value, so that we consciously practiced it as an art, but it was a frontier inheritance.

The quality of all this scarlet was its irrelevance. And that is precisely my point: the West's scarlet, the frontier's violence, was episodic and irrelevant. Our elders and their elders had been lifelong addicts of civilization and community building. The cowboys arriving at Trail's End, who liquored up and shot one another, were an inconvenience, like the breaking of a water main, and had nothing to do with the life of Dodge City. The schoolmarm took the children out to look for mayflowers through that intermittent barrage. Bat Masterson, on the prowl for a kill, stepped out of the way of matrons of the Eastern Star carrying crullers and chicken patties to a church supper. Just across the Weber River (a very small stream) from my grandfather's south field, the Morrisite war produced three days of rifle and artillery fire. Civil revolt and its suppression get one line in his journal, being subordinated to the record of his plowing. A cattle war, a battle of miners, the rape of a bank or a stage coach was just what it is to-day, a violent interruption of a peaceful process, and was met in the same way, with the same despatch. Only, the frontier, being a large country and insufficiently policed, had few community safeguards for life and property. That fact put such safeguards up to the individual: if his safety and his property were threatened he had to defend them himself. "The law west of the Pecos" was what one wore on one's hip or carried on one's shoulder. When someone stole your horse or dynamited your ditches you could not send east of the Pecos for a cop. The frontiersman sighed, dropped his plow, went for his arsenal, attended to the horsethief, and then came back, got his crop in, and became a private citizen. He gladly made a peace officer his vicar as soon as one was available, and if he sometimes showed a preference for one who had got his training among the outlawed, megalopolis shows the same preference to-day. Organization achieved, he promptly forgot his earlier phase. It is not in the West where a tradition of personal responsibility and violence persists. I have seen more pocket pistols at a single party in Georgia than in any ten years' travel in the entire West.

II

Ogden had seen a deeper violence than casual outlawry. From its first settlement on, Utah was constantly rocked by the deadliest of all warfare, economic and religious. The Church of Jesus Christ of Latter-Day Saints was a semi-co-operative society governed by an oligarchy who claimed divine sanction and exercised absolute power. It had reached Utah after a series of expulsions which proved that the American social system could not adjust itself to it. Once in the mountains, the Church did its best to establish its system in defiance of experience. Fifty years of economic war between Mormons and Gentiles, intensified and made picturesque by the religious idiom of its expression, ensued before the compromises which finally permitted the adjustment. In the course of that campaign the national government once sent an expeditionary force against the Church and at another time, in flagrant violation of the Constitution, confiscated the Church's property, dissolved its corporations, proscribed some hundreds of its leaders, and attached a test-oath to the franchise. On its part, the Church expropriated the property of many Gentiles, with and without process of law, maintained a Gay-pay-oo [a reference to the Soviet GPU or secret police] for the immemorial purposes of dictatorships, and ruled by terrorism such of its own members as it had to and such Gentiles as it could. If the principles of the warfare were economic and if its strategy was political, the actual frontline tactics necessitated a long series of murders and one massacre in the grand manner.

Yet this gaudy era too was over in that transition period during which I grew up. Ogden, as the railroad center of the State, had an actual majority of Gentiles and so had achieved a working compromise, a forced equilibrium, long before the rest of Mormonry. The violence of neighbors at one anothers' throats, calling upon God, morality, and the national sovereignty for vindication, had subsided, and very little strife found its way to children. Mormon and Gentile, we grew up together with little awareness that our fathers fought in hostile armies. The child of a Catholic father and a Mormon mother, I myself was evidence of the adjustment. One of my earliest memories is of a little girl's prophecy that the Wasatch mountains would be shaken down upon the plain in the imminent Last Days, and that I, as a Gentile, would be destroyed whereas she, as a Saint, would be saved for glory. Her prediction showed the smug self-righteousness as the Lord's chosen that characterizes all Mormons. Children had, even at four or five, a vivid feeling of membership in a unity, a secret and exotic way of life which entitled them to privileges denied the rest of us. They had also an array of duties, organizations, and badges that set them off, but, being children, frequently found them a bore and could be as skeptical of "primary" as we of St. Joseph's parish were of communion class. But this exclusiveness was less marked in Ogden than in other Utah towns, and far less marked than in the farming country where Mormonry was unalloyed.

The Irish priests of my own communion never preached against the heretics. Protestant ministers were less amiable, but it was only an occasional Gantry in the evangelical sects who bellowed excerpts from the filthy and preposterous anti-Mormon literature of the earlier age. We even mingled in Sunday School without shock. A Mormon meeting house was the place of worship nearest my home, and I was sometimes sent there for instruction until I was about seven, when Rome idly exercised its claim. (Somewhat to my relief. No Puritan divine in the Bay colony ever equalled the long-windedness of any Mormon bishop.) As we grew toward high-school age the lines tightened a little — surprisingly, by the formation of castes. The rudimentary aristocracy of Ogden tended to be Gentile, and a good many people began to feel superior on the simple ground that they had been baptized or married not for eternity but only for this world. As we grew still older, as the efficient Mormon system began to select its missionaries among the boys and point the girls toward marriage in the faith, the cleavage grew distinct. But even then it was unimportant and often humorous. I remember a debate when my high-school class selected a baccalaureate speaker. The Mormon contingent, a minority, proposed one of the Twelve Apostles. An opponent solemnly put Jesus Christ in nomination, and Catholic, Presbyterian, and Baptist united to vote down the Saints.

Polygamy, the sole symbol of Mormonism in the outside world, meant almost nothing to us. The truth of history, which historians have not yet understood, is that to the Mormons themselves it was only a religious symbol, lacked the coercion of economic logic, and was slowly and insensibly found to be a mistake. More briefly still, Mormon polygamy was a caste privilege. "The hierarchy" is the Mormon term for the governing class, the hagiocracy or plutocracy as distinguished from the body of the Church. In general only the hierarchy was permitted to practice polygamy; only the hierarchy could afford to practice it. Thus there were never enough polygamists to establish the tone of any community; there were fewer of them in Ogden than in other towns, and the institution had been driven underground by the persecutions of the 'Nineties. Some of our playmates were known to be polygamous children and the number was increased as we grew up and learned the open secrets of the town. So far as I can remember, that fact meant absolutely nothing to us except as it gave them a certain distinction. By the time we were adolescents some of them, especially the girls, felt, I believe, a kind of embarrassment or social inferiority which the training of the Church did not always transform to fervent superiority. It was, however, frequently compensated by the fact of plutocracy: a polygamist's child was likely to be a well-to-do child. Adolescence also informed us about the furtive practice of polygamy. We saw conspicuously monogamous Mormons paying regular parochial visits to conspicuously unmarried women. But there was no persecution to make such secrecy romantic and, unhappily, they were dreadfully ordinary people. We were just ribald about them. They were easily associated with the folklore that clustered about Brigham Young.

The way in which Mormonism did influence our daily life was to spice it with miracle. In few societies are angels as common as policemen and heaven rather more familiar than a city park: I have had a lifelong tenderness for the world's delusions because I grew up amid prophecy and the glories of the Lord. The whole aim of Brigham Young's policy, after one disastrous experiment, and that of his successors was to abandon the supernatural. The leaders tried to repress the impulses of their people, but the Church had been founded during the Apocalypse by a prophet of God and had always been recruited from the naturally ecstatic. Miracle might be officially denounced but it was a fundamental condition of daily life. Hired girls in my mother's kitchen looked into heaven. God spoke to ditch-diggers and garbage-collectors. On any day, at any corner, any Saint might meet an angel on his way. Patriarchs, prophets, and even deities nightly visited each block in Ogden when the Saints slept. The conversation of all Mormons was predominantly theological, and exegesis might at any moment change to prophecy—and when I say prophecy I mean not only the hosannas of the chosen but literal, detailed soothsaying by qualified seers and revelators under immediate inspiration of God.

Miraculous healing, of course, was commonest. The Lord sustained his people in all ailments from cancer to the common cold, from snakebite to St. Vitus dance. The Mormon elders had their sacred oils and liturgical pantomime, like all priests, but it was extempore miracles by individual Mormons that impressed us. In time of epidemic these were intensified to the classic symptoms of mass hysteria till terror and ecstasy walked the Ogden streets. But other miracles were more picturesque. The widow's cruse had an exact parallel in a miraculous flour sack owned by a widow in my block. All but empty in the fall, it fed her family through a hard winter and when spring came was fuller than it had been in October. The Three Nephites are the Mormon variation of the Wandering Jew, three survivors of the earlier church doomed to wander the earth till the Last Days. Rumor of their presence sometimes spread through the back lots; there were omens and queer sequels of their passing, and I knew several Saints who had seen them. Piety was rewarded by a legacy which paid the mortgage, by the miraculous provision of clothes or horseflesh or quails or manna. Sin received equally direct action: an accident that removed a "bad Mormon" was the judgment of an angry God, and drouth, plagues of grasshoppers and disastrous forest fires meant that the Saints were not living their religion—usually by skimping their tithes.

The destruction of one village by cloudburst and of another by a snowslide was incontrovertible evidence of communal sin.

Deliverance from the plots of the Gentiles was common. The missionaries went forth without purse or scrip throughout the world and they were not always loved. But God's providence went with them. Sandy P., for instance, had been persecuted by the Austrians. One night a mysterious stranger, bearded and dressed in shining white, woke him from sleep and told him that Satan had prompted the villagers to take his life. Sandy rose and fled, the pursuit swiftly gathering behind him. It grew nearer as he labored through the night, and at last he came to a river too wide and rapid for him to cross. With the Mormon readiness for martyrdom, Sandy commended himself to the Lord. But a deep sleep came upon him. When he waked he was on the far side of the river and the frustrated lynchers were cursing him from the other bank.

That miraculous slumber and that white-clad stranger were constantly with us in Mormonry. Portentous words thundered out of silence. The skies above Twelfth Street opened and Olaf Olafson, teamster or swineherd, saw unfolded the future course of his life. In the deep night Granny Gudmanson heard a sonorous, semi-Biblical apostrophe telling her how to improve a granddaughter's morals, how to treat an ailing cow, or how to build an extension on the chicken house. Celestial messengers overtook wayfarers and told them to turn back or armed them against danger on the route. Angels snatched one back from a train fated to be wrecked or came at night to bid one withdraw money from a shaky bank. And anything might be an omen or a portent. Dreams and visions made all the neighbors rapt. A configuration of the clouds, an egg with two yolks, a blight on the radish bed, even a nightmare had been inspired above and could either be interpreted at home or taken to some neighborhood seer for explanation. The Sandy P. I have mentioned was greatly gifted in divination. He kept his large family in a continual tension of miracle—and of terror; for do not suppose that communications from God are always conducive to a peaceful life. At about the age of five one of his grandchildren was repeatedly visited in dreams by another one who was dead. Through Sandy's interpretation the dead child's message was seen to be a warning that a third child was soon to die; and before long they took that third child to an asylum for the insane, which showed that Sandy hadn't missed it far. Sandy's youngest daughter was a classmate of mine at high school, and it was once my privilege to console her when a Mormon swain took some other maiden to a dance. She wept on my shoulder, most enjoyably to us both, but that night an angel visited her in a dream, and she laid the apparition before her prophet-father. Sandy interpreted and Sally sought me out. The Lord, Sandy decided, had pronounced her swain unworthy and had then given her a warning. "The Lord says," Sally told me, "that I must not let a Gentile kiss me any more."

Childhood on the Mormon frontier seems to me a rich heritage. It prepared me for the economic and governmental miracles of these days. It gave me a good many yardsticks for the behavior of the race. It dissuaded me from asking much rationality in human affairs, and it made my faculty of surprise abnormally inactive. It gave me laboratory experience in dictator-ship. . . . And there was also my Mormon grand-father's revelation. The Bishop of Uinta once came to Grandfather's house and told him that the Lord had revealed an intention to bestow his daughter on the bishop as a plural wife. Grandfather was a devout man, a man who had lived his religion, followed the priesthood, and built up the kingdom. So now his piety was rewarded, in miracle. The skies were opened to him and he said, "I prophesy that if you don't get out of here, Brother L., and if you ever mention the revelation to any-one, I will shoot hell out of you."

III

The greatest influence on childhood of the vanished frontier was the freedom we enjoyed. It was an all-inclusive freedom that touched every aspect of our lives. Perhaps I can best suggest it by the relations of the sexes in adolescence, and of this the most vivid symbol I have is a memory from my last year at high school. Toward noon one day a girl and I were coming back toward Ogden over the foothills when we reached a barbed-wire fence. Helen stopped and modestly bade me look the other way lest I glimpse her calf when she climbed the fence. It was a request absolutely in accord with the Ogden folkways—and yet she and I had been alone in the mountains since one o'clock that morning, had climbed a peak and cooked our breakfast on the top.

This, in 1914. It was the privilege of young people, in groups or in couples, to wander in the mountains unchaperoned and unsuspected of misbehavior—and, let me say, rightly unsuspected. At a time when elsewhere in America stringent restrictions were put on all such intercourse outside the home, we were quite free to go where we liked at any hours that pleased us. The form which the convention took is amusing: if we went into the mountains to cook supper we must be back before dawn, and if we wanted to cook breakfast we must be careful not to start till after midnight—otherwise we should spend the night together, which was unthinkable.

The mountains were a force in our freedom. By the time we were eight we went on day-long explorations of the foothills, miles from home, unsupervised by older people. Two or three years later we were beginning to climb the peaks, and by the time we were fourteen we were camping out for days at a time, with or without tents, in canyons a hundred miles up the range. I remember, at fifteen, spending a Christmas vacation in a deserted log cabin deep among the peaks and, with several companions, practicing the not inconsiderable skill that such a stay implies. The frontier had left this impress on us, and when the Boy Scout movement reached Utah just as we grew too old for it, we were contemptuous of its sterilized and evangelized woodscraft. Toward the supervised outdoor-life of the Boy Scouts and of the summer-camp movement which followed we felt a frontiersman's disdain for the counterfeit. At fourteen we were able to take care of ourselves in the wilderness. We wanted no lectures on the hazards of cliffs, poison ivy, and rattlesnakes, and no exhortations about the beauties and purities of nature. As for nature, we were realists—and that, I think, is one of the deepest values we experienced.

But be sure we also paid a tax. This was a time, let me repeat, between two ages. The frontier organization had collapsed and the organization of the industrial order had not taken its place. In this very matter of outdoor skills we suffered. We were practicing a frontier craft but practicing it as an art—survival value had gone from it and so nothing vital depended on it. For instance, I have deeply regretted my ignorance of the native botany and natural history. A generation earlier I should have learned the seasons, qualities, and uses of all native plants and woods, the habits of birds and animals, the use of traps, and the crafts of taxidermy and tanning quite as naturally as I did learn camping and mountain climbing and marksmanship. A few years later I should have learned them from the paid instructors supplied by a community grown suddenly solicitous about its young. I would rather have had the first training than the second certainly, but the second rather than none at all.

Frontier society disciplined children within its necessities; the industrial order taught them from a new sentiment of humanitarian responsibility. Our order granted them the frontier freedom and then, omitting discipline, disregarded them. In some ways it was not a bad system. Psychology approves its impersonality, and it taught children a practical Darwinism—they learned, earlier than children elsewhere, immediate implications of the struggle for existence. But it was a handicap in many ways, since the terms of that struggle were changing and we were not equipped for the new phase. Also, it had its immediate pangs. A regret that has lasted to my thirty-eighth year springs from my inability to become a really good swimmer. I never saw the crawl stroke till boys just older than I began coming home from college—the first generation of college men in Ogden. Now the crawl stroke is probably not universal in Utah even to-day (no river there has more than a thirty-yard stretch deep enough for swimming and there are only a half-dozen lakes in the whole State), but at least the new order teaches it. There was no one to teach me, and that fact has, I think, its significance. A boy who was not born with a knack for boys' skills was simply out of luck. To-day playgrounds and schools swarm with specialists who teach the awkward the approved technics of all games, sports, crafts, skills, and arts. In the Ogden of my time one had them or one never got them. No doubt the preferential treatment of to-day has been carried too far; but one would like to ask analysts and social pathologists how much maladjustment, inadequacy, and frustration they have traced to the wounds inflicted by its lack. Whole areas of experience, whole classes of social adjustment, may well have been thrown out of balance. Certainly it showed in the experience of my generation when we ventured away from Ogden. We had the rituals of our own society, but when we got away from it we had an ineptness that proper supervision of children would have prevented. The elders had brought us into the tribal house, but they had not fitted us to deal with the outlanders.

But one will have to go still deeper into the mind to appraise the basic fact of that frontier remnant. We learned as children, I say, implications of the struggle of existence. Frontier children always learned them, but the industrial order, at even its most squalid levels, delays that instruction and, above those levels, delays it perhaps too long. Among frontiersmen and those who succeeded to their heritage, such a realization has conditioned the entire climate and physiology of thought. The significance of that fundamental has been insufficiently realized and so has been grotesquely distorted by the students of American society. Make of it what you will, to the despair of the hopeful or the apprehension of the merely liberal, one whole division of the Americans was conditioned by it. To that people the struggle of existence is not something that can be repealed by Act of Congress or demolished by rainmakers, philosophers, or the community meeting in prayer.

IV

There remains one frontier-fossil which I touch on with reluctance because, though one of the ideas which students of American life have been most voluble about, it cannot be clearly phrased or adequately defined here. It relates to that cliché of editorial writers—individualism, and its implications in the action of the frontier on the national history.

If as a critic of historical writing I have challenged the simplicities of certain historians about the American frontier, it is because I know of my own experience that frontier life was infinitely complex and not reducible to formula. Consider: I was the child of an apostate Mormon and an apostate Catholic, which suggested that the religious culture of the frontier was far from simple. Across the street from me lived a prosperous miner who made his cross on all documents because he could not write, whose wife could not read, and who did not send his children to school till the town forced him to. He was the type-frontiersman of many thinkers. Yet the book in which I was taught to read was a Pope's *Iliad* of 1781 and, chanting the couplets while I played with the miner's children, I was a laboratory specimen of frontier relationships which no literary or academic formula could express. One of my grandfathers was an English mechanic turned farmer, another was an Italian cavalry officer turned commission merchant. I played with the sons and grandsons of Hawaiian princes, Scandinavian murderers, German geologists with duelling scars, English poets, Spanish mathematicians, French gamblers, Virginia slave-owners, Yankee metaphysicians—of men who came from everywhere, who had every conceivable tradition, education, and canon of taste and behavior. On Memorial Day one ancient hung the Stars and Bars on his front door and mounted guard on it in butternut; the King's birthday was celebrated three doors away; a pastry cook made a Dauphinist of me at ten; down the street Kriss Kringle was venerated instead of Santa Claus; in the next block manuscript letters of Emerson created a whole ritual of behavior; beyond that house a fiercely silent dignity protected a national but locally unmentioned disgrace. Here, God knows, was none of that deadly uniformity of thought, habit, belief, and behavior which books about the frontier detect *in absentia*. I grew up in a culture much more various than I have found anywhere else.

Such a society could have no such coercive singleness of opinion, no such dictatorial and puritanical absolutism, as the books describe. Quite the contrary: it could survive only by the utmost latitude of thought, expression, and personal behavior. We learned to sing "What was your name in the States?" and we sang it in derision, but it had a meaning which the community taught us to respect. We learned that what a man thought about God, the government, the banks, the social revolution, women, sex, alcohol, or the Dauphin, Kriss Kringle, or separation for Ireland was most definitely his own business and not subject to our own views. More, we learned that what he did about them was, within the farthest possible limits of community elasticity, even more his business and not ours. We learned this from our parents and ourselves and from the daily practice of our community. The frontier had lapsed just so far that the lesson was not occasionally italicized by gunfire. We learned, in short, that the frontier had existed as a community, and could have existed, only by the constant exercise of the freedoms, individualisms, and eccentricities which the absentee critic finds it never had.

I may say too that we saw these conditions end. As my generation grew up, industrialism and megalopolis made us their benefactions. Luncheon clubs arrived, and Chautauqua, the Y.M.C.A., the syndicated

press, booster movements, the hysterias and compulsions of wartime
and prohibition, and the liberal point of view and national prosperity.
We had been boys in the despotic uniformity of the intellectuals; we
did not know what uniformity was till their Utopia gathered us in.

At the same time a boy who had once risen from bed at three of a
spring morning with an arctic wind blowing out of the canyons, to irrigate his grandfather's fields with icy water, at just such times as the
community chose to allot—such a boy understood another widely denied quality of the frontier. For the books have struck the frontier
paradox and solved it exactly wrong. They find that the frontier rigidly
suppressed individualism in personal opinion and behavior, whereas
frontiersmen could live together only by virtue of a greater latitude in
such matters than any other part of America permitted. And they find
that the frontier enforced an even greater individualism in economic
and governmental affairs, whereas the very conditions of frontier life
imposed co-operation. When glacial water seeped down my boots in a
canyon wind at hours dictated by the water commissars, I was working in the earliest tradition of the pioneers, locally sixty-five years old
and ninety years earlier than Mr. Ickes. Who but the economic individualist was the proverbial victim of frontier violence? It would be unfair
to allude to the stage-robber and the horse-thief; but surely the rustler,
the claim-jumper, and the fraudulent homesteader were lynched by
co-operative effort; surely the stock-detective, the wolf-hunter, and the
fence-rider were agents of a frontier economy which the individualism
of the critic had small part. How indeed did the frontier community
exist at all except by means of a close-knit co-operation? Especially,
how did a frontier community in the desert exist?

The first job I ever held for a length of time was in a land-title office
and it took me deep into territorial organization. I found the intricate
network of a co-operative system. Not the co-operative merely, for the
frontier had its share of communistic experiments which went the way
of communisms and, it may be, left some skeptical deposit on the
minds of Westerners. Even Mormonism, whose co-operative society
ruled in the name of God by a superior hierarchy, a privileged class, is
a practical answer to the enigma of government, had once quaintly investigated communism. There in the records I digested was the United
Order of Enoch and its melancholy teachings, with the Prophet John

Taylor instead of Stalin to change its alignment. But in the routine of business I had to master the water laws, the grazing laws, the mining code—I had to re-create the frontier's co-operative reduction of chaos. Do not wonder if I have, in print, sometimes suggested that metropolitan authorities on frontier life go and do likewise. Or if I commend to them such casual items from frontier journals as this: "To-day our water committee waited on Stark and Stevens and told them to close up their dams until they come into the agreement." With its entry of a week later that Messrs. Stark and Stevens, kulaks of rugged frontier individualism, have been liquidated.

Well, Ogden of those days was the damnedest place. We were really *fin de siècle,* we were the frontier's afterglow. We saw that glow fade out. We stood, as it were, on a watershed, and also we went down the other side. In the class of 1914 at the Ogden High School there were three girls each of whom had one pair of silk stockings. By the class of 1918 there was no girl who had ever worn cotton stockings to the school, and the town had broken out with something that looked like a bucolic variant of the Junior League. Children of parents who had been conceived in cottonwood lean-tos, with their older brothers looking on, had suddenly become a plutocracy with a mistaken belief that they were a fashionable caste. But the sagebrush debutante is without interest to history and is hereby abandoned to literature, which so far has left her out.

The West: A Plundered Province

(*Harper's Monthly Magazine,* August 1934)

The Westerner remains a bewildering creature to the rest of the nation. Socially he has never blended with the energetic barbarian that for many decades symbolized the Middlewesterner to the appalled East. Politically, also, he has remained distinct from the Middlewesterner, to whom our cartoonists give a more genial grin, a better filled-out frame, and a neater suit of overalls. To cartoonists, the Middlewesterner is the Dirt Farmer and he lives in the Corn Belt and, except occasionally, he is admitted to be a person of some consequence. On the contrary, it is established that the Westerner is gaunt, ragged, and wild-eyed; also he a mendicant and rapacious. Under one arm he clasps a concrete dam or a bundle labelled Government-Built Hard Roads. Other labels dangling from his pocket announce that he has grabbed a lot of pork. They allude to Reclamation Projects, Forest Reserves, Experiment Stations, Grazing Acts, the Desert Land Act, Crop Surveys, Home Loan Banks, and similar privileges. Sometimes, with a quaint candor, they mention Land Grant Railroads, and nearly always a caption informs the reader how much Massachusetts paid in federal taxes and how many miles of concrete in Idaho were laid by the sum. The mendicant's mouth is open: you are to understand that he is bawling for more Privilege and Paternalism. This is his routine appearance when the cartoonists are merely amused, are even willing to tip him a dam or two for the sake of quiet as you would give a child a nickel to go play somewhere else. When, however, the spectacle of human greed dismays the artist the Westerner ceases to be a mere beggar. Gaunt and wild-eyed still, he now rides a whirlwind or rushes over a cliff, invariably dragging the Republic with him, and the lightning round his head is labelled Socialism, Bolshevist Daydreams, or National Bankruptcy. Instead of being merely a national pensioner, he is now a national danger.

This is the symbolism of the Westerner in our metropolitan press—the national wild man, the thunder-bringer, disciple of madness, begetter of economic heresy, immoral nincompoop deluded by maniac visions, forever clamoring, forever threatening the nation's treasury, forever scuttling the ship of state. And yet there is a queer thing: a mere change of clothes gives him a different meaning on quite as large a scale. Put a big hat on his head, cover the ragged overalls with hair pants, and let high heels show beneath them, knot a bandana round his neck—and you have immediately one of the few romantic symbols in American life. He has ceased to be a radical nincompoop and is now a free man living greatly, a rider into the sunset, enrapturer of women in dim theaters, solace of routine-weary men who seek relief in wood-pulp, a figure of glamour in the reverie of adolescents, the only American who has an art and a literature devoted wholly to his celebration. One perceives a certain incompatibility between these avatars.

The land he inhabits has a further symbolism. The West is the loveliest and most enduring of our myths, the only one that has been universally accepted. In that mythology it has worn many faces. It has meant escape, relief, freedom, sanctuary. It has meant opportunity, the new start, the saving chance. It has meant oblivion. It has meant manifest destiny, the heroic wayfaring, the birth and fulfillment of a race. It has, if you like, meant what the fourth house of the sky has meant in poetry and all religions—it has meant Death. But whatever else it has meant, it has always meant strangeness. That meaning may serve to reconcile the incompatibles.

Much energy has been spent in an effort to determine where the West begins. The definitions of poetry and the luncheon clubs are unsatisfactory: vagueness should not be invoked when a precise answer is possible. The West begins where the average annual rainfall drops below twenty inches. When you reach the line which marks that drop— for convenience the one hundredth meridian—you have reached the West. And it is a strange country.

The first part of its strangeness is that it was the last frontier to fall. The American migration leaped across it and in part returned to it from beyond, Californians and Oregonians invading it eastward from their region of plentiful rain. It lingered on invincible after all other frontiers had disappeared, into a time when pioneering was only a memory already shimmering with the rainbow of the never-never. The pioneers' grandchildren were now citizens of orderly manufacturing towns, and when they read of to-day's happenings over the hill they had to think of them as belonging to grandfather's romance. It must clearly be a strange country where the legendary saga of redskins and first-fruits was going on.

It was strange too in that the westward-making Americans, when they came to their last frontier, found that what they had learned on the way there would do them little good. They were the world's great frontiersmen. The whole continent had been frontier, and in subduing it they had learned an exquisite craftsmanship, an exquisite technic, round which much of the national culture had formed. Yet four-fifths of their travel had lain among trees, and the forests had conditioned their craftsmanship. Was not the first chapter in the heroic legend called The Cabin in the Clearing? The roadways through the wilderness were forest-fed streams down which produce could be floated to market and up which the pioneers could make their way by canoe. It was a hard labor, but the very core of American significance was that its results were certain. A man made a clearing with his axe, raised his cabin, fenced his fields, and grew old in security. During the last fifth of the westward journey craftsmanship had had to be somewhat modified, for the Americans had reached the prairies. Yet the problems here differed in degree rather than in kind, for the rivers were still navigable, there was wood for fuel and for the cabin and the fences, and the pioneers could count on even greater security, since this was the richest land in the world. But when they reached the West a craftsmanship refined through more than two centuries, and now felt to be a hereditary way of life, was simply useless.

There could be no cabin in the clearing, for there were no trees to clear and no logs to shape into walls: the pioneer's axe, his greatest tool, was as ineffective as its prototype of the smooth-flint age. The rivers ran contrariwise, most of them ran too shallowly to float a barge or even a canoe, ran brackish water, and in summer sometimes did not run at all. The redskins of the forest had been cruel, pestiferous, and obstinate, but they had never been a match for the Americans. Whereas the mounted Indians of the plains for many years exercised a boisterous superiority over their invaders, easily dominating them because of superior equipment and superior adaptation to the land's necessities. Even the fauna gave the pioneer problems his legendary technic was not adequate to solve. Bear and venison were not to be butchered in the dooryard but had to be followed over the horizon and perhaps could not be met with at all, and the buffalo, the West's beef, had had no precedent in the forests. Not only the fauna was unfamiliar—the tightfisted land would not grow most of the crops which the pioneers had grown to the eastward, would grow little dependably, and nothing at all except under methods radically different from anything the East had known.

It was a strange land, and all its strangeness came from the simple arithmetic of its rainfall. A grudging land—it gave reluctant crops only. A treacherous land—its thin rain might fail without reason or warning, and then there were no crops at all and the pioneer, who had been ignorant of drouths, promptly starved. An inventive land—besides drouth it had other unprepared-for plagues: armies of locusts and beetles, rusts and fungi never encountered in the forests, parasites that destroyed grains and cattle which had been habituated to an Eastern climate. A poisoned land—it was variously salted with strange earths which must be leached away before seeds could germinate. And in the end as in the beginning, a dry land—so that all problems returned to the master problem of how to get enough water on land for which there could never be water enough. In sum, conditions that made unavailing everything that the pioneers had learned, conditions that had to be mastered from scratch if the last frontier was to be subdued.

And, therefore, the final strangeness of the West: it was the place where the frontier culture broke down. The pioneer's tradition of brawn and courage, initiative, individualism, and self-help was unavailing here. He could not conquer this land until history caught up with him. He had, that is, to ally himself with the force which our sentimental critics are sure he wanted to escape from: the Industrial Revolution.

Professor Webb's fine book *The Great Plains* catches the era in the actual process which can only be alluded to here. The country had no rivers for the transportation of goods—so settlement had to await the railroads. It had, except for the alpine regions, no forests. The pioneer might cut sod or mold adobe bricks for a shanty, but he could not fence his claim until industrialism brought him barbed wire. The Plains Indians were better equipped than he for the cavalry campaigns that had to be the West's warfare—so the Industrial Revolution had to give him repeating rifles and repeating pistols, especially the latter. So far as the Winning of the West was a war of conquest, victory waited upon the Spencer, the Winchester, and especially the Colt. And always the first condition: to grow crops where there was not water enough. The Revolution's railroads had to bring westward the Revolution's contrivances for deep cultivation, bigger and tougher plows, new kinds of harrows and surfacers and drills, and its contrivances for large-scale operations, new harvesters and threshers, steam and then gasoline group-machines which quadrupled cultivating power and then quadrupled it again. Finally, the problem of the water itself. The axe-swinging individualist had farmed his small claim with methods not much different from those of Cain's time. The Western pioneer could not farm at all until the Revolution gave him practicable windmills, artesian wells, and the machinery that made his dams possible. When he crossed the hundredth meridian, in order to be Cain at all he had first to become Tubal-Cain.

II

The West, then, was born of industrialism. When the age of machinery crossed the hundredth meridian the frontier, which had so long resisted conquest, promptly came under the plow. But industrialism has other products than machines. Drawn to his heritage partly by advertising, which is one of them, the pioneer found prepared and waiting there for him the worst of all, financial organization.

In one sense the California gold rush won the Civil War, and that has its importance for history; but a greater importance is that it developed a mechanism for the exploitation of the West. The inventive men who devised ways of preventing gold-washers from retaining any outrageous profit from their labors slipped eastward into the true West with a perfected system. From 1860 on the western mountains have poured into the national wealth an unending stream of gold and silver and copper, a stream which was one of the basic forces in the national expansion. It has not made the West wealthy. It has, to be brief, made the East wealthy. Very early the West memorized a moral: the wealth of a country belongs to the owners, and the owners are not the residents or even the stockholders but the manipulators. Gold, silver, copper, all the minerals, oil—you need not look for their increase in the West, nor even among the generations of widows and orphans thoughtfully attached to them by trust companies. The place to look for that increase is the trust companies, and the holding companies.

All this was demonstrated by the mines even before the Westerners arrived in force. The demonstration was repeated on a magnificent scale by the railroads, which added refinements in their ability to loot the Westerner directly as real-estate agencies and common carriers. Meanwhile the government, the press, the whole nation were expediting the rush of settlement. It was *Zeitgeist,* by God! The continent had to be occupied—a bare spot on the map was an affront to the eagle's children. The folk migration, now in its last phase, was speeded up. Manifest destiny received the valuable assistance of high-pressure publicity. Congress, even less aware than the rail-splitters that this was a strange country, helped out by passing, over fifty years, a series of imbecile laws which, even if no other forces had been working to that end, would have insured the West's bankruptcy. To inconceivably stupid government was added the activity of the promoter, who in the West had his last and greatest flowering as a statesman. Able to invade the last wilderness after fifty years of frustration, the migrating folk settled on the West like locusts. And they found finance—the finance of the East—waiting for them.

The catch phrase is "a debtor section." This was not, let me repeat, a problem of shouldering an axe and walking into the forest. The country had to be developed with the tools of the Industrial Revolution, and these cost money. The fencing, the wells, the canals and the dams, the windmills, the gang plows, the cultivators, the tractors had to be paid for. The pioneers have been a debtor class all through history, and the Westerners as debtors differed only in having to pay more. What distinguished them from the rail-splitters was the fact that history had got ahead of them. They had to pay for the development of the country because the financiers were there first, whereas on the earlier frontiers that development had paid for itself.

Costs are not always apparent on the surface. The financing of an expertly wrecked and re-wrecked railroad may be like the salesman's overcoat—you don't see it on the expense account but it's there just the same. The railroads have been made symbolic; but in comparison with some of the other devices of exploitation, their watered capitalizations, rigged bankruptcies, short-and-long-haul differentials, and simple policy of getting what they could seem socialminded and almost sweet. There were the water companies, the road companies, the land companies, the grain-storage companies. There were the mortgage companies. There were the banks. All of them learned from the mines and railroads, improving on instruction, and all of them looted the country in utter security, with the government itself guaranteeing them against retributive action by the despoiled. There was also the Deacon Perkins formula which, because it contains the basic principle, will suffice to describe the whole process.

When money was easy, Deacon Perkins got three per cent for it in his little back room bank at East Corner, Massachusetts. When money was tight, he raised the rate to three and a half or four per cent. So from a thousand East Corners, a thousand Deacon Perkinses sent a nephew West, trusting him just so far as it was impossible to find further legal safeguards. Then borrowing from his own bank at three or four per cent, the Deacon had Nephew Jim lend it in the West at twelve per cent. I say twelve per cent but it was more likely to be sixteen or eighteen per cent, and in the newest districts it went to two per cent a month. If Nephew Jim wanted to kite the rate a little by charging his client a commission for getting the loan, that was his own affair and had nothing to do with the system, which was concerned solely with the spread in interest rates, East and West. A good many Deacon Perkinses got rich on the system. A good many of them also got into the real estate business but, with both government and tradition sending the come-ons West in a steady stream, it was an easy business to get out of with another profit. The point, however, is that this system, a little complicated by the law of corporations, was precisely that of the manipulators. They were Eastern corporations and they financed themselves at two per cent in order to charge twenty per cent interest against the West, over and beyond the profits of trade, finance, monopoly, combination, and the normal increase of development. They had learned how to make the country pay. Their system was automatic and self-adjusting, an excellent system—for the East.

Besides taking over the country, then, the East added direct usury. The customary justification has mentioned empire-building—this tax was merely the fee which the strong men, the leaders, assessed for opening up the country. The explanation sounds sufficiently like that of other empire-builders who got theirs without risk of loss to sound convincing, and it probably satisfies the principles of imperial expansion in the textbooks. It has not, however, had a wide popularity in the West. The Westerner has seen palaces rise on Fifth Avenue and the endowments of universities and foundations increase with a rapidity that establishes the social conscience of his despoilers. The water company that took a mortgage on his farm grew into a bank, joined a network of interlocked pilfering agencies, changed into a holding company, and ended as an underwriter of railroad bonds and a depressant of farm prices in the interest of someone's foreign trade. In his whole country no one has ever been able to borrow money or make a shipment or set a price except at the discretion of a board of directors in the East, whose only interest was to sequester Western property as an accessory of another section's finance. He has contributed to those palaces and endowments just precisely what his predecessors in the pioneering system were enabled to keep for themselves. Meanwhile, the few alpine forests of the West were leveled, its minerals were mined and smelted, all its resources were drained off through the perfectly engineered gutters of a system designed to flow eastward. It may be empire-building. The Westerner may be excused if it has looked to him like simple plunder.

Meanwhile the *Chicago Tribune,* the *New York Times,* and similar organs of his despoilers have maintained their amusing howl about those federal taxes. Look how New York and Illinois, Massachusetts and Pennsylvania contribute fifty- or a hundred-fold to the national treasury, and look how their money is commandeered to build roads and maintain bureaus in the begging West. So long as this appears to be mere cynicism, the West enjoys the show, having had an experience that begets an enjoyment of cynicism. But sometimes the spokesmen seem really to believe what they are saying, seem really to be protesting against a form of confiscation, and then one hears above the sage the sound of prolonged and acid laughter.

III

So far as there is any theory in the politics of sectional warfare beyond the simple one of "them who can, gets," it is this: that the plundering of one section for the benefit of another is justifiable if the prosperity of the second spills over enough to compensate the first for what it has been robbed of. The theory sanctioned the tariffs, trusts, and service charges that the dominant East used as implements of exploitation. Since, however, the West flouted theory by going and staying bankrupt, it has for fifty years been customary to supplement the theory, which may be described as the horse-feathers school of thought, with occasional backshish. The West has sometimes been tipped a fractional per cent of its annual tribute in the form of government works or social supervision. This backshish is what the Eastern press so regularly laments, and yet it is the time-honored way of dealing with agrarian unrest. Throughout history, governments have found it expedient to buy off the farmers when they grow troublesome in order to sell them out at a profit later on. East of the hundredth meridian the agrarians have satisfactorily responded to that method. It has failed in the rainless country because the manipulators took too large an equity to begin with—they set the empire-builder's fee too high. The West has never had enough to come back on. It is the one section of the country in which bankruptcy, both actuarial and absolute, has been the determining condition from the start.

Newspapers are practicing relativists. A proposal to widen the scope of the horse-feathers policy has always been statesmanship. If you are

a creditor seeking by tariffs or mergers to expedite the plundering of
the West you become ipso facto a person of patriotic vision. If, however, you try to slow up the rate of exploitation, you are just an anar-
chist pushing the Republic over the cliff in the name of Utopia. Fair
enough, but at least it may be explained that the cartoonists are wrong
about Utopia. The West exists only by rigorous adaptation to a realistic climate. It has no vision of perfection and has been unable to sprout
belief in planned economies. Millennial visions in America are native
to areas of forty inches annual rainfall or above. Nevertheless, the accepted symbol is accurate: throughout its existence the West has produced much of the agitation known in the East as radical and has
wholeheartedly supported all it did not produce. Most notably, schemes
to debase the currency. Greenbackery, bimetalism, proposals for the
cancellation of mortgages, for the reduction of usury, for even more
direct methods with debt—all of them have either been born in the
West or have had their apogee there. Nothing can exceed the horror
of a banker who owns the mortgages or receives the usury or has participated in the mergers at which the reduction would be aimed. He
knows that the Republic would be brought down by the collapse of
its cornerstone, the sanctity of property; and in his way he is quite
right. Only, the Westerner in his madness has experienced the fall of
the Republic. It was property private to him that proved to lie outside
the churchyard. The Republic crumbled fifty years ago, about the time
a bank took over his first co-operative water company, and his radicalism consists of inability to see wherein lies the heinousness of trying to get back some part of what was stolen from him at the muzzle
of a gun.

   The late flurry of doom, which agitated literary folk and frightened
customers' men and young communists, anticipated a revolution so
vague that one could make out little except that it would be bloody
and soon. The prospect was stimulating but uncorrected by the historical approach. Agrarian revolutions in America, as I have pointed
out, have always yielded to simple bribery, and our political revolutions have been hamstrung by the more economical method of enlist-
ing their leaders on the side of the virtuous. If American history shows
anything, it makes clear that revolution by means of the class struggle
is inconceivable. The one revolution that did come to actual warfare in

America was a sectional revolution, and it is likely that any new one would take the same form. If the nation weakened sufficiently, conceivably it might split along the cleavage-lines of the sections. (Perhaps intrasectional revolution could then follow the classics. While the united soviets of the steel country marched out to liquidate the kulaks of Western Pennsylvania, we might find General Dawes' Minute Men arming themselves with castor oil to extirpate the LaFollettes, take over the co-operative creameries of the Green Bay region, and exile the last socialist councilman of Milwaukee.) The prospect of such fission would not appall the West. When empires crumble it is the provinces that go first, and the plundered province would slide into the sea with a definite exhilaration. Imagine repossessing the mines, the oil, the power-lines, the cattle-ranges and the wheatfields—imagine going into the first conference of independent sections prepared to bargain as proprietors, not as tenants or peons! The West could correct the interest-spread and realign the tariffs on a basis of realism. It could demand something more than the *pourboire* of a dam or some hard roads. Conceivably, Massachusetts and Pennsylvania would learn something from federated bargaining that they have omitted to infer from federal taxes.

This, however, is a virtual movement, an economic pipe dream kin to the editorials in liberal journals but unrelated to the actual pressures exerted by people who are carrying on economic struggles. The West has no hope of such a dissolution, being able to estimate the strength of chains from their weight. It anticipates neither a breakup of the American economy nor any substantial readjustment of its part in that drainage system. It can fight the battle only on the terms laid down. If you can't win the campaign you try to win the individual engagement; if you can't reduce the salient you make a sortie against a limited portion of the front line. Reversal of the intersectional system is beyond hope, no return to the West of its equity in the nation is conceivable. In effect, no matter how the exterior alters, the East will go on producing protected goods for the West to buy in produce which the East's protection has depreciated. The West cannot modify the conditions but will continue to make sorties against the front line. The equity is not recoverable, but here and there the forced debt may be in part reduced. Cartoonists may as well dig in for a long winter; the West will remain radical. Necessarily, it will always be shoving the Republic over the same old cliff, bellowing one or another insanity. The actual form of insanity will change with chance and opportunism, but the force behind it will remain constant, a desire to rob the robbers of some fraction of their loot. That is part of the West's strangeness: it has always had an inexplicable hankering to get back its own.

Those of its spokesmen who resisted purchase have always been regarded as near relatives of the wild jackass. This too has an irony of its own, considering the politicians who have been the West's governors when they have not been simply the agents of its despoilers. With the greatest kindness, Congress has frequently taken time off to help the West develop institutions fitted to its conditions. Amiable thinkers, who had the traditions of the well-watered country to guide them, produced a series of inconceivable stupidities for the formation of the West—and had the power to convert stupidity into law. Hence another part of the West's strangeness: its lawlessness. Quoting Professor Webb: "No law has ever been made by the Federal government that is satisfactorily adapted to the arid region."

The West soon realistically phrased the Homestead Act under which the government invited occupation: Uncle Sam bets you a hundred and sixty acres that you'll starve in less than five years. It was a safe bet and all alterations made in the odds were just as safe. Two only of such alterations need be mentioned. Congress, perceiving a generation too late that the country could not be farmed but might be grazed, authorized patents fully one-tenth the size of the minimum that would permit grazing. But that was enlightened vision compared to another bounty—one of Pennsylvania's little gratuities to Wyoming—under whose terms the Westerner might occupy his land provided he would grow trees on it. God's forestry had not been that ambitious, but it was just lawlessness that withheld the West from complying. The Homestead Act itself provided for units of settlement that had made forests and prairies productive but just one-eighth the size required in the region of thin rain.

The Westerner had his choice. He could become a social producer by occupying and developing the country illegally, in flat defiance of the law, or he could become a social charge by obeying the law and pauperizing himself. He did both. Survival in the West has been won at the price of actual or constructive illegality; beyond the hundredth meridian, the basic social institutions have always been beyond the law of the land, which catches up with them slowly and only in part. And of course, governmental stupidity co-operating with promotional skin games, hundreds of thousands of Westerners have failed in their pioneering efforts. These bankrupts form the unlovely finale of the westward wayfaring, the squalor in which the folk movement ended. Brought West by *Zeitgeist* and advertising, they were asked to make the country produce what it could not produce and to do the job under regulations that doubled the grim humor of the farce. They are the West's paupers, victims of the East's advertising campaign for unearned increment; and both government and the East have forgotten them except as exasperating dependents who must be fed at someone's expense. Probably at the expense of the land-grant railroads or those federal taxpayers in Pennsylvania.

Government's prodigal stupidity abetted them throughout. They were brought to a country unfitted to produce the crops they were asked to grow—a country which, under the conditions Congress laid on them, could support them at best only two years in five and, one year in five, would wipe them out altogether. It was among these foreordained victims of a country which Congress could not understand that Pennsylvania's *pourboires* were expended. Here the dams and canals were built and the whole stupendous asininity of Reclamation enacted. God couldn't grow trees in this country but Congress would.

So now, after sprinkling those taxes on the alkali, Congress, we hear, proposes to buy back the land and let the alkali have its turn at reclamation. The dams and canals built, the generations bankrupted, the land is discovered to be what the maps label it, desert. It was, we are told, sub-marginal land all along. This discovery, in view of its history, is hardly of this world—belonging rather to the cosmic reaches. But let it go: the West is a strange country.

IV

Remember that this sub-marginal land, the sage and greasewood of the West's ultimate barrens, witnessed the end of a historic process. The rainless country was the last frontier, and in its poisoned areas, without dignity, the wayfaring Americans came to the end of their story. Reclamation is a shining image of something or other—aspiration, it may be, or futility. Confronted by the last acres of the tradition and finding them incapable of producing, the Americans wasted millions trying to enforce their will on the desert. The impulse and the glory of the migration died hard but, when the desert was conceded to be desert in spirit of will-power, they died at last, in something between pathos and farce. So here ends ingloriously what began gloriously on the Atlantic littoral, below the falls line; and the last phase of the westward wayfaring has the appearance of a joke.

Yet, this having always been a country of paradox, there is something more than a joke. Before that ending the Westerner learned something. Implicit in the westward surge, both a product and a condition of it, was the sentiment that has been called, none too accurately, the American dream. It is a complex sentiment not too easily to be phrased. The plain evidence of the frontier movement, from the falls line on, indicated that there could be no limit but the sky to what the Americans might do. The sublimate of our entire experience was just this: here was a swamp and look! here is Chicago. Every decade of expansion, every new district that was opened, backed up the evidence till such an expectation was absolutely integral with the national progress. There was no limit but the sky: American ingenuity, American will power, American energy could be stopped by nothing whatever but would go on forever building Chicagos. It was a dream that, in the nature of things, had to be wrecked on reality sometime, but in actual fact the West was the first point of impact. Just as the pioneer had to give up his axe and learn mechanics when he crossed the hundredth meridian, just as he had to abandon his traditional individualism, so he had to reconcile himself to the iron determinism he faced. In the arid country just so much is possible, and when that limit has been reached nothing more can be done. The West was industry's stepchild, but it set a boundary beyond which industrialism could not go. American ingenuity, will power, and energy were spectacular qualities, but, against the fact of rainfall, they simply didn't count. The mountains and the high plains, which had seen the end of the frontier movement and had caused the collapse of the pioneer culture, thus also set the first full stop to the American dream. Of the Americans, it was the Westerners who first understood that there are other limits than the sky. To that extent they led the nation. It may be that to the same extent they will have a better adjustment to the days ahead.

There at least, and not in the symbolism that has attached to them, is to be looked for the national significance of the West. They learned adaptation: they built their institutions, illegally for the most part and against the will of their plunderers, in accordance with the necessities of a climate that rigorously defined the possible. It was the necessities of the mining codes that first gave the clue of collectivism, and these codes were the nucleus round which the commonwealths coalesced. The law of real estate in part and the law of water rights in entirety followed this lead; the axe-swinger's individualism, in the desert, yielded to an effort much more co-operative. There was no other way in which the land could be occupied; this was determinism, and the Westerners accepted it, and not even their manipulators could do much against the plain drift of necessity. To the dismay of bondholders and cartoonists, the West is integrated collectively. It will stay that way while climate is climate. That also may be a portent for the nation whose dream has receded.

Looted, betrayed, sold out, the Westerner is a man whose history has been just a series of large-scale jokes. That comicality has helped to form the image which the dominant East has chosen to recognize. But it is not altogether a comic image. The wild-eyed figure of the cartoons attests to a certain Eastern uneasiness, and there is the strangeness of the chaps and sombrero. It is wise to end on that strangeness. For the romantic clothes are only occupational garments, a work suit, the sign of the Westerner's adaptation to the conditions of one of his trades. Their true symbolism is not romance but intelligent acceptance of the conditions. The American dream was ended, but cattle could be grazed in this country, and these were the best outfit for the job, so he put them on. So dressing himself, he became a romantic symbol to people who live in areas of greater rain, but do not be fooled. He is a tough, tenacious, overworked, and cynical person, with no more romance to him than the greasewood and alkali in which he labors. He is the first American who has worked out a communal adaptation to his country, abandoning the hope that any crossroads might become Chicago. The long pull may show—history has precedents—that the dispossessed have the laugh on their conquerors.

The Anxious West

(*Harper's Magazine,* December 1946)

The West is plains, mountains, and desert. Its landscape is dramatic, its climate violent. Its history is dramatic and paradoxical, and parts of it important to both East and West never happened. Its natural wealth is enormous and belongs mostly to the East and the national government. Its inhabitants, products of its landscape, climate, and history, are a volatile, expansive people, energetic extroverts at the base of whose consciousness are tensions and conflicts. They are the fall guys of the United States and have been victimized by everybody, most disastrously by themselves. They have repeatedly scared the nation at large and now dream of seceding from it but have never been able to work together or trust one another. They have worked out an adaptation to their incredible environment which is one of the pleasantest ways of life ever known and this culture holds a shining promise for the United States, a promise which is countersigned by world movements. They are the only Americans today who look toward the future with hope and confidence and they ignore the elements in themselves which bring both in question. They are children of paradox and begetters of paradox.

The first clue to them is their language. They speak standard American and speak it with fewer local tunes and shadings than any other section. The Western voice has none of the nasality and flatness of the
Midwest. There is a Western drawl and it is on the increase but it is a
phony. It is part Southern and part Hoosier. The Southern ingredient
arrived with deserters from the armies during the Civil War—their
trail can be traced on the map in various Virginia cities, Richmonds,
Davisvilles and the like, and innumerable Secesh Creeks, Confederate
Bars, and Rebel Gulches. It was supplemented after the war by a migration that amounted to a stampede and is still known in the West as
the left wing of Price's army. There was a third increment when the
cattle began to move to the northern range. All three, however, were
soon diluted to the vanishing point and there was no revival of the
drawl till the West began to succumb to the most damaging of its illu-
sions, the notion that it is universally a race of cowpokes.

That revival was self-conscious and originally it was for comic purposes only—which brought in the Hoosier tune by affinity, the Hoosiers
having dedicated themselves to bucolic humor unto all eternity. But
the illusion has proved so comforting and has received such support
from the movies and the radio that the future looks ominous. Whereas
twenty-five years ago switching on the drawl notified the listener that
a joke was in process, now it is histrionic. Westerners, too many of
them, have an urge to dramatize themselves to strangers as the Old
Ranger or the Old Trail Boss. So far it is only drama but the role is
taking hold. Increasingly the West sees itself as a congeries of big
cow outfits before the freeze of 1886. It has always been facile at self-
deception; that it has chosen this illusion to erect into a myth may be
comic to outsiders but could end by being tragic to the West.

A good ear can make out some Westernisms. The habitual use of
"home" for "house" is not confined to the West and neither is a characteristic handling of *eg* sounds, but the universal substitution of "lady"
for "woman" comes close to being diagnostic and the Westerner gives
himself away by the mayhem he commits on the sounds represented
by *au* and *ol*. You can compose a shibboleth that will unmask him at
the passages of Jordan—any such sequence as "Aunt Augusta's naughty
daughter and her autumnal doll." He may have been educated at Ox-
ford and lived for fifty years in Brooklyn but when he speaks such
words he reverts to his childhood on Nine Mile.

Western speech is poetic, shot with fantasy, running over with metaphor. The figures of all the tongues in the melting pot and all the romantic occupations that are commonplace in the West have left a deposit on the common speech, superimposed on a similar deposit from the violent frontier. The common humor is also specific. Southern humor is oratorical and anecdotal; as the world knows, Yankee humor runs to dryness and underemphasis; Midwestern humor is nervous and hyperbolic—but Western humor is self-depreciating, disparagement suspended in a medium of irony. It is partly explained by the fundamental fact that the West is at the mercy of the physical environment but the rest of the explanation is more revealing still: much Western humor expresses an inner chagrin.

Westerners are big men, according to the Army the biggest in the country. Also they are heavy men; an extraordinary percentage of them are fat. Elsewhere metropolitan America has adopted a diet proper to the sedentary life, but the Western city dweller eats a cowhand's meals. His breakfast egg is plural and is usually accompanied by meat, frequently a steak, and always by fried potatoes. Fried potatoes are the West's seasoning, in fact; they are served with practically everything except ice cream. The breakfast steak is likely to be served with pancakes as well and they are likely to be a side dish at lunch. The excellence of Western pastry increases the consumption of starch. You may know that you have reached the true West when you are served salads embedded in gelatine or cottage cheese and when you begin to encounter good pies in restaurants. Public or private, Western pies and cakes are the best in the country; so are Western breads and, in spite of the literary cliché about the South, Western rolls and biscuits too. They help to produce the Western waistline.

Western cooking has vastly improved in the past quarter of a century. But the West only reluctantly gives up the idea that the thing to do with a steak is to fry it—fry it hard—with the result that hostesses and waitresses habitually set out several kinds of bottled sauces to make it edible and there is a big business in bicarbonate of soda. A sense of the salad has grown too. You seldom encounter the mixtures of cold veal, grapes, and boiled dressing that meant salad when I was a boy in the West, but you seldom encounter a plain green salad either. Only an occasional restaurant carries it on the menu and at some of those that do you may still have to explain that you don't want boiled carrots and lima beans in it. Western vegetables and fruits, which the unexhausted mineral soil makes the best in the country, have come into their own during the past generation; Westerners now eat them passionately. But they have added them to, rather than substituted them for, the proteins, fats, and starches which they have always eaten passionately. The word is revealing: Westerners are passionate eaters, and this passion may be a displacement of others.

The diet is proper for ranch hands, farmers, and outdoor workers in general, who really have the lean, muscular look that is Western to illustrators and the movies. But it tends to bring the townsman's chest down to his waist at thirty and to pad his neck with fat at forty. I should like to speak more agreeably of Western women, young women, and girls—to call them buxom, deep-breasted, strong-thewed, fit to be the mates and mothers of big men. Mathematics forbids; too high a percentage of them are just fat. Overeating gives them thick ankles, cylindrical calves, big behinds, wide waists, heavy breasts. They must be the bulwark of the corset industry but all in vain. Elizabeth Arden could make a killing by establishing a chain of her Maine Chance reducing farms from the Missouri to the Pacific.

The cosmetic end of Miss Arden's business is a more fundamental necessity in the West than elsewhere, for the environment levies a heavy tax on women. There is no escape from or alleviation of Western sun, wind, and dryness. Women's hair fades and grows brittle. Their skin dries, coarsens, and wrinkles. They tend to look older than they are and this effect is progressive. A girl of eighteen may look matronly only because she eats too much, but by the time she is forty she may look fifty because the climate has had its way with her.

II

Sun, wind, aridity—they condition life in the West, where men and society are more dominated by the natural environment than anywhere else in the United States. That Western society has survived at all is proof of a successful adaptation to them, and it is an engaging adaptation. The Western way of life is a good one. Westerners, I think, have a better time than any other Americans: they enjoy themselves more. The paradox is that mastering their environment has not given them self-confidence. They brag, they are obsessive and coercive and gang-minded; an awareness that something is wrong gnaws at them.

Basic in the Western way of life is the naturalness of living much in the open. You do not need the weather forecast in order to set the date for a picnic, a camping trip, a hunting or fishing or skiing expedition; for a calendar will do. The climate is violent but it is also stable, and in the seasons when rain is not to be expected there will be no rain. Winters are short except in the high country, which lengthens the season for summer sports, and the high country is so accessible that the season for winter sports lasts through June and in some places all year. The great fact is the mountains. Mountains are within the driving range of all Westerners, even those on the eastern edge of the high plains who can reach the Black Hills. They are a refuge from heat and dust, from the aridity that dehydrates you and the intensity of sun that shrinks the ego. The forests are in the mountains, with the fish and game, the trails, the creeks, the ski runs, and the cliffs that need rope work. More important still, they put solitude and silence at the disposal of everyone. Western life has come to incorporate mountain living. A national forest near large towns—the Wasatch Forest for instance, which straddles the range it is named for just above Salt Lake City—will have a million or more visitors in the course of a year, practically all of them from the immediate vicinity.

As a result most Westerners are hunters and fishermen and campers. Most of them are in some degree mountain climbers, naturalists, geologists. They know nature at first hand and intimately, are adept at outdoor skills, can maintain themselves comfortably in the wilderness. Furthermore, since they have grown up to these things naturally they have not romanticized or stylized them—except, that is, for the myth of the cattle business. There are no rituals. A Westerner cooking a meal in the forest is simply cooking a meal in the best way with the means at hand—there is none of the high-church nonsense that accompanies outdoor cooking in Westchester or Long Island. Westerners are habituated to firearms and the right to bear them has not been abridged, but not even the movies have succeeded in tricking out Western firearms with the twaddle that has developed about them in the South.

Such folkways have produced the West's happiest contribution to architecture. I do not mean the bungalow, which is an eyesore, but the mountain cabin. It is made of logs, usually lodgepole pine, which are peeled and varnished with clear shellac; sometimes for the exterior surfaces a little burnt sienna is added to the shellac. The logs are chinked with concrete; chimneys and fireplaces are made of stones ("rocks" in the West) from the nearest creek. The result is a charming, comfortable, functional dwelling which blends with the landscape, warm in winter, cool in summer, almost vermin-proof. It is excellent everywhere except when the resort business parodies it by covering steel and concrete hotels with a veneer of logs.

An astonishingly large number of Westerners own such cabins or still more inexpensive camps in the mountains. They visit them at all seasons, not only for the annual vacation and at weekends but on momentary impulse. Similar cabins and camps can be rented everywhere. And almost no one is too poor to own an automobile and a camping outfit; those who use them, in fact, get farther into the wilderness and come to know it better than those with fixed camps. So the frontier's mastery of the outdoors has remained a part of Western life. It has contributed alike to the realism and the mysticism that make so striking a mixture in the Western consciousness. Familiarity with the skills of Western occupations is also widespread; most Westerners know something about mining, prospecting, engineering, lumbering, sheep growing, and cattle raising. The Westerner is the best American outdoorsman and he is almost the only remaining American who rides a horse naturally, not as one practicing a cult.

All these sports and occupations have pleasantly vivified Western dress, especially the cattle business. The working cowpoke, of course, wears levis, a Big Yank shirt, and a pair of nine-dollar Acme boots. But the dress-up tradition of his trade, supported by the same tradition in lumbering and mining, has given Western clothes a moderate, satisfying flamboyance: half-gallon hats, saddle-shop belts with silver buckles, bright but not insistent colors in shirts and scarves, a species of riding trousers better than breeches or jodhpurs and for women much more attractive. (Turquoises, ninety-dollar boots, boots anywhere away from the presence of horses, hats beyond a gallon, and purple, orange, magenta, and vermilion shirts mean dudes or professional entertainers.)

The cattle business has also supplied the West's autochthonous festival, the rodeo. (Accent the first syllable.) It has been so commercialized and stylized that the pure form is to be seen only in small towns where cowhands from neighboring ranches do the riding. Nevertheless, the circuit shows, whose performers are as much professionals as baseball players, are an important contribution to entertainment. Their spectacles and skills are derived from a still living reality and their roots go down to an authentic past.

Not so much can be said for another Western festival whose generic name might be Frontier Week. It is the property of the Chamber of Commerce, a bad custodian for the expansive spirit. It is aimed at the tourist trade and retail sales. It is a fake and it is objectionable. (Montana, the most urbane and most skeptical of Western states, is least given to it.) There is no harm in people's dressing up in the costumes of their ancestors, though silk coats, flowered vests, black mitts, and hoopskirts are tolerably grotesque. There is no harm in growing beards, though the vehemence with which the modern West grows them suggests a fear that it has not inherited all the frontier masculinity they are supposed to signify. There is no harm in celebrating the past if the celebration involves some knowledge of what it was or some respect for it, but Frontier Week seldom involves either. It is conducted without reference to history, it is empty of idea and emotion, its data are anachronistic and preposterous. Unlike a rodeo or a country fair, it has no cultural validity. Even its much-advertised release from restraints is pumped-up and cold.

It is, however, extremely revealing. Western towns by the hundred submit to Frontier Week and make a big noise about it at the direction of the Chamber of Commerce, for business reasons. They grow beards as an assist to sales—at the same command. They submit to being fined, ducked, or otherwise penalized if the beards won't grow. The kind of Westerner whom Frontier Week is supposed to commemorate would have slugged or if need be taken a shot at anyone who ventured to tell him how to wear his hair. He was an individualist with all that individualism implied in the West for both good and ill, but the contemporary beard-grower is just a coerced advertiser. He accommodates his behavior to sales talk and gang dictation and what is worse, he is advertising a myth. He symbolizes several of the unhealthiest forces in Western life.

In twenty-five years the celebration of the Western past has grown enormously. It has grown, however, chiefly in business sagacity and in

noise; little increase in knowledge or understanding is visible. The West
has found its history a valuable asset but remains widely uninterested
in doing anything about it beyond hoking it up for tourists. Western
antiquarians, local historians, collectors, and annalists are as enthusias-
tic and expert as those anywhere else, but they are few and forlorn; the
historical societies (several of them very distinguished), societies for
the preservation of antiquities, and similar groups, are small, handi-
capped by poverty, and under some public derision. Apart from advertising or at most ancestor worship, public feeling for the past is lethar-
gic. In three months of Western travel I saw only one private enterprise
devoted to celebrating local history which was both sincerely intended
as a public service and likely to succeed. That was the work of Charles
A. Bovey, who began by making the amazing collection at Great Falls,
Montana, that is called Old Town and has gone on to restore Virginia
City. I cannot praise it too highly, but what struck me was not only Mr.
Bovey's success but the fact that he had been privileged to use his own
money exclusively. Practically all the other non-utilitarian efforts to
recover the Western past or to preserve its vestiges are the work of the
federal government, and they are usually conceived and carried out by
Easterners.

The effort to expand the tourist business is not, however, the only explanation for the uninformed noise which the West is making about its
past. Much of it shows the influence of the horse operas, which are the
West's favorite movies, and of the radio programs which alternate sup-
posedly Western songs and allegedly frontier dramas all day long, with a
large part of the West listening. But the ultimate responsibility cannot be
charged to Hollywood and Tin Pan Alley, for the urge they satisfy originates in the West itself and reveals a tension in the Western consciousness. The past quarter century has transferred the myth of the old West
from fiction and the screen square into that consciousness, where it is beginning to show resemblances to the myth of the Old South.

The most significant aspect of this revelation is that the West has
chosen to base its myth on the business that was of all Western businesses most unregardful of public rights and decencies, most exploita-
tive, and most destructive. The Cattle Kingdom did more damage to
the West than anything else in all its economy of liquidation. As a
mythology it will do even worse damage hereafter.

III

Much other evidence suggests psychic conflicts. For instance, Jesus is advertised in the Northwest as insistently as in southern California and if possible more vulgarly. Innumerable small crank religions saturate Oregon and Washington and fan out across the neighboring states. They range from simple but extreme evangelism far into mental disease. Their emotional content is squalid and their compulsiveness attests a widespread inner frustration. Or take public attitudes toward liquor, which in the Northwest, Idaho, and Utah are downright schizophrenic.

These states desire drinking to be surreptitious, excessive, and un-civilized and have preserved all the evils of prohibition. In Utah this is understandable, since teetotalism is a tenet of the Mormon Church and all drinking has to be officially attributed to the Gentiles, though inquiry develops that the state liquor stores do their highest per capita business in purely Mormon communities. (The hamlet of Wendover is trying to secede from Utah and attach itself to the franker if frowsier culture of Nevada.) Idaho somewhat reduces the worst absurdities of the common system—the prohibition of liquor with meals and the re-fusal to sell it in less than bottle lots—by licensing cocktail bars at ho-tels so long as they pretend to be under a different management. It nevertheless refuses to let you drink less than a bottle in a hotel room; and it requires a temperate person to seek out the institution called a private club.

That institution is the worst result of the liquor laws in Washington and Oregon, where the system is most vicious—and most characteris-tic, since both states have always done some of the most brutal drink-ing in the United States and both had prohibition societies before they had local governments. The club is the customary answer to prohibitory laws: it is a speakeasy. It is unregulated, protected, frequently gang-owned, a place for getting drunk, and it serves prohibition liquor. Ro-mantic Easterners nostalgic for the indecencies of the Incredible Era are advised to try Portland or Seattle.

The attitude thus revealed is pointed up by another one. Nothing is more shocking to a resident of the East than to come out of the speak-easy where he has had to go for his six o'clock cocktail and enter a restaurant, hotel, grocery, drugstore, railroad station, barber shop,

beauty parlor, or department store where the natives are lined up by
the dozen playing slot machines. They are universal from the Dakotas
on, though of course in Utah they are more or less under cover, and
they are in all public places except churches. And in a town which
shall be nameless I saw the Episcopal rector dropping a stack of half-
dollars into one, no doubt in the hope of increasing his poor fund—
a vain hope since the slot machine is the most openly crooked and
cynical of all gambling devices, in fact is not a gambling device at all.
The machines are owned by syndicates, which implies widespread corruption of police officials and occasional gang wars, and they are
played constantly and obsessively by everyone more than four feet tall,
male or female. The obsessiveness is what strikes a visitor. The universal patronage of admittedly crooked machines cannot be explained by
the Westerner's traditional eagerness to take a chance or by his liking
for being treated as a sucker. It stems from unconscious anxiety and
dissatisfaction.

Genuine gambling is wide open in the West (again Utah requires a
veneer of hypocrisy) but appears to be conducted with decency everywhere except in Nevada. I am not referring to such places as Reno and
Las Vegas which are organized to trim Easterners who can afford to be
trimmed and which, I suppose, maintain the institutional honesties of
gambling as rigorously as Monte Carlo. As a Westerner I cannot weep
at the sight of Eastern dudes leaving their money in the West, nor re-
frain from reflecting that the take is only a small percentage of the sum
lifted from well-heeled Westerners by New York alone. I am referring
to the repulsive little dives in unknown Nevada hamlets which are pa-
tronized wholly by local residents.

No town is too small to have a combination lunchroom, bar, and
gambling joint where a fish-eyed house man sits at his frowsy table
dealing for a handful of customers—a couple of high school girls, a
couple of phony cowpokes and a couple of real ones, some machinists
from the railroad, a grade school teacher, and a bum who has cadged a
dollar from a tourist. They absorb a percentage of the town's earnings
every day. And they have a discernible relation to the signs set up along
the roads leading to Fernley, the only signs I have ever seen advertising the desirability of getting drunk. In those signs there may be expansive Western humor and in the squalid dives there may be some of

the Western freedom which the State of Nevada itself advertises at all its borders, adding that it has no sales tax, no income tax, no inheritance tax, and no corporation tax. But also they testify to the West's inner awareness that something is lacking in the way it lives.

IV

To Eastern eyes Western cities, most of which are just big towns, seem clean, neat, glistening, even new. Part of this shininess is due to the fact that few have slums and very few have industrial slums, and part to the thin air. Most of it, however, comes from the drama of the Western landscape. You cross a long stretch of treeless country and suddenly you reach such a town as Pierre or Miles City which has been growing shade trees ever since the first settlers came. The overwhelming Western sun is diffused, the wind is splintered, there are coolness and dampness. The shade has a spiritual, even a mystical quality, and as it assuages you it give you a vivid sense of the desperate and dogged aspiration that produced it. Or the drama may be the mountains where they seem to rise straight out of the town square—at Missoula, Ogden, Colorado Springs, dozens of other places. But the greatest drama comes from the miracle on which the entire life of the West rests, irrigation.

Climb, for instance, out of the valley of the Snake at Glenn's Ferry and head into the desert. For those who love the desert there is great beauty here but it is a beauty of sterility, in the imminence of death, sagebrush flats leading the eye across nothingness till barren mountains put a bound to space. Eventually you will come to a river and will instantly understand why it was named the Boise—and how infinitely more worthy its valley is of the name now because its waters have been diverted across the land. You cross the great canals with a kindling awareness of the achievement they represent and the tremendous imagination they realize. So you come into the town of Boise. After such a prologue, against such a backdrop, a drab and obsolescent town would seem resplendent, but Boise is neither. Its trees and lawns, the contemporaneousness of its hotels, its shop windows, its inbound and outbound freight traffic, the multifarious matériel of ranching, farming, mining, lumbering, and engineering which it is busily distributing—well, a complex culture is at work in circumstances that never permit you to forget that that culture has been created in a land originally lifeless. This touch of miracle might suggest to a newcomer that Boise is an extraordinary town, but it is a typical Western town, like Carson City, Billings, Walla Walla, Pendleton, like any town where irrigation has made a dead land live.

Such settings and such achievements, with the violent drama of the climate, have shaped the Western consciousness. Moreover, the towns are set not only in drama but in vastness. Enormous distances have been a master-condition of Western life from the beginning and they have altered conceptions of space and therefore of time, too. The reduction of space began with the railroads but its conquest awaited the automobile, which has reoriented Western society, business, and thinking.

The Western orientation always startles even the most mobile Easterner. Your hostess is going to make a three-hundred-mile round trip tomorrow to buy a blouse she has seen advertised in a big-town paper. Your host will be going to his ranch, fifty miles away, after breakfast but will be back for lunch and glad to take your son to a rodeo, fifty miles in the opposite direction, and have him back well before dinner. Your friend won't be in San Francisco over the weekend, having decided to go fishing on the Madison River at the edge of Yellowstone Park, or the Salmon River in Idaho, or the Deschutes in central Oregon. To take you picnicking at the cabin the family will drive a distance equal to that between New York and Buffalo and while there will drive you the width of Massachusetts to take in a movie or a dance. And why not? The family income probably derives from a business whose routine transport is done by truck at distances elsewhere thought proper only for railroad freight, in areas where a railroad could not possibly penetrate, at a steady reduction of the ratio of space to time.

The conquest of space is not enough, however, and the West is now in a fair way to annihilate it by means of aviation. Where sowers, foresters, prospectors, surveyors, vermin-exterminators, and even cow-punchers adapt the airplane to their daily job it is natural for all kinds of businesses to turn to it. Even before the war municipalities down to village size were building excellent airports, and the war compressed the development of a quarter of a century into five years. There are airports everywhere in the desert now and landing fields in the most inaccessible mountains. The interior West is less than twenty-four hours from the Atlantic coast and much less than twelve hours from the Pacific coast.

This alteration of time-space is one leg of the tripod—electric power and war industries are the other two—on which the West rests the glorious vision that it may at last emancipate itself from absentee control and compete with other sections. Moreover, if markets are only fractions of a day away, littoral fashions, clip-joints, luxury shops, theaters, and smart gossip are at the same radius. Hayseed America has practically ceased to exist everywhere, of course, and the West was never hayseed in terms of "The Old Homestead." It has always had a cosmopolitan overtone and has always been nearer the Atlantic than the Midwest. But the airplane is an additional reason why Boise and Missoula seem so spruce and why the girl at the slot machine seems to have stepped in off Fifth Avenue.

Airplane and automobile underscore the historic role of technology in the development of the West. Technology made the West possible, revolutions in firearms and mining machinery, the technology of railroading and conservation, of wells and dams, of windmills and barbed wire. It is another reason why Western towns are so clean. In the past quarter-century a network of natural-gas mains has crisscrossed the West and wiped the grime of bituminous coal from many towns. The girl in the Fifth Avenue dress cooks on an electric range, heats her bath water by electricity, and has filled her air-conditioned bungalow with more labor-saving gadgets than the bourgeois household has anywhere else. During the war she added to them a deep-freeze unit, which her husband keeps filled with meat bought at wholesale and at the bottom of the market, and with the fish, elk, deer, and game birds he gets at the mountain camp. She is living in an approximation of the America of tomorrow as the fantasies of engineers describe it.

These Western towns would be, thousands of tourists must decide, excellent places for the children to grow up in. So much space, so much sparkling air, so much lawn and forest, so much sunlight, so much natural beauty, such easy access to wilderness and silence, such facilities for recreation. Moreover, their social system is uncomplicated. If the Westerners are not quite free they are at least free and easy, spontaneous equalitarians, open-hearted if not precisely open-minded, friendly, buoyant. There is no anti-Semitism. Though Jim-Crowism appeared during the war, there is very little of it. (The West has always had its own color lines: Chinese and Japanese on the coast, Indians in the upper interior and the southwest, Mexicans everywhere.) It would be good, so the day-dream runs, for the children to have such things from their earliest years. And it would be good for them to acquire the West's feeling for the mountains, deserts, and forests, and especially its ever-present, dualistic awareness of the struggle between man and nature, the tension between survival and disaster, the conduct of life under the threat of flood, drought, forest fires, and insect plagues. Western realism and Western mysticism, in both of which the idea of man's fate is objectified as the Western environment, make an equipoise that promises much for satisfaction in life.

I have heard this reverie many times from Easterners whom the West has taken by storm. They are right. The West always was a good place for children to grow up in and has steadily become a better one. How good a place it is and will henceforth be for them to stay in when they are grown, however, is a different, not necessarily related question.

v

How important the West is to the post-war United States is insufficiently realized in the West and hardly realized at all anywhere else except at the centers of industrial and financial power.

New Deal measures, war installations, and war industries have given the West a far greater and more widely distributed prosperity than it has ever had before. Moreover, during the war a fundamental revolution took place: power and industrial developments in the West have made a structural change in the national economy. That change is certain to increase and have increasingly important results, for if the developments that have occurred are revolutionary those already planned and sure to be carried out are even more revolutionary, and some of those which so far are only dreams but may be achieved stagger the mind. Finally, the world movements which are working out a long-term reorientation of human societies whose focus is the Pacific Ocean will be increasingly favorable to the West.

The West sees all this in terms of its historical handicaps: colonial economic status and absentee control. The ancient Western dream of an advanced industrial economy, controlled at home and able to compete nationally, is brighter now than it has ever been before. For the first time there are actual rather than phantasmal reasons for believing that the dream can be realized. I will discuss them in a later article. But the West cannot escape history and especially its own history. Nor can it escape psychology, its own historic psychology. If the dream is to be realized at all it must be realized within the Western culture and the limits of Western consciousness. Psychology will have quite as much to do with it as economics. I have described here certain ambiguities in the culture and psychology of the West which at least tinge the dream with doubt.

For some kinds of people the West is something of a paradise and those who have worked out an effective adaptation to it seem to be happier than the average run of Americans. Even they, however, show symptoms of psychic insecurity. That insecurity shows most plainly in the two kinds of Westerners who are most obviously unhappy and most obviously out of harmony with Western culture, the intellectuals and the rich. It must be significant that both are obsessed by a feeling of inferiority and that the Western colonialism by which they explain it is not economic but cultural.

The rich are easily explained. In the overwhelming majority they are either local representatives and managers of, or else are necessarily allied with, the system of absentee exploitation that has drained the West's resources eastward and channeled its wealth in the same direction. As parties to or dependents on that system they are really adversaries of the West. Their intellectual and spiritual loyalties are to its enemies. They have no function in the indigenous culture but they must live in the midst of it as remittance men, émigrés, and expatriates. Forty years ago Harry Leon Wilson described them as Spenders, and a generation has only made their phantasy-life sillier and more vulgar. In that phantasy-life they see themselves as exiles from reality, but their reality is only the advertising pages of *Vogue*. They are the silliest (and one observer of them is here substituting that adjective for "most hoggish") members of that class for whom the clip-joints of the Atlantic and

Pacific Coasts are run: the gaudy restaurants, the vulgar shops, the meretricious resorts, the whole falsely-veneered world which has been expertly designed to take them in and whose phoniness they understand to be Elegance and Fashion. Their ambition may be summed up as to be mistaken for the kind of millionaire who was born within this world either in Hollywood or better still New York, night-club New York. It is hard to manage in the desert and impossible in New York. They are America's stupidest fall guys and the West's only hicks.

The rich derive no sustenance from Western culture and contribute nothing to it. There would be no particular significance in that, since it is by their own choice, if it were not for the fact that the West's intellectuals come out much the same, if for reasons as different as possible, reasons which are seldom their fault.

Effective radicalism in the West has originated in the economic struggle, as a direct product of the exploitation. The West's intellectual radicals, however, have been and remain something else. They are charming, as the millionaires assuredly are not, but theirs is a charm of irresponsibility. They are at once fiery and sweet—red in tooth and claw and buoyed up by the knowledge that they will never have to do anything at all about it. The barricades they fight on are imaginary and the deaths they undergo are mere formulas. Their radicalism is a species of aesthetics. But the point is that if it were anything else they could not survive in the West.

Intellectuals have always been a Western export. In the United States at large the professions—the learned professions—journalism, literature, and the arts contain a disproportionate number of men and women who grew up on Nine Mile over against Dead Man but whose address is now Westport or Winnetka or Palo Alto. They found the going too hard and so they got out. They refused to waste their strength fighting an unfavorable environment.

In the past generation that environment has become somewhat more favorable but not much. Let writers stand for them all. Only a small handful of first-rate writers have stuck it out in the West—men who write as Americans without Western provinciality or who write about Western experience without neuroticism. I do not know what inner resources have been required of such men as, say, Edwin Corle,

Thomas Hornsby Ferril, Vardis Fisher, and Joseph Kinsey Howard, but that such achievement as theirs requires unusual strength is obvious from what has happened to the generality of Western writing. It has got mired in the spongy, self-conscious regionalism that has devitalized American writing wherever it has broken out, though for the South's forty acres and a poet the spacious West has substituted six hundred and forty acres and a mystic. Or else it has fled into coteric literature, with the result that the little magazine is making its last stand in the sagebrush and the writer who stayed there is trying to be Eugene Jolas. He has his own *Vogue* and *Spur* and is trying to erect a Left Bank on Nine Mile. This escapism is pathetic rather than vulgar because it is forced on him, but if escapism is a means of survival it nevertheless ranges him with the millionaire. He has found no roots in the common culture and so regards it as colonial.

What has denied him roots, however, is not a colonial state of mind but the state of mind of the vigilantes, the vigilantes who were always as useful for suppressing nonconformity as for getting rid of stagerobbers. I have suggested that the coercive beard-growing of Frontier Week, the developing myth of the Old West, and the compulsive mass-hypnotism of the slot machines are not casual surface-phenomena of Western life but symptoms of conflicts that come close to being organic. They go back in history as far as the West goes but they are more important now than ever before, because the fulfillment of the great dream will depend on whether the West resolves them as it undertakes to seize its hour.

Western freedom has always been extended to certain kinds of behavior only; freedom has always been denied to other kinds of behavior and has hardly existed at all in thought and opinion. Western individualism has different appearances in different lights but it has always been less a matter of letting my neighbor go his way as he chooses than of waiting for him to make some mistake that will allow me to jump his claim. That Chambers of Commerce have taken over the gang function of the Vigilance Committee has only made Western business more timorous, an easier setup for absentee exploitation. It has only increased the West's historic willingness to hold itself cheap and its eagerness to sell out. The West has certainly been raped by the East but its ads and its posture have always invited rape.

Thus the basic problems are internal. The West has always suppressed domestic criticism, while cringing before criticism from outside, and has treated non-conformity of idea and innovation of any
kind, especially in business, as dire social evils. Forever in rebellion
against exterior exploitation, it has nevertheless always co-operated
with the exploiters against itself when the chips were down. Worst of
all, its own interior exploitation has always worked to the same end.
No destruction by absentee-owned corporations of the West's natural
resources—all it has—has ever been forestalled, because anything that
could forestall it would also forestall the West's own destruction of
those same resources. At this moment there is intended an assault on
the public resources of the West which is altogether Western and so
open that it cannot possibly be called a conspiracy. It is an assault
which in a single generation could destroy the West and return it to the
processes of geology. That such an intent publicly flourishes and may
succeed—at the very moment when the West is undertaking, with
some possibility of success, to emancipate itself and establish an advanced industrial economy—is plain proof of schizophrenia.

Will the effort to achieve the status of an equal in the national economy turn out in the end to have been just one more Western boom? Is
the West's contemplated secession from the union premised on getting
the federal government to subsidize the secession and Wall Street to
pay the carrying charges? Will the revolution now gathering momentum end with the same old masters at the throttle still?

The issue will be settled in terms of steel, aluminum, water, electric
power, freight rates, and credit. But the determinant will be the Western consciousness. Westerners have always thought of the East as their
worst enemy, but they have always acted as if their worst enemies were
the Westerners who wanted their children to live in the West, who
wanted to make something of the country and keep it. They have been
chary of trusting one another and with good cause: what has always
wrecked co-operation has been their willingness to sell one another
out. Unless that changes in the course of the revolution, Wall Street
can view the future of its Western satrapy with detached calm.

[Mr. DeVoto will continue this discussion
in a second article.—The Editors].

The High Country
(*Woman's Day*, December 1952)

*For everyone there is a place where the meaning of life is crystal
clear and the heart finds its home*

The ancients believed that every place had its genius, a spirit with
power to influence anyone who came there. We say much the same
thing today when, using a trite phrase, we speak of the spell a place
casts on us. For spells were part of the practice of magic and were supposed to transform people from what they were to something else. We
are speaking more truly than we realize, for most of us periodically seek
out a particular place in order to be renewed, and renewal is a kind of
transformation.

The geniuses of place are individual. Everyone must find his own
country, the place whose spirit speaks to him, perhaps in a voice none
of his friends can hear. Thus, I find the Everglades desolate and even
frightening, though I know people who go there rejoicingly and come
away remade. I have never learned to love the sea, though I have spent
most of my adult life on the Atlantic coast. My trade sometimes takes
me to the southwestern desert, but I find its vast pageant of chromatic
stone a dead land and am always glad to come out of it. My place is the
high country. There is no way of analyzing love—I cannot tell you the
secret of its mysterious power; I can only describe it.

Find Denver on a map, and draw a line west across the Rocky Mountains. Most of the country I am talking about lies north of that line, in Colorado, Utah, Wyoming, Idaho, and Montana. The cities and towns of the mountain West, its farms and ranches and industries, are located in long, broad valleys. We call them valleys, that is, for they lie between ranges of mountains, but actually they are high plateaus. Commonly they have an altitude of at least four thousand feet, sometimes much more; one of the steps of the state capitol at Denver bears a brass plate which states that it is exactly a mile above sea level, and some distance out of Colorado Springs a hill beside the highway is exactly the same height as Mount Washington, the tallest peak in the White Mountains of New Hampshire. The high country is in the mountain ranges back of these valleys.

Some of those ranges have names so evocative that they, too, have a spell: the Wasatch and the Uinta Mountains in Utah, the Wind Rivers and the Absarokas in Wyoming, the Bitterroots in Montana, the Sawtooths in Idaho. There is one in Colorado (not far from another called the Rabbit Ears) so much of which is above the line of permanent snow that it is called the Never Summer Range. I do not know Indian grammar, but a National Park naturalist once told me that the name is a translation of a Ute phrase which has a double negative in it, so that they are really the Never No Summer Mountains, and when you see their peaks in summer sunset, you feel that the emphasis is right. Well, to reach the high country, you head your car into such mountain ranges as these.

The road takes you into a canyon, and if the valley was hot, you are cool here, and from now on you breathe the tingling air of the mountains, electric and exhilarating, aromatic with the evergreen forest, perfumed with the sweet and poignant river smell. A western mountain range is not a single row of peaks connected by a ridge. Usually it is a succession of such rows and ridges with valleys in between, smaller valleys than those where the towns are, of higher altitude, sometimes with farms or stock ranches in them, though soil is poor and the growing season short. Climbing steadily but gently, the road leads deeper into the mountains. The canyons are twisting and narrow, usually no wider than the stream and the road that has been built along its bank. The mountainsides slope up gently or sometimes rise vertically as cliffs.

These small valleys, canyons, and peaks are all part of the high country, but there is a place that has always seemed to me its very heart.

The mountains move back, and you come into a kind of intervale, an open space after the confining canyon walls. It is a mile or so wide, or perhaps several times as much, and it has a floor of grass broken by little groves. There are no ranches; there may be a few log cabins, summer camps of people who live in the nearest towns, but they are probably hidden from view. If you see a cabin near the road, it is likely to be a ranger station or a fire-guard station belonging to the Forest Service, for most of the high country is included in national forests. The forest marches up the mountainsides that ring you round, an evergreen forest broken only by cliffs and outcrops of rimrock. It ends at a line so straight that it seems almost to have been made by surveyors: timberline, above which the gray or rose-pink rock of the peak is sharp against the sky. The peaks wear surplices of snow till August, the highest ones all year. Back of them you see the lines of other peaks and ridges, growing fainter with the distance till the farthest ones seem clouds or mirages. The gulches on the mountainside brim with violet shadow. And at the far end of the opening you have come into, the mountains draw together again and the canyon the road enters is hung with purple that deepens as the afternoon wears on.

Such intervales have various names, but when I was a boy in the West I learned to call them mountain meadows. As I write this in a Massachusetts city, drab today with blowing sleet, I can summon many such meadows to mind, all of them bright with summer sun. They seem to me the essence and climax of the high country. It is here the genius of the place says to me in Hamlet's words, "Rest, perturbed spirit"—and peace comes.

Tranquility of mind and heart is something none of us feels often or for very long, and surely the power to confer it is what makes a place our own. And for me, the power does not depend on my doing anything but merely on my being there. The chemistries of the spirit work their transformation without active help from me.

The quiet is a large part of the transforming power. We forget how torturing the noise of cities is till we become aware again of the wilderness serenity, and forget how we have protectively deafened ourselves to it till we realize that we are hearing little sounds again. The mountains have a special quality of quiet, not the full silence of the desert but a stillness in which the sounds that nature makes are carriers of peace. The movement of an animal in the underbrush or the splash of a leaping fish is a slight accent that points up the enveloping soundlessness. In the city we never hear the wind; here it is a day-long sibilance in the cottonwoods or a distant organ music in the evergreens. There is no note so peaceful as the voice of the Western mourning dove—unless it be the voice of the Western meadow lark. But the sound that brings completion is that of running water, the mountain creek that is always a background music in your ears.

Mountain sunlight is intense. It will blister your back and burn your photographic films black with overexposure till you learn to allow for it. But it is another element of the serenity the high country brings. It thins the primary colors till they seem newly washed, and thins the shadows to transparency. It is infinitely spacious and it is always changing, so that, moment by moment, no vista ever stays the same. Haze softens the peaks in the early morning and comes again when evening sets in, but in the midday hours everything has a sharply chiseled outline. Shapes and colors change as you watch. A cliff flattens, stands out in relief, sharpens. The forests that march rank by rank into the distance over the curves of mountainsides are dulled or highlighted, are massed together without form or cut by slanting planes of light. Those near at hand range through all the shades of green, but on the sides of distant peaks they are black. The distances are enormous, they seem too vast ever to end, and over them, over forests, mountainsides, cliffs, and canyons, the mile-long shadows of clouds move with infinite slowness. Space is so great and time has so slow a pulse that surely nowhere in the world can there be haste.

But if it were possible to analyze the influence the high country exerts—the healing or magical or restorative power—I think we would find the rivers at its core. They are always in my remembrance of it, and I can sit here at my desk now and visualize scores of them and hear their voices. Only in the West, where water is precious, would they be called rivers—they are creeks, but they are like no other creeks. They run cold and swift and shining over beds of stone, so clear that you expect the water to be luminescent when you scoop some up in your hand.

I have no need to fish a mountain creek, no need to do anything but sit or lie beside it. One watches the always changing curve the water takes where it rises in ripples, or the different curve where it divides around boulders. Foam from upstream rapids drifts by, tree shadows shift and shimmer across the surface, sun glints strike and fade. It is easy to fall asleep or to sink into a reverie so deeply contented that it is like a dream. But mostly one merges with the place, passive, aware, and at peace. And always there is the music of the running water. It is not like the roar of a waterfall, or the sliding rush of plains rivers with a deep bass undertone, or the high note of big rivers such as the Columbia and the Snake that these creeks unite to form. It is clear, soft, swift but unhurried, a chord rather than a single note, and scored for the woodwinds rather than the strings. It transports one out of time.

Or rather it transports one into a different order of time. And this, I feel sure, does much to explain the serene well-being we feel in the wilderness. The intervals of time are not marked by schedules, appointments, a prescribed ritual of necessity. They are nature's intervals marked by the ebbing of color and the lengthening of shadows, the course of seasons, the centuries of a tree's growth, the epochs of an eroding rock. We become aware again of the natural order we had lost touch with, just as we recover subtle senses there is no use for in town and can feel a shift in the wind or detect an approaching storm.

There is another clue in mountain night. The sound of the creek draws nearer and seems to increase. The wind is louder, too; you hear it thrashing in the trees overhead and walking the mountainsides miles away. A deer leaps in the brush; down the canyon coyotes are barking. As the cliffs cool, small fragments of rock fall with a minute sound and perhaps start miniature slides of pebbles or sand. Hearing such microscopic sounds, you become isolated in an enormous silence. The systems of the stars wheel on their axes almost within reach of your fingers. The air is bitter cold, but not at the campfire—whose fluctuating light comes back from trees, streams, and cliffs. Night, fire, the wind overhead, the flowing water; silence and warmth; endless space beyond the circle of firelight, and within the circle one's friends or family—everything is here, nothing else need be considered, no harm can come. At the deepest level of personality a primitive fear has been assuaged by a primitive sense of safety. We have responded to a feeling

of our earliest ancestors, who knew the wilderness as awe and fear but
were part of it themselves and forged from it as much security as human
life is ever granted to know. A pinpoint of light in a great darkness,
warmth and affection enveloped by cold and the unknown—it is a
moving symbol.

We say instinctively that these periods of solitude and simplicity are
healing, though we might be hard put to it to explain just what they
heal. It is less a healing than a restoration and rediscovery, no matter
whether we think in terms of sport and pleasure, of the beauty of nature, of living at a simpler level, or of putting away for a time the re-
sponsibilities and anxieties of our usual life. A part of us that had got
lost is found again; a part that was wandering has come home. We use
that very phrase, saying when we get back briefly to our own place that
we feel we have come home. It is, I think, a feeling of being made
whole again, of being harmonious as a person, of relearning the secre-
cies of ourselves which we forget in town. For a time we join the order
of nature and are open to the sun; for a time we live free.

To everyone his own place. I will not propagandize for the pleasant
place where the lines have fallen to me, but say only that I wish everyone could know the high country. Do not visit it in winter, for it is a
hostile land then and only experienced, expert outdoorsmen can travel
it. It is a land for summer, which comes late and departs early. June is
overcast, cold, sodden with rain and sleet. But the rest of summer is,
like all brief seasons, passionate and intense. The crest has passed by
the middle of August, and then there comes a period which I find the
most poignant of all. A new brightness comes into the air and the colors. The underbrush is splashed with scarlet, poplar and cottonwood
leaves are gold, and the aspens have bleached to a high, shining silver.
Mist hangs blue and lavender gauzes across the canyons and the distances almost till noon; twilights are early and long. There is a hush, an
expectancy in the clean air—a portent of winter, a premonition of
death, but the world is resolved to reach its fullness first. There is an
illusion that no one is here but you, and you respond to it with a delight so deep, so moving, so complete that it is wrapped round with
sadness. Above all others, this is the time to visit the high country.

TWO
The Western Land Grab, 1940s

The plan is to get rid of public lands altogether, turning them over to the States, which can be coerced as the federal government cannot be, and eventually to private ownership. . . . This is your land we are talking about.

"The West Against Itself," 1947

The West Against Itself

(*Harper's Magazine*, January 1947)

In Harper's for August 1934, I called the West "the plundered province." The phrase has proved so useful to Western writers and orators
that it has superseded various phrases which through generations of
Western resentment designated the same thing. We must realize that it
does designate a thing; that, whatever the phrases, there is a reality behind them. Economically the West has always been a province of the
East and it has always been plundered.

The first wealth produced in the West was furs, mainly beaver
furs. It made a good many Easterners rich. Partnerships and corporations sent technical specialists—trappers and Indian traders—into the
West to bring out the furs. No producer ever got rich; few were ever
even solvent. The wealth they produced—from the West's natural resources—went east into other hands and stayed there. The absentee
owners acted on a simple principle: get the money out. And theirs was
an economy of liquidation. They cleaned up and by 1840 they had
cleaned the West out. A century later, beaver has not yet come back.

In the early 1840's emigrants began to go west. They leapfrogged
over the plains and mountains, which were settled much later, in order

to get to Oregon west of the Cascade Mountains and California west of the Sierra. Their settlements were the first permanent local interests in the West and (with Mormon Utah) for decades the only ones. The emigrants expected to stay in the West and expected their descendants to go on living off the country. They made farms and set up local systems of production, trade, export of surpluses, and even manufacture. The interests of these people, the permanent inhabitants, have always been in conflict with the interests of transients, of those who were liquidating the West's resources. Their interests have not been in conflict with those of the East, in fact have been worth more to the East than all other Western sources of wealth put together—so long as the East has been able to control and exploit them, that is from the beginning up to now. The East has always held a mortgage on the permanent West, channeling its wealth eastward, maintaining it in a debtor status, and confining its economic function to that of a mercantilist province.

The development of the mineral West began in 1849. Mining is the type-example of Western exploitation. Almost invariably the first phase was a "rush"; those who participated were practically all Easterners whose sole desire was to wash out of Western soil as much wealth as they could and take it home. Few made a stake. Of those who did practically everyone carried out his original intention and transferred Western wealth to the East. The next and permanent phase was hard-rock mining or mining by placer or dredge on so large a scale that the same necessity held: large outlays of capital were required and the only capital that existed was Eastern. So the mines came into Eastern absentee ownership and control. They have always channeled Western wealth out of the West; the West's minerals have made the East richer. (The occasional Westerner who fought his way into the system—called a "nabob" in his era—became a part of that system, which is to say an enemy of the West.)

Mining is liquidation. You clean out the deposit, exhaust the lode, and move on. Hundreds of ghost towns in the West, and hundreds of more pathetic towns where a little human life lingers on after economic death, signalize this inexorable fact. You clean up and get out— and you don't give a damn, especially if you are a stockholder in the

East. All mining exhausts the deposit. But if it is placer mining, hydraulic mining, or dredging, it also kills the land. Nothing will come of that land again till this geological epoch has run out.

In witness of what I said last month about the West's split personality, consider this: that in the West no rights, privileges, or usurpations are so vociferously defended by the West—against itself—as the miner's. The miner's right to exploit transcends all other rights whatsoever. Even the national government is unable to effect enough control over mineral rights to harmonize them with conflicting or even merely different rights.

Oil and natural gas follow the pattern of the mines. Because their development is comparatively recent the national government is able to exercise some control over them in the common good, by using the lease system instead of the patents which it must issue to miners. But just because that development is recent, Eastern capital has been able to monopolize oil and gas even more completely than ever it monopolized mining. The wells, pipelines, and refineries belong to Eastern corporations. They pump Western wealth into Eastern treasuries. It is possible for a Western independent to make a mineral discovery, finance it, and maintain his local control in defiance of the absentee system; it has happened occasionally in the past and it happens occasionally now. But the wildcatter in oil, the independent, has no chance at all except to submit to the system. He may find oil without its assistance; in fact the system hopes he will. But he cannot refine or transport or sell oil except to the system, on the system's terms.

Western psychology prevents him from desiring to do anything else. Last summer I talked with the manager of a small, locally owned refinery which, with much good luck but mostly because the necessities of war had set up exactly the right conditions, had cleared its debts, secured contracts which seemed to guarantee it permanent independence, and built up an impressive surplus and reserve. It was a minute item of fulfillment of the West's great dream, the dream of economic liberation, of local ownership and control. And what had been done with that surplus and that reserve? They had been invested in Standard Oil of New Jersey. The West does not want to be liberated from the system of exploitation that it has always violently resented. It only wants to buy into it, cumulative preference stock if possible.

So we come to the business which created the West's most powerful illusion about itself and, though this is not immediately apparent, has done more damage to the West than any other. The cattle business. Now there was stock raising along the Pacific Coast before there was agriculture there, even before there were American settlements. But the cattle business of the West as such has been conducted east of the Cascades and Sierra and mostly east of the Rockies, and it began when cattle were brought to the open range—first to the Dakotas, Wyoming, and Montana, then elsewhere. Its great ear lasted from about 1870 to the terminal winter of 1886–87, which changed its conditions forever. Changed them, I repeat, forever. But the practices, values, and delusions developed in that era, the Cattle Kingdom of romance, dominate the cattle business today.

The cattlemen came from Elsewhere into the empty West. They were always arrogant and always deluded. They thought themselves free men, the freest men who ever lived, but even more than other Westerners they were peons of their Eastern bankers and of the railroads which the bankers owned and the exchanges and stockyards and packing plants which the bankers established to control their business. With the self-deception that runs like a leitmotif through Western business, they wholeheartedly supported their masters against the West and today support the East against the West. They thought of themselves as Westerners and they did live in the West, but they were the enemies of everyone else who lived there. They kept sheepmen, their natural and eventual allies, out of the West wherever and as long as they could, slaughtering herds and frequently herdsmen. They did their utmost to keep the nester—the farmer, the actual settler, the man who could create local and permanent wealth—out of the West and to terrorize or bankrupt him where he could not be kept out. And the big cattlemen squeezed out the little ones wherever possible, grabbing the water rights, foreclosing small holdings, frequently hiring gunmen to murder them. And, being Western individualists and therefore gifted with illusion, the little cattlemen have always fought the big ones' battles, have adopted and supported their policies to their own disadvantage and to the great hurt of the West.

Two facts about the cattle business have priority over all the rest. First, the Cattle Kingdom never did own more than a minute fraction of one per cent of the range it grazed: it was national domain, it belonged to the people of the United States. They do not own the range now: mostly it belongs to you and me, and since the fees they pay for using public land are much smaller than those they pay for using private land, those fees are in effect one of a number of subsidies we pay them. But they always acted as if they owned the public range and act so now; they convinced themselves that it belonged to them and now believe it does; and they are trying to take title to it. Second, the cattle business does not have to be conducted as liquidation but throughout history its management has always tended to conduct it on that basis.

You have seen the Missouri River at Kansas City, an opaque stream half-saturated with silt. A great part of that silt gets into it from the Yellowstone River, above whose mouth the Missouri is comparatively clear. The Yellowstone is fed by many streams, of which those from the south carry the most silt, the Tongue, the Rosebud, especially Powder River, and most especially the Big Horn. Above the mouth of the Big Horn the Yellowstone is comparatively clear. These plains rivers are depressing and rather sinister to look at, and they always have been helping to carry the mountains to the sea. But one reads with amazement descriptions of them written before the Civil War. They were comparatively clear streams, streams whose gradual, geological erosion of the land had not been accelerated—as it was when the cattle business came to Wyoming and Montana. The Cattle Kingdom overgrazed the range so drastically—fed so many more cattle than the range could support without damage—that the processes of nature were disrupted. Since those high and far-off days the range has never been capable of supporting anything like the number of cattle it could have supported if the cattle barons had not maimed it. It never will be capable of supporting a proper number again during the geological epoch in which civilization exists.

That should be, though it mostly isn't, important to the citizens of Wyoming, whose heritage the West's romantic business in part destroyed. It is directly important to everyone who lives in the lower Missouri Valley or the lower Mississippi Valley, and only a little less directly important to everyone who pays taxes for flood control, relief, or the rehabilitation of depressed areas. For when you watch the Missouri sliding greasily past Kansas City you are watching those gallant horsemen out of Owen Wister shovel Wyoming into the Gulf of Mexico. It is even more important that their heirs hope to shovel most of the remaining West into its rivers.

There remains lumbering. It perpetrated greater frauds against the people of the United States than any other Western business—and that is a superlative of cosmic size. It was a business of total liquidation: when a tree is cut, a century or two centuries may be required to grow another one and perhaps another one cannot be grown at all. Also it killed the land. A logged-out forest does not take so much geological time to come back as a place where a gold dredge has worked but during the generations of men it is even more evil. The effects of denuding a forest extend as far as fire may go and beyond that as far as any of the streams on the watershed it belongs to may be used for human purposes or are capable of affecting life, property, or society.

Lumbering, however, shows several deviations from the Western pattern. First, though the greater part of the timber came into Eastern ownership, with the consequent disregard of Western interests and the usual transfer of wealth out of the West, nevertheless an important fraction of it came into the hands of Westerners. Second, the national government got on the job in time to protect vast areas of forest from liquidation—and to protect the heart of the West from geological extinction. Third, a good many of the big operators got the idea in time and it is mainly they who are now trying to maintain privately owned Western forests as a permanent source of wealth, whereas the drive to liquidate all forests comes most vociferously from small operators, who have neither the capital nor the timber reserves for long-term operation. But with lumbering as with the cattle business we see revealed the psychic split that impels the West to join its enemies against itself.

These then, with power and irrigation which we may skip for the moment, are the businesses founded on the West's natural resources. While these businesses were developing, the rest of the West's economic structure, the parts which are like similar businesses everywhere, was also developing. There came to be in the West agriculture, transportation, wholesale and retail distribution, all the multifarious activities necessary to society. As I have already said, they are in sum much more important to the East than the basic businesses it owns—so long as it can control them in its own interest.

II

We lack space to describe the system by which the East maintains the West as an economic fief. It has been described many times and several recent books discuss it in relation to the current Western hope of breaking it up. Mr. A. G. Mezerik's *The Revolt of the South and West* is sound but in some contexts emotional rather than factual and commits the fallacy of assuming that the modern Far West can have the same relation to the South that the Midwest had before the Civil War. Mr. Wendell Berge's *Economic Freedom for the West* is more analytical and much more realistic. Mr. Ladd Haystead's *If the Prospect Pleases* is less comprehensive than either but Mr. Haystead deals with the Western psychology that imperils the Western hope, as Mr. Mezerik and Mr. Berge do not.

The bases of the system are simple. In a startling analogy to eighteenth century mercantilism, the East has imposed economic colonialism on the West. The West is, for the East, a source of raw materials for manufacture and a market for manufactured goods. Like the colonies before the Revolution the West is denied industry. Natural evolution concentrated industry and financial power in the East but the same evolution gave all other sections but the West a sizable amount of both. By the time the development of the West began it was possible to control the evolutionary process—to finance the West in such a way that the growth of locally owned industry became all but impossible.

The control of capital is, of course, the basic process. There is an amazing spread of interest rates between the East and the West. For such purely individual financing as real estate loans the West pays from two to three times as high a rate as the East. For the ordinary conduct of business it pays exactly what the East cares to charge and always enough to constitute a handicap in competition. But also as Western business becomes large enough to compete the Eastern financial network can either dictate to it absolutely or destroy it. This at the simplest level. Above it is the inter-connected structure of finance: the monopolies, cartels, inter-industry agreements, control of transportation, the many other instruments of power.

Take freight rates. They are devised so that the East pays lightly for the transport of Western raw materials but the West pays heavily for the transport of Eastern manufactured goods—and is prevented from manufacturing its own goods. The cowpoke on a ranch fifty miles from Sheridan, Wyoming, does not wear boots made at Sheridan. He wears boots made of leather from hides shipped from Sheridan to Massachusetts, processed and manufactured there, and then shipped back to Sheridan. The business man of an Oregon town does not buy a desk made where the lumber is made, but in Grand Rapids whither the lumber is shipped and whence the desk is returned to his home town, paying two freight charges where he should pay none at all. The wheat rancher in Washington or Montana has to buy agricultural machinery made not in rational proximity either to his ranch or to Western deposits of iron and coal but in Illinois, Ohio, or Pennsylvania—and is mentioned here because he pays not only that tax to Eastern control of business but another one, the tariff that protects the manufacturer but builds no wall round the wheatgrower. Finally, the business man who erects an office building in Denver or the county commissioners who build a bridge in northern Utah may indeed use steel produced within a hundred miles of the operation—but they pay on it, for the maintenance of the system, a tax assessed by the "basing point" principle that makes a satisfactory substitute for the outlawed "Pittsburgh plus."

The West is permitted to engage in preliminary operations that reduce the bulk of raw material so that the East can save freight costs in transporting them to the mills where the finishing operations are performed. It is not permitted to perform those finishing operations, to manufacture finished materials into consumers' goods, or to engage in the basic heavy industries which would give it the power to blow the whole system wide open. So far as the West is industrialized, it has a low-level industry. But there are necessarily loopholes in the system: kinds of industry which cannot be prevented from developing in the West. Such loopholes do not disturb the Eastern masters. Control of credit enables them to buy them out or dictate the terms on which they may be operated. Or they manipulate patent rights or trade agreements to the same end. Or they establish a branch plant of their own which cuts the throat of the Western-owned plant. Or they merely mention these possibilities and the Western industrialist, a fiery secessionist in his oratory, joins the system.

The result is an economy altogether bound to the industrial system of the East even where it is not in fact owned and managed by that system. That is to say, the West is systematically looted and has always been bankrupt.

There has never been a time when the West did not furiously resent all this nor a time when some elements in the West were not trying to do something about it. All the furious agitations that have boiled out of the West and terrified Eastern *rentiers* (but have seldom caused the actual engineers of plunder to turn a hair) have had the sole purpose of securing for the West some fractional control over its economic future. None of them have ever succeeded except when they could perform an ancillary service to the absentee system—like the permanently inflated price of silver, as outrageous a robbery of the American people as any ever devised by the steering committee of a patent pool. At most they have got the West an occasional tip amounting to a nickel or a dime, tossed back out of the millions drained eastward. There was never a chance that they could accomplish more. That is, there was never a chance till recent years. But now there is.

The New Deal began it. New Deal measures slowed the liquidation of resources and substituted measures of permanent yield. They operated to rehabilitate depleted resources, halt and repair erosion, rebuild soil, and restore areas of social decay. They eased credit, opened small gaps in the master system, and created much local prosperity. Such things improved the economic system and more important measures widened its base. Rural electrification dented the power monopoly which I have not touched on here but which is a basic tool of the system. A great expansion of reclamation projects increased agricultural wealth and, what is more important, made a start toward the production of surplus electric power. Finally, with such enterprises as the Central Valley Project and the stupendous, integrated plans for the development of the Columbia River basin and the Missouri Valley, the New Deal laid the groundwork for a fundamental attack on the system.

The West greeted these measures characteristically: demanding more and more of them, demanding further government help in taking advantage of them, furiously denouncing the government for paternalism, and trying to avoid all regulation. But the measures began to make possible what had not been possible before. They would provide electric power so cheaply and in such quantity that great industrial development must follow in the West. The Western economic structure must be revolutionized and reintegrated—which would imply tremendous changes in the national economic structure. And for the first time the West had a chance to seize control over its own economic destiny.

The war came and the process begun by the New Deal was telescoped and accelerated. Factories of many kinds sprang up everywhere. (Except in Montana, the private fief of Anaconda Copper and Montana Power, which succeeded in preventing any serious threat to their control of labor and production.) Mr. Berge has shown how, even in the stress of war, the absentee Eastern masters were able to direct much of this development in the old pattern, to restrain it to plants that performed only preliminary or intermediate processes. But not altogether. The West got airplane plants, shipyards, plants that manufactured such complex things as tanks and landing craft, heavy machinery, packing plants, innumerable processing plants. At Fontana in Californian and Geneva in Utah it got basic and partly integrated steel production. The war also produced something else the West had never had, a large body of skilled industrial labor. Also, by building landing fields and modern airports everywhere it made at least a fissure in the monopoly of transport and took out of transport much of the handicap of time which the West has always had to carry. Finally, it exhausted the new surplus of electric power and so hastened the already contemplated production of more power.

In short, the West now has an industrial plant and the conditions for its use are favorable—and certain to become more favorable. That is the fact on which the reinvigorated dream of economic liberation rests. The plant is too heavily concentrated along the Columbia, Puget Sound, the Willamette Valley, and the Pacific Coast—more so than it would have been if the development had been more gradual—but it does extend through most of the West. And with the production of, for instance, ingots and rolled steel and aluminum, heavy industrial goods, and many kinds of finished consumers' goods, and with the certainty that the production of power will increase, the terms are changed forever. The West can at last develop a high-level economy with all that that implies: stability, prosperity, rising standard of living, successful competition with other sections, a full participating share in an expanding national economy.

Realization that the dream can be fulfilled has made the West all but drunk. It is, I said last month, looking forward to the future with hope and confidence. I cannot list here the sectional and interstate associations and committees engaged in implementing the dream, the plans they are working out, the measures they are preparing, or any other specific details that have been born of a strange wedlock—the dynamics of boom which any trigger whatever has always been able to release in the West and the unique opportunity which the last few years have brought about. Enough that the West understands the opportunity, understands the possibilities of success and of failure that are inherent in it, and is taking every conceivable measure to avert failure and insure success.

With a conspicuous exception. The West seems unaware of one possibility of failure, the one that is inherent in its historic psychology.

III

Some doubts will occur to anyone. Thus if the upheaval should merely transfer financial power from Wall Street to Wall Street's California branch office, the basic system would be changed no more than it was years ago by the entrance of Chicago finance into the Western exploitation that had previously been monopolized by New York and Boston. A coastal dictatorship would merely be substituted for a trans-Mississippi one. Certain assurances will also occur to anyone and of these the principal one is that the Northwest has a better chance of pulling it off than the West as a whole. Its natural resources are more compactly concentrated and have been less impaired. The Northwest

is a more self-contained unit with fewer internal frictions and the Columbia system is more uniform and manageable than the Missouri system or any other focus of future development. Most important of all,
the Northwest seems to have got the idea that sustained use of natural
resources—which is to say simply, the future—is incompatible with
the liquidation of those resources in the present.

I have described a basic split in the Western psyche. Whether the
great dream will fail or be fulfilled depends on how that split works
out. Western individualism, I said last month, has always been in part
a belief that I stand to make more money from letting my neighbor
down than from co-operating with him. Westerners have always tended
to hold themselves cheap and to hold one another cheaper. Western resentment of its Eastern enslavement has always tended to be less a dis-
like of the enslavement than a belief that it could be made to pay.

The oil refinery that invested its surplus in Standard Oil was hardly
warring on absentee control and the same thing is to be seen throughout the West. The Wolfville Chamber of Commerce which is campaigning almost rabidly for local investment, local manufactures locally
owned, integration of the local commercial system—all surcharged with
violence about Wall Street, "foreign" corporations, the freight rates,
and the East as such—that Chamber of Commerce is also campaigning by advertisement and paid agents to bring Eastern corporations to
Wolfville. At the moment when its rhapsody of insurrection is loudest
its agents are spreading out their charts on the desks of Eastern industrial managers. Look, we've got this cheap power at Wolfville and a
labor surplus, too. The unions are feeble in Wolfville and in fact
throughout the state—it's not Paterson, it's not Akron, it's a setup.
We'll give you a site free and build your spur. Now as for tax abate-
ment, just what do you need? Just what additional advantages do you
need, that is, over the locally owned businesses of Wolfville we are trying to build up in order break the stranglehold of the East?

The symptoms of the division in the Western mind show more clearly
in the Western press, the newspapers, and the specialty journals of mining, lumbering, cattle and sheep growing, engineering. It is, to begin
with, an astonishingly reactionary press. The Western radical who occasionally scares the East usually turns out to be advocating on his native

plains something a couple of decades earlier than Mark Hanna. An average Democratic newspaper in the West would seem in, say, the advanced
liberalism of the Pennsylvania state machine, to be expressing a point of
view much too backward for Boies Penrose. A typical Republican editorial page in the West is written out of the economic and social assumptions of avalanche capitalism just after the Civil War. The point is
that these conceptions, assumptions, and values are improperly labeled
when they are called Democratic or Republican. They are Western.

One image of the West that the East accepts is that of the West not
as economic peon but as pensioner of the East, as beggar. The West
with its hat held out beseeching the expenditure on its behalf of federal money which must be raised from Eastern corporation and income taxes. Considering how much of that income is plundered from
the West, the image is both comic and profoundly ironical. But there
are ways in which it is also true. You can hardly find an editorial page
in the West that is not demanding as Western right, as compensation
for the West, and as assistance toward Western liberation, the expenditure of more federal funds. More government money for public health,
hospitals, inspection, treatment; for schools; for service by the Bureau
of Mines to the mining industry; for the improvement of Western agriculture, the replenishment of soils, the instruction of farmers; for the
instruction and protection of cattle and sheep growers, the improvement of stock and range, quarantine, research; for fire protection in the
logging business; for drainage; for reseeding and reforestation of private lands; for roads; for weather service; and always for dams, canals,
and the whole program of reclamation.

But at the same time: hands off. The West has been corrupted, its
press believes all but unanimously, by a system of paternalism which is
collectivist at base and hardly bothers to disguise its intention of deliv-
ering the United States over to communism. The second column of the
editorial page is sure to be a ringing demand for the government to get
out of business, to stop impeding initiative, to break the shackles of
regulation with which it has fettered enterprise, to abjure its philosophy of suppressing liberty, and to stop giving money to people who
will only fill the bathtub with coal. The editorial is certain to have a few
lines about bureaucrats in desk chairs, impractical theorists, probably
professors and certainly long-haired, who are destroying the West by

interfering with the men who know how. Also it is certain to be horrified by the schools, which the bureaucrats are using to corrupt our young people with Russian propaganda.

An editorial typical of scores I read this summer begins, "Next to getting over our complex that we have to appease labor and give it more money every Monday A.M., our next task is to go over to the schoolhouse." It denounces a handful of revolutionary notions, including the dreadful one that "the people should own the water power and the forests," and goes on to suggest measures, of which the first is, "we would call in the principal, or the president of the university, and quiz him on why do his teachers recommend socialism. And if his answer was dubious we would get a pinch hitter to take his place."

It shakes down to a platform: get out and give us more money. Much of the dream of economic liberation is dependent upon continuous, continually increasing federal subsidies—subsidies which it also insists shall be made without safeguard or regulation. This is interesting as economic fantasy but it is more interesting because it reveals that the Western mind is interfusing its dream of freedom with the economic cannibalism of the post-Civil-War Stone Age. It is still more interesting as it reveals the West's attitude toward the federal intervention which alone was powerful enough to save Western natural resources from total control and quick liquidation by the absentee Eastern ownership.

For that preservation the West is grateful to the government. But there was and still is a fundamental defect: federal intervention has also preserved those resources form locally owned liquidation by the West itself. So, at the very moment when the West is blueprinting an economy which must be based on the sustained, permanent use of its natural resources, it is also conducting an assault on those resources with the simple objective of liquidating them. The dissociation of intelligence could go no farther but there it is—and there is the West yesterday, today, and forever. It is the Western mind stripped to the basic split. The West as its own worst enemy. The West committing suicide.

IV

The National Parks are composed of lands that were once part of the public domain (plus a few minute areas that had previously passed out of it). Exceedingly small in total area, they are permanently reserved and dedicated to their present uses: the preservation of wilderness areas, the protection of supreme scenic beauties, and the pleasure and recreation of the American people. By the terms of the original dedication and by policy so far kept inviolate they are to be maintained as they are, they are not to be commercially exploited at all. But they contain timber, grazing land, water, and minerals. And that, in the West's eyes, is what is wrong with them.

The Olympic National Park contains a virgin stand of Sitka spruce, which yields a wood that is essential for airplanes. During the war a violent agitation was conducted by logging interests (unobtrusively backed by other interests with an eye on natural resources) to open these forests to logging. It presented itself as patriotism and skillfully assimilated itself to the emotions of wartime. There was more than enough Sitka spruce in privately owned and national forests to take care of the end in view but no matter: victory depended on our opening the Olympic National Park to logging. The persistence and power of the agitation and its accompanying propaganda (some of it conducted in the public schools, which are supposed to be poisoned with collectivism) would be unbelievable to anyone who had not looked into them.

The Park Service, backed by conservation associations and by Eastern lumbering interests which have seen the light, was able to hold fast—the Olympic Park was not logged. But immediately the war ended the same interests, augmented by a good many others, began an even more violent campaign of agitation, commercial pressure, and political pressure. We must now house the veterans and clearly we could not do so unless we opened all the national parks to logging.

That onslaught has been held in check and it will not win this time. But it will be repeated many times and the West intends it to win.

This campaign had nothing to do with Sitka spruce, winning the war, or housing veterans. Its purpose was to make a breach in the national parks policy with the aid of war emotions and to create a precedent. Once that precedent should be set, the rest would follow. Lumber companies could log the parks. Cattle and sheep associations could graze them. Mining companies could get at their mineral deposits.

Power companies could build dams in them, water companies could use their lakes and rivers. Each of those objectives has been repeatedly attempted in the past and the sun never sets on the West's efforts to achieve them. Success would mean not only the destruction of the national parks but, as we shall see, far worse.

The parks are trivial in extent, though the destruction of their forests, many of which have critical locations, would have a disproportionately destructive effect on the watersheds—the watersheds which must be preserved if the West is to continue to exist as a society. They are trivial—the main objectives of the Western assault on the natural resources are the remnants of the national domain, the Taylor Act grazing lands, and the national forests.

I have heard this assault called a conspiracy but it is in no way secret or even surreptitious; it is open and enthusiastically supported by many Westerners, by many Western newspapers, and by almost all the Western specialty press. Openly engaged in it are parts of the lumber industry (though other important parts of that industry are opposing it), some water users (though water users would be its first victims), the national associations of cattle and sheep growers and an overwhelming majority of the state and local associations as such and of their members individually, large parts of the mining industry, the U.S. Chamber of Commerce (some of whose local chambers are in opposition), and those Western members of Congress who represent these interests. Obscure but blandly co-operative in the background are Eastern interests perennially hostile to the West and concerned here because they greatly desire to halt and reduce government regulation and to open further Western wealth to liquidation—notably the power companies.

Right now the stockmen and woolgrowers are carrying the ball. We must confine ourselves to them and their principal objectives—remembering that the organized assault aims at many other objectives which would benefit other groups. Their limited objectives are:

(1) Conversion of the privilege which cattlemen and sheepmen now have of grazing their stock on Taylor Act and Forest Service lands—a privilege which is now subject to regulation and adjustment and for which they pay less than it is worth—into a vested right guaranteed

them and subject to only such regulation as they may impose upon themselves.

(2) Distribution of all the Taylor Act grazing lands, which is to say practically all the public domain that still exists, to the individual states, as a preliminary to disposing of them by private sale. (At an insignificant price. At an inflammatory meeting of committees of the American National Livestock Association and the National Woolgrowers Association in Salt Lake City in August 1946, the price most commonly suggested was ten cents an acre.)

(3) Reclassification of lands in the national forests and removal from the jurisdiction of the Forest Service of all lands that can be classified as primarily valuable for grazing, so that these lands may be transferred to the states and eventually sold. Immediately in contemplation is the removal of all government regulation of grazing in about 27,000,000 acres of forest lands and their distribution to the states — and to stockmen and woolgrowers as soon thereafter as possible.

These tracts compose the Minidoka and Caribou Forests in Idaho, all the forests in Nevada, most of the forest land in the southern half of Utah, and some ten or twelve million acres in Arizona and New Mexico. But that is just a start: a further objective is to wrest from Forest Service control all lands in all forests that can be grazed. And beyond that is the intention ultimately to confine the Forest Service to the rehabilitation of land which lumbermen and stockmen have made unproductive, under compulsion to return it to private ownership as soon as it has been made productive again. The ultimate objective, that is, is to liquidate all public ownership of grazing land and forest land in the United States. And the wording of the resolution in which the U.S. Chamber of Commerce came to the support of the program *excepted no government land whatever.* That certainly represents the desire of most of the leaders of the assault.

The immediate objectives make this attempt one of the biggest land grabs in American history. The ultimate objectives make it incomparably the biggest. The plan is to get rid of public lands altogether, turning them over to the States, which can be coerced as the federal government cannot be, and eventually to private ownership.

This is your land we are talking about.

The attack has already carried important outposts. Regulation of the use of Taylor Act lands, the vast public range outside the national forests, was vested in the Grazing Service. That service has been so systematically reduced in staff and appropriations that some cattlemen and sheepmen are now grazing the public range just about as they see fit. Violation of the Taylor Act is widespread, flagrant, systematic, and frequently recommended to their members as policy by various local cattle and sheep associations. The Grazing Service was organized to assist grazers and to protect the public interest. When it took the latter purpose seriously it was emasculated by Western members of Congress, and for this emasculation Senator Patrick A. McCarran of Nevada has been willing to take credit in speeches to cattle and sheep associations and in newspaper interviews. But Senator McCarran is by no means so extreme as the majority of the big stockmen whose interests he serves so brilliantly in Washington. His more limited purpose is to get the public lands away from those he calls "the swivel-chair oligarchy," that is federal officials who cannot be coerced, and into the hands of the states, that is officials who can be coerced. His model is his own state government, a small oligarchy dominated by stockmen. At the Salt Lake City meeting I have mentioned he warned the associations that demands for private ownership were premature and might embarrass his efforts, and he is understood to have been furious when, after he had left, the combined committees declared for ultimate private ownership of all public lands.

Senator McCarran has been the ablest representative of cattle and sheep interest in Washington, against the West and the people of the United States. But from time to time he has had the help of more than half the Western delegation in Congress—most surprisingly of Senator Hatch—and especially of Congressman Barrett and Senator Robertson of Wyoming. (New Mexico and Wyoming are the only states whose delegates to the Salt Lake City meeting were unanimous for the program.) Let us look at some of the measures they have proposed.

Senator McCarran has fathered a number of bills aimed at small or large objectives of the program. The one in point, however, is the "McCarran grazing bill" (S 33 in the last Congress) which has now been defeated four times but will certainly be reintroduced in the next Congress. This measure would give present owners of grazing permits in the national forests fee simple in those permits, on the theory that if you have leased an apartment from me (at half price or less) you have become its owner. The purpose was to convert a privilege (and one that is subject to regulation) into a vested right, to confine the use of grazing rights in the national forests to the present holders of permits or those who might buy them from the present holders, and to deny the Forest Service the greater part of its present power to regulate the use of grazing lands.

The Barrett Bill of last session (HR 7638) provided for the sale of disconnected tracts of unorganized Taylor Act grazing land, up to four sections per tract and to the total of over 11,000,000 acres. Priority in purchase was to be granted to present lessees of those tracts. Its purpose was to let present users of public grazing lands, who pay less than a fair rental, buy that land at less than it is worth—and to get public grazing land out of public regulation and control.

But the most revealing bill was last session's S 1945, introduced by Senator Robertson. The Senator is, it should be noted, the owner of one of the largest and finest sheep and cattle ranches in Wyoming. He holds a grazing permit in his own name in the Shoshone National Forest for 2,400 sheep, has a financial interest in an association that grazes 1,200 sheep there, and acts in various ways as agent for individuals and associations that graze nearly 8,000 more sheep in the same forest. His bill is a sweetheart.

The Robertson Bill would transfer to thirteen Western states all unappropriated and unreserved lands, *including the minerals in them;* all oil and mineral reserves; all minerals, coal, oil, and gas and all rights related to them in the public lands; and all homestead lands that have been forfeited to the United States. It would empower the states to dispose of these lands as they might see fit—that is, to sell them—except that coal, oil, and gas lands must be leased, not sold, and the federal government would retain power to pro-rate production.

The guts of the bill, however, are the provisions which set up in each state a commission ordered to re-examine every kind of reservation of public land—national forests, national parks and monuments, Carey Act (irrigation district) withdrawals, wildlife reserves, *reclamation reserves,*

power sites, and certain less important ones. The commission's duty
would be to determine whether parts of the national forests in its state
are more valuable for grazing and agriculture (practically no Forest
Service land can be farmed at all) than for timber production, and it
should decide that any were, to certify them for transfer to the state—
that is, the commission is intended to get forest grazing land into private ownership. The commission's duty in regard to other reservations
is to do the same in regard to grazing and agricultural land—and also
to determine whether the original purposes of the reserve can be
achieved by state ownership or "individual enterprise," and whether
the reserves may not have lost their importance or perhaps do not justify national administration.

The Robertson Bill is both transparent and carnivorous. It would liquidate the public lands and end our sixty years of conservation of the
national resources. And this single bill would achieve all the main objectives of the whole program of the Western despoilers at one step, except that purely timber lands in the forests would still be protected and
would have to be attacked by other means. In some respects it goes beyond anything that had been publicly advocated by the despoilers.
Nowhere else, for instance, has it been proposed to turn public power
sites or reclamation reserves over to private hands. But it expresses the
program.

    The public lands are first to be transferred to the states on the fully
justified assumption that if there should be a state government not
wholly compliant to the desires of stockgrowers, it could be pressured
into compliance. The intention is to free them of all regulation except such as stockgrowers might impose upon themselves. Nothing in
history suggests that the states are adequate to protect their own resources, or even want to, or to suggest that cattlemen and sheepmen
are capable of regulating themselves even for their own benefit, still
less the public's. And the regulations immediately to be got rid of are
those by which the government has been trying to prevent overgrazing of the public range. Cattlemen and sheepmen, I repeat, want to
shovel most of the West into its rivers.

    From the states the public lands are to be transferred to private
ownership. Present holders of permits are to be constituted a prior and

privileged caste, to the exclusion of others except on such terms as they may dictate. They are to be permitted to buy the lands—the public lands, the West's lands, your lands—at a fraction of what they are worth. And the larger intention is to liquidate all the publicly-held resources of the West.

Everyone knows that the timber of the United States is being cut faster than replacements are being grown, that the best efforts of the government and of those private operators who realize that other generations will follow ours have not so far sufficed to balance the growth of saw timber with logging. Everyone knows that regulation of grazing is the only hope of preserving the range. Open the public reserves of timber, the national forests, to private operation without government restriction and not only the Western but the national resources would rapidly disintegrate. (And presently the government, on behalf of our society as a whole, would have to wipe out private property in forests altogether.) Turn the public range over to private ownership, or even private management, and within a generation the range would be exhausted beyond hope of repair.

But that is, by a good deal, the least of it. Most of the fundamental watersheds of the West lie within the boundaries of the Taylor Act lands, the national forests, and the National Parks. And overgrazing the range and liquidating the forests destroys the watersheds. In many places in the West today property in land, irrigating systems, and crops is steadily deteriorating because the best efforts of the government to repair damage to watersheds—damage caused by overgrazing the ranges and overcutting the forests—has not been enough.

Stream beds choke with silt and floods spread over the rich fields on the slopes and in the bottoms, always impairing and sometimes destroying them. Dams and canals and reservoirs silt up, decline in efficiency, have to be repaired at great expense, cannot be fully restored. Fields gully, soil blows away. Flash floods kill productive land, kill livestock, kill human beings, sometimes kill communities.

Less than a month before the joint committees met in Salt Lake City this summer, a hundred and twenty-five miles away in the little town of Mt. Pleasant, Utah, the annual parade was forming for the celebration of July 24, the greatest Mormon feast day. That parade never got started. A heavy summer storm struck in the hills and gulches above town and what marched down Mt. Pleasant's main street was not a series of decorated floats but a mud flow that, in a town of twenty-five hundred people, did half a million dollars' worth of damage in ten minutes. The range above town had been overgrazed and the storm waters which would have been retained by healthy land could not be retained by the sick, exhausted land. They rushed down over Mt. Pleasant, bringing gravel, stones, and boulders with them, depositing several feet of mud, damaging many buildings and much of the town's real estate, leaving much of the grazing land above town ruined and much more damaged and dangerous.

This destruction had been predictable—and predicted; in a small way it had happened before. The government had been working for many years to restore that range but had not been able to begin the infinitely slow process soon enough. It knew and had repeatedly said that such a catastrophe might happen just as and where it did happen.

The same thing has happened repeatedly in Utah, in some places more destructively, in others less so. It has happened and goes on happening throughout the West wherever the grazing land of watersheds has been exhausted or their forests overcut. Mud flows and flash floods are dramatic but only occasional, whereas the steady deterioration of the watersheds and the slow destruction of their wealth go on all the time. Overgrazing and overcutting—and fire, the hazard of which is greatly increased by heavy cutting—are responsible. The program which is planned to liquidate the range and forests would destroy the Western watersheds. Which is to say that it would destroy the natural resources of the West, and with them so many rivers, towns, cities, farms, ranches, mines, and power sites that a great part of the West would be obliterated. It would return much of the West, most of the habitable interior West, to the processes of geology. It would make Western life as we now know it, and therefore American life as we now know it, impossible.

There you have it. A few groups of Western interests, so small numerically as to constitute a minute fraction of the West, are hellbent on destroying the West. They are stronger than they would otherwise be because they are skillfully manipulating in their support sentiments that have always been powerful in the West—the home rule which means basically that we want federal help without federal regulation, the "individualism" that has always made the small Western operator a handy tool of the big one, and the wild myth that stockgrowing constitutes an aristocracy in which all Westerners somehow share. They have managed to line up behind them many Western interests that would perish by their success. And they count on the inevitable postwar reaction against government regulation to put their program over.

To a historian it has the beauty of any historical continuity. It is the Western psychology working within the pattern which its own nature has set. It is the forever-recurrent lust to liquidate the West that is so large a part of Western history. The West has always been a society living under threat of destruction by natural cataclysm and here it is, bright against the sky, inviting such a cataclysm.

But if it has this mad beauty it also has an almost cosmic irony, in that the great dream of the West, adult economic development and local ownership and control, has been made possible by the developments of our age at exactly the same time. That dream envisions the establishment of an economy on the natural resources of the West, developed and integrated to produce a steady, sustained, permanent yield. While the West moves to build that kind of economy, a part of the West is simultaneously moving to destroy the natural resources forever. That paradox is absolutely true to the Western mind and spirit. But the future of the West hinges on whether it can defend itself against itself.

The Western Land Grab

(*Harper's Magazine,* June 1947)

The January issue of *Harper's,* which contained my article about the assault on the public lands in the West, reached the stands on the closing day of the annual meeting of the American Livestock Association. The caballeros were grieved to find someone attributing to them any but the most patriotic motives in their effort to destroy the national resources but, being men of action and not (as they put it) "intelligentsia," they needed more time than was left to find words that would express the full measure of their sorrow. About all they could do was to load their six-inch guns with the epithet "New Deal" and fan them at *Harper's.* Then they remembered the Alamo and the *Maine,* declared themselves the last thin line defending the private enterprise that made America great against the communism of government interference, and adjourned. Not, however, till they had called on the government to go on interfering with the importation of Argentine beef, lest free enterprise and unfettered competition perish.

The National Wool Growers Association met immediately afterward. Maybe sheepmen are more articulate than cattlemen, maybe California produces better oratory than Texas, or maybe the explanation is merely that there had been time to compose set speeches. At any rate, *Harper's* and I got a thorough working-over and American initiative died at our hands so loudly that all San Francisco shuddered. Communistic New Dealers had slain it by upholding the government regulations that were preventing sheepmen from appropriating huge areas of the public lands. Once that was made clear, the woolgrowers got down to business. There were proposals in Congress to do away with the government regulations that have artificially supported the price of wool and those proposals had to be stopped cold. They have been.

Meanwhile the Joint Committee on Public Lands of the two associations had been at work, and the first steps in the program which I described in the January *Harper's* have now been made public. Changes in tactics and long-term strategy have been made. The joint committee is concentrating on the first steps and holding the rest of the program in abeyance.

As this is written the McCarran grazing bill, the Barrett bill, and the Robertson bill, all described in my January article and defeated in the last Congress, have not been reintroduced in this session. They probably will not be and so some egregious frauds will not come up this year. Thus we are not currently threatened with state commissions whose duty would be to inquire into all federal reservations of Western land and, if their fitness for grazing could be established, to turn, say, the Custer battlefield park and the national cemetery on the Little Big Horn over to the states for sale to stockgrowers. (The U.S. Chamber of Commerce, however, has not modified its original referendum. The language has the usual looseness of embattled business men denouncing government interference but if I read it correctly Jamestown, the Wilderness, and the Salem Custom House would eventually have to pass into private hands if free enterprise could establish an economic use for them.)

The joint committee has decided that the shotgun charge of the Robertson bill will not do just now: it alarms people and it tries to do too much, thus taking steam out of the drive to get the public grazing lands into private hands. The committee believes that the best tactics are to go after the grazing lands in a different way, by amending the Taylor Act. That was the act which brought practically all the unappropriated grazing lands in the West under regulation by the Grazing

Service. For years both the cattle and the sheep interests have been trying to gut the Taylor Act and get rid of the Grazing Service. They have
about succeeded with the latter: their representatives in Congress have
understaffed and underappropriated it into practical paralysis. Now
the idea is to amend the Taylor Act out of existence.

The committee, as I pointed out in January, is an instrument forged
by the two associations to get all the usable public range into private
ownership—into the ownership of the present holders of grazing permits. It wants to turn the privilege of leasing grazing land, a privilege
now subject to both regulation and revocation, into fee simple, thus
making a privileged class of the present lessees and shutting everyone
else out. The committee's proposals call for the land to be classified for
sale at preposterously low prices, ranging from nine cents to $2.80 an
acre—classifying to be done by the Bureau of Land Management, to
which the remnants of the Grazing Service have been attached and
which the committee believes will see the light. Purchasers are to pay
ten per cent down. They are to have thirty years to pay off the rest of
the purchase price, with interest at one and a half per cent. The federal
government is to get ten per cent of the money raised by sales; the rest,
in a bid for local support, is to go to the states.

But there is a lot of good grazing land in the national forests which,
since it does not come under the Taylor Act, cannot be grabbed in this
way. So, already glancing toward the Robertson bill, the committee
demands that the forests be surveyed and "that all lands determined to
be not of timber value be removed from the national forests and be
turned over to the Division of Range Management for their management until final disposal" by private sale.

There you have it, simple, clear, and stinking. Many epithets have been
fired at me for calling this an attempt at a land grab, but it makes any
earlier land grab in our history (the Oregon timber frauds, for instance)
seem picayune. Cattlemen and sheepmen are trying to get exclusive
possession of the public resources in Western grazing land. The interests that are running interference for them are trying to get exclusive
possession of all other public resources in the West. What is a land grab?

I am happy to report that currently it is not succeeding. Congress is
not co-operating—and some of the most vigorous non-co-operators

are certain Western representatives who have unexpectedly got religion. Publication of the joint committee's proposals revealed to a lot of
small stockowners that they were being taken for a ride, that they had
been supporting a movement which was dangerous in general and
highly dangerous to them. They began saying so to their congressmen.
Resolutions denouncing the proposals have come in from local cattle
and sheep associations and from other groups all over the West—especially Colorado, Utah, and Idaho. They shoot from the hip. "The endorsement of this proposal by the American National Livestock Association," a typical one says, "was done *without the knowledge or consent of
the membership at large* and our [local] association, as a member organization, repudiates that endorsement."

Worse still, some highly important bodies have joined the opposition. In January the Governor of Idaho was calling me a liar for what
I had said in *Harper's*. But in March the legislature of his state adopted
a memorial to Congress denouncing the whole program of the joint
committee and demanding "that the public lands remain in their present ownership status." The legislature said that the rights of sportsmen and vacationers would be obliterated over an enormous area if
the proposals were adopted. It said that private ownership could not
protect the natural resources from fire, depletion, or mismanagement.
It pointed out what the stock business itself has got to realize if it is to
survive: that private ownership of the range lands now publicly-owned
and regulated would cut the throat of the stock business in a short
time, since production would decline because soil and forage would decline. It went on to express what the whole West has got to realize if it
is to remain a healthy society: that the interests of the Western economy as a whole cannot be sacrificed for the temporary profit of a single part of that economy, and that success in the land grab would mean
the destruction of the watersheds by which alone the West survives. Finally, said the Idaho legislature, which is certainly no corrupt instrument of the New Deal, "private ownership of the remaining public
lands would result in a feudal ownership and restriction of human lib-
erties similar to those that now exist in European countries."

In short, influential portions of the West are opposing the assaults
on the Western economy and a lot of small stockgrowers have realized
that they have been stooging for the bigshots to their own loss. The

national associations have got a harder fight on their hands than they expected last summer. They intend to make it, regardless. They have a war chest that will pay for a lot of pressure and propaganda. Some of that propaganda will be directed at you.

I can touch on only a single specimen of it this month. The United States Chamber of Commerce is supporting the joint committee's program and in fact wants all the publicly-owned lands in the United States whatsoever that are capable of being worked profitably turned over to private ownership. At the San Francisco meeting of the Wool Growers Association, the chairman of the chamber's subcommittee on public land policy, Mr. Frederick P. Champ, made a speech which, to judge by the number of copies sent me by stockmen, expresses the party line. Because Mr. Champ's speech is a good deal longer than an Easy Chair I can touch on only a couple of parts of it, but they are the stuff that you, Congress, and the West are going to be fed.

Mr. Champ gives his remarks a historical background which any historian would repudiate—which, apart from references to the heroic spirit of American enterprise, consists of appalling misreadings or misrepresentations. It is untrue and perverted, and his historical logic is just as bad: for instance, "the public lands belong to the people and should be transferred to private ownership as soon as possible." But even in his own terms his conclusions are applicable to the early nineteenth century only, without relevance to the facts of life in the West today. In reaching one of them he calls to his support a Senator Benton speaking in 1799. If he means Thomas Hart Benton, he has him speaking at the age of seventeen, twenty-one years before he was a Senator, but 1799 is not a bad date for Mr. Champ's ideas, so let it go. Old Bullion is dragged into the discussion in order to introduce the word "tenantry" and in order to record his belief that we should "pass the public lands cheaply and easily into the hands of the people."

All the public lands it was possible to talk about before 1890 long ago passed easily and cheaply into the hands of the people. They do not figure in the present problem at all. We are talking about the reserved grazing and timber lands and the fundamental watersheds of the West, whose preservation as public lands under our historic conservation policy is indispensable not only to the West and the United

States as societies but to the heroic individualists for whom Mr. Champ is speaking. But "tenantry"—there you have a useful word. Americans never will be tenants, and a vision of the hopeless misery of Southern sharecroppers is supposed to rise before our eyes. (Not, of course, the West's tenant farmers, displaced by huge corporate holdings and called communists by the Chamber of Commerce because they don't like their own status.) But the miserables whom Mr. Champ has in mind are the biggest owners of cattle and sheep in the West, as the current opposition of small owners testifies. They are tenants only as they lease from you and me the right to graze on our lands for part of the year herds and flocks too big to be grazed for a full year on their home ranches. They are trying, for sweet justice's sake, to convert their leases into fee simple ownership at a fraction of their worth, to the exclusion of all other owners of sheep and cattle, to the extinction of the public interest, to the irreparable damage of the Western economy. They are not tenants to Mr. Champ the banker when he finances their business, but maybe they will be tenants in our eyes if he can throw enough loose topsoil from the dustbowl in them.

Mr. Champ turns from the Americans' unwillingness to be slaves to geology and produces the hoariest of all anti-conservation arguments: that erosion is a natural process and that overgrazing (which, besides, no stockman could be guilty of because in other parts of Mr. Champ's speech stockmen are the best conservationists) can have no effect on it. At a distance no one can tell whether this is naiveté, ignorance, or dishonesty but it is certainly nonsense. The mountains have indeed been running into the sea ever since they became mountains—but at a rate no mortal can perceive. We are talking not about geological processes but about the kind of man-accelerated erosion Mr. Champ has seen innumerable times in the Cache Valley where he lives. The erosion which occurs because overgrazing has so reduced the plant cover that the land cannot hold the runoff, which frequently telescopes five thousand years of natural erosion into five minutes of flash flood and a geological epoch of it into a few years of topographical degradation, which has brought a terrifyingly large part of the West to the edge of ruin and pushed some of it over the edge forever. Which has so depleted the ranges in Mr. Champ's own state that whereas in 1900 they supported

3,800,000 sheep, by 1940 2,300,000 sheep were overtaxing them. That is a thirty-nine per cent reduction in forty years—and it is also an inadequate measure, for the process of depletion is pyramiding.

It was January 28 when Mr. Champ told the woolgrowers that the canyons of the Southwest were eroded before there were any cattle in the West. Three weeks later at the University of Utah, a hundred miles from Mr. Champ's bank, Dr. Walter P. Cottam, a professor of botany who has not been communing with the New Dealers, delivered the eleventh annual Reynolds lecture. The university has printed his text under the title "Is Utah Sahara Bound?" Dr. Cottam says, yes, Utah is certain to return to the desert unless the overgrazing of its ranges can be stopped and those ranges can be restored to health—two *if's,* not one. The history of overgrazing in Utah, he says, "suggests ultimate defeat for man unless more brains . . . are used in the battle" with the forces of nature. He says that the joint committee indicated in June that the issue of overgrazing lies "solely between the western stockgrowers and Washington" but that actually it lies between the livestock interests and the public. He characterizes the ranges before the Taylor Act brought them under regulation as "at the mercy of unrestricted grazing use," a return to which is the joint committee's end in view. He votes against the unfettered freedom of stockgrowers to destroy the West and he speaks of "the social wickedness of passing on to an unborn generation a land impaired by selfish exploitation." That is what we are talking about, Mr. Champ.

The ultimate objectives of the biggest land grab in our history are to extinguish the public interest in all lands now held by the government that can be used by cattle, sheep, mining, lumber, or power companies. The immediate objectives of the joint committee are to get the publicly-held grazing lands into private ownership and to add to that monopoly all portions of the national forests that can be grazed. A good many Westerners have begun to protest to their congressmen. Wherever you live, your interests and those of your grandchildren are endangered. You, too, have representatives in Congress and a stamp.

U.S. Forest Service and the Western Land Grab

(Harper's Magazine, January 1948)

New England had a drought in 1947. So it also had big forest fires. Everyone has read about the destruction of Bar Harbor but the public at large does not realize how many smaller communities in Maine and New Hampshire and how many farms and isolated homes were burned. Thousands of firefighters were mobilized and they worked heroically. But they were facing an emergency which they did not know how to deal with. They were inexperienced, untrained; a tragic line is repeated over and over in the press and in private letters, "We didn't know what to do." It is clear that if anything like the United States Forest Service's organization, plans, and methods for fighting fires had been in existence in New England on an adequate scale, great damage and great suffering would have been prevented. A realization of that fact has spread across New England. Advertisement to Western congressmen: The Honorable Frank A. Barrett's attack on the Forest Service is not likely to pick up Yankee votes in Congress.

It is time to remind you again of the Western land grab. I described it in the January *Harper's* and in the June issue I told you that, as a result of publicity and outraged public opinion in the West, the tactics had been changed and the immediate objectives had been restricted. As I extend the record here bear in mind four facts.

One: the first objective is to get into state ownership as a step toward private ownership, or into private ownership directly, all publicly owned grazing lands; success would mean the destruction of the fundamental Western watersheds. Two: the ultimate objective is the conversion to private ownership of all the public lands in ten Western States; this would mean the end of conservation in the United States and, within a generation, the destruction of the intermountain West. Three: the drive is spearheaded by the national associations of cattlegrowers and woolgrowers, is conducted in the interests of a relatively few large-scale operators, is clearly detrimental to the interests of cattlemen and sheepmen in general, is being vigorously opposed by an increasing number of them and by other Westerners. Four: invisible so far behind the spearhead are other, larger, more powerful interests which will profit enormously if the public lands pass into private ownership or private control, if conservation practices are stopped or even weakened, if the precedents are broken, or if government regulations can be ended or even reduced.

While New England was burning, Congressman Barrett of Wyoming was taking his subcommittee of the House Committee on Public Lands across the West, holding a series of "public hearings." The announced purpose of those hearings was to inquire into the administrative methods of the Forest Service in its regulation of grazing in the national forests. From where I sit, however, the subcommittee's junket looks like an assist to the program I have just described. I am sorry that headlines dealing with Senators Ferguson and Brewster and Mr. Howard Hughes and other headlines dealing with Congressman Thomas and his Hollywood troupe deprived Congressman Barrett's circus of the newsprint it was entitled to. I have written "Congressman Barrett's circus"; what the Denver *Post* called it was "Stockman Barrett's Wild West Show." To the *Post,* to a good many other Western newspapers, to Western newspapermen and other observers with whom I have been in correspondence, and to the representatives of various conservation organizations, the hearings looked like an attempt to discredit the Forest Service, like a smear. My desk is piled high with reports from them which say so. Many of them believe that the true purpose was to inflame public opinion. Why? So that support could be gained for reduction of Forest Service appropriations, to the end that the Forest Service might be intimidated into conformity with the stockgrowers' proposals or else starved into acquiescence or paralysis—as, by exactly this method, the Grazing Service was. Some incautiously elated stockgrowers agree with my correspondents.

(At these hearings Mr. Barrett repeatedly attacked my articles in *Harper's* and two by Lester Velie in *Collier's* on related subjects, though he refused to let them be entered in the record. He also alleged, so my correspondents say, that my articles had been written at the instigation of the Forest Service. If he did, he was mistaken; considering how easily he could have got the facts, "mistaken" is not the exact word. All that the Forest Service had to do with my articles was to supply me, at my request, with certain information in its possession. As a stockman Mr. Barrett may forget, though as a congressman he knows, that public agencies are required by law to supply such information to whatever citizens may ask for it.)

It has been said publicly, and my correspondents say, that the committee's hearings looked as if they had been rigged. In advance, stockmen's journals had called for complaints against the grazing regulations of the Forest Service to be used at the hearings, and had suggested useful forms and specific content for such complaints. Mimeographed statements were distributed at some of the meetings. The committee required preliminary statements about what witnesses expected to say and then numbered the witnesses. Somehow neither conservationists nor the Forest Service officials under attack got called till most of the time had been used up. After listening to vilification of themselves for many hours (some of it by the chairman or by a couple of his committeemen) they were given only a few minutes to reply. It was not pretty. It would not have been pretty even outside the United States.

From an official transcript of the hearing at Rawlins, Wyoming, September 2 and 3, Mr. Barrett speaking: "My colleague, Mr. Rockwell, says this is going to be very mild compared with the hearing we're going to have at Grand Junction [Colorado, Mr. Rockwell's state: observe that Mr. Rockwell knew in advance what was going to happen there] . . . so I might warn my friends Mr. Watts and Mr. Dutton [Chief Forester and Chief of Range Management for the Forest Service] that they're having a nice time, yesterday and today, compared with what's coming next Friday." Does that appall you? Does it look like gloating by a prosecutor who was instead supposed to act impersonally as an inquirer? Does it look like a threat made by a congressman, a public servant, against a public agency?

One of the most prominent citizens of Mr. Barrett's state writes me that in his opinion, tremendous as the conservation issue is, the committee's behavior raises the even greater issue of democratic procedures. "Upon what T-bone steaks has this our Caesar Barrett fed?" he writes. "Who the hell do these senators and congressmen think they are? And what the hell does this growing arrogance among them mean? . . . If it wasn't for Congressional immunity they'd get . . ." Here my correspondent, a Wyoming cattleman, lapses into a robust Western idiom denoting anatomical violence from the rear which these Eastern pages may not reproduce.

I should like to print here much similar comment that has been published in the Western press or distributed by conservation societies or written to me by eyewitnesses who are trained reporters. I should like to devote a whole article to this material, to the evidence of the committee's star-chamber methods, its attacks on those who protested them, its violations of what we hold to be the just principles of public inquiry. But now let me call your attention to the wholesome effects of publicizing things that were not intended to be publicized.

Both Congressman Barrett and Senator Robertson of Wyoming (who was not on the committee of course but had fences to repair) vociferously denied that they knew of any desire of anyone, or had themselves participated in any attempt, to turn public lands over to private ownership. This was in direct response to my articles, Mr. Velie's articles, articles and editorials by Mr. Arthur H. Carhart, and other articles and editorials in the Western press. It was also in direct response to the uproar raised in the West by the publication on February 2, 1947, of an article by Mr. J. Elmer Brock, the vice-chairman of the joint livestock committee on public lands of the two national associations. Mr. Brock's article revealed that his committee's immediate aim was to transfer the

Taylor Act grazing lands to private ownership and, as soon as possible, to do the same with grazing lands in the national forests, national parks, and national monuments. (I had reported exactly that aim in *Harper's* five weeks earlier.)

A letter from Senator Robertson has been entered in the official record of the Rawlins meeting. In that letter Mr. Robertson flatly denies that legislation favoring such transfers was introduced in Congress. He also forcibly asserts that he believes the national forests should remain under federal control, that he believes the same applies to "the great forage-producing and recreational areas," and that the national parks "must remain under the administration of the federal government." There is room for a weasel even in this statement, since it leaves Senator Robertson free to support attempts to reduce any or all of the areas in question or to turn over to stockgrowers permanent grazing rights in them or even control of grazing there. However, the statement is for Senator Robertson something of a conversion. Let us hold him to it when the voting comes.

But Senator Robertson and Congressman Barrett, who also dissociated himself from the transfer of public lands, were doing some delicate footwork behind some dust. They were actually saying that no such legislation was introduced in "the last session" of Congress, the first session of the 80th Congress. But they were implying "any session."

I quote from the "Easy Chair" of last June: "The McCarran grazing bill, the Barrett bill, and the Robertson bill, all described in my January article and defeated in the last Congress [the last session of the 79th Congress], have not been reintroduced in this session. They probably will not be and so some egregious frauds will not come up this year." I also quote the title of S. 1945, the Robertson bill just mentioned, introduced by Senator Robertson in the 79th Congress: "A bill to provide for the granting of public lands to certain states, for the elimination of lands from national forests, parks, monuments, reservations, and withdrawals in connection with such grants, and for other purposes." This bill is analyzed in my article of January 1947. Presumably the Senator did not introduce it in his sleep. And, however inattentive he and Mr. Barrett may be to what goes on in the West, there is some chance that they may have previously heard of proposals to implement the land grab I have several times described here. If not, they will find them on the record now.

How much the Wild West Show accomplished is open to question. Montana proved cool and some of the most conservative papers in the state denounced it. In Nevada it was thrown for a loss by mining and other organizations that would suffer from impairment of the forests. The going in Utah was not too smooth. The hearings scheduled for Arizona were called off, either because time was short or because conservation societies there intended to try replying in kind. But it broadcast a lot of abuse of the Forest Service and the landgrabbers may find that helpful.

For the assault on the public lands continues and the idea is to keep plugging away, breaking a ball-carrier into the open for a long run when possible but counting a yard or two through the line a satisfactory gain if a given play carries no farther. A habit of stockgrowers, especially bigshot cattlemen, the habit of talking loudly, enables anyone who may be interested to work out the pattern.

In the last Congress Senator Robertson's bill S. 91, his S. 815, and Representative Fernandez's H.F. 1676 would all have helped undermine the established conservation policies of the United States. They would have prevented any further permanent reservation of the public lands, or required Congressional action instead of Executive Order, or required six months' public notice in the State where a reservation was to be made—time enough, in emergency, to ruin an area and time enough to put on a bigger and better Wild West Show. Mr. Barrett's H.R. 206 was more to the point. It provided for the admission of Alaska as a state—and turned over to the proposed state all public lands within its boundaries, *reserved or unreserved,* except those in use by the government (chiefly military) and a national park and a national monument. The sharp edge of this is the precedent it would set. If the national forests and all other public lands in Alaska were to become state lands, to be disposed of as the state might see fit, then the way would be open for every Western state to demand all the public lands within its borders, forests, Taylor Act lands, what you will. Down that road, clearly to be seen, is the ultimate destruction forever of the public domain, the public ownership of the land held in common for us all.

Mr. Barrett's H.R. 1330, last year's attempt to abolish the Jackson Hole National Monument, is even more important. I cannot here go into the tangled history of that controversy but the crux is, again, the precedent to be set. Abolish one national monument and the way will be open to abolish any other that anyone can find a use for. (This is the point too of the repeated efforts to reduce the area of the Olympic National Park.) Mr. Barrett's bill will be reintroduced in the coming session of Congress. Its loudest supporters expect it to be passed and vetoed; they hope to make it law in 1950.

More urgent is the recommendation of Mr. Barrett's committee for a "moratorium" on cuts in grazing permits in the forests. The immediate effect would be to safeguard current hoarding of sheep and cattle; the ultimate effect would be twofold, progressive degradation of the watersheds and a precedent sanctioning stockgrowers to hold up conservation measures. Even more important is the continuing effort to establish "advisory" grazing boards composed of stockgrowers—to give the men who use the national forests for grazing control of the grazing regulations, and to turn the grazing privilege on public lands (now held permissively and under regulation) by individual stockmen into fee-simple ownership of absolute rights which no one could regulate, curtail, or terminate.

As I said in June, the tactics have changed. The small minority of stockgrowers who are now agitating are quite open about it, and they can pick up at least a hint from the Barrett Wild West Show. Intimidate the Forest Service if you can; if you can't, then bleed it to death by cutting down its appropriations. The vision extends to the National Park Service, the Soil Conservation Service, the Fish and Wildlife Service, the Office of Indian Affairs—to all government agencies that are concerned with the public lands. A lot of the boys are betting blue chips that it can be done this way. They need, so they say, to control just three posts in Congress. Better keep an eye on them: the chairman of the House Committee on Public Lands, the Western member of the subcommittee for Interior Department appropriations of the House Appropriations Committee, and the Western member of the subcommittee for Department of Agriculture appropriations of the same House committee. It can be done, the boys say, by appropriations. Maybe, at least one of them says, by 1950.

Well, yes, maybe. But it cannot be done by Western votes alone. After all, the active landgrabbers are only a small minority of Western stockgrowers, a still smaller minority of Western citizens, and an infinitesimal fraction of the American electorate. The crisis is national— and you are represented in Congress too. These babies can be stopped: your senators and representatives can help stop them.

Sacred Cows and Public Lands

(*Harper's Magazine*, July 1948)

The Constitution of the United States does not provide for Congressional blocs, pressure groups, and corporate lobbies but under our unwritten Constitution they have become organic in our government. They are instruments for applying political power in the solution of specific political problems and by now it would be impossible to govern a hundred and forty million people without them. But their development has given journalism an additional political function, that of keeping their operations publicized.

This article describes the application of political pressure to a specific problem of administration. It shows a committee of the House of Representatives acting in response to a pressure group. The committee is the Subcommittee on Public Lands of the House Committee on Public Lands. The pressure group consists of certain Western cattlemen and sheepmen operating through various of their State associations, their two national associations, a joint committee of the national association, their agents and lobbyists, and their trade press. The immediate objective of the activities described here was to prevent the U.S. Forest Service from making certain reductions in the number of livestock permitted to graze on certain portions of the national forests.

That was the immediate objective but various long-term objectives must be borne in mind. Permits to graze stock in national forests are licenses, not rights, and are subject to regulation, modification, and revocation: for years the pressure group we deal with has been trying to invest the present holders of such permits with permanent rights. It has also been trying to secure such vested rights to present holders of grazing permits on other publicly owned ranges administered by the Bureau of Land Management. Associated with both efforts is a recurrent one to open both kinds of public land to private purchase and to give present holders of permits priority over other buyers, a long period to decide whether or not they want to buy, and the right to buy at the value of the grazing privilege alone, without regard to other uses of the land. In the background are still more astonishing aspirations. The pressure group has periodically undertaken to convert first to State and eventually to private ownership whatever land can be grazed that now belongs to other public reservations, for instance the National Parks. It has thereby attracted the sympathy of more powerful interests whose ultimate hope is to destroy the established conservation policies of the United States.

That larger hope interests us here only indirectly. We deal with a small minority group of stockgrowers, with the Subcommittee on Public Lands, and with the hearings which that committee held in the West in August, September, and October 1947. The records of those hearings have been printed. I use ten volumes of them here, two being records of preliminary hearings in Washington in April and May of 1947. I can touch on only a small part of them: eight of the volumes contain more than twice as much reading matter apiece as is printed in an issue of *Harper's*. Some things that happened at the hearings were kept from print by the standard device of declaring them off the record. In addition I suspect that sometimes the printed record may not do the facts full justice. A witness at one of the hearings sent me the part of the typed transcript that contained his testimony: in some respects it differed from the corresponding passage in the printed record. I may be wrong in supposing that there may be important differences between the transcript and the records. If I am, I shall be glad to make amends whenever I can get hold of the transcripts.

II

The pressure group dealt with here consists of only a small fraction of the Western livestock industry. For the most part it consists of large operators who hold government permits to graze cattle and sheep on publicly owned land. By no means all the large operators who hold such permits and only a small minority of the large operators in the Western industry belong to it. The group claims to speak for the industry as a whole but it does not. When you inquire what percentage of Western stockgrowers belong to the two national associations, for instance, you get not figures but polite evasions: it is a small percentage. Many local cattle and sheep associations have officially repudiated the objectives of the group, asserting that they were not consulted about the pressure campaign and have had no part in it. Since the ultimate objectives of the group were publicized in the early part of 1947, the number of stockgrowers who had opposed them has steadily increased.

The group claims that the entire livestock industry of the United States is in deadly peril because the Forest Service is reducing the number of stock grazed in national forests. Well, all told something more than a third of the sheep raised in the United States and about one-seventh of the cattle are raised in the West. Of these by far the greater part are not grazed in the forests at all: ninety-one per cent of the cattle and seventy-three per cent of the sheep. Those that are grazed there spend, on the average, less than four months of the year on forest ranges. In other words the national forests supply a little more than two per cent of the grazing for Western-owned cattle and a little less than seven per cent of the grazing for Western-owned sheep. And of these small numbers only a microscopic fraction are affected by the Forest Service reductions that produced all the uproar.

Grazing in the national forests is wholly permissive. You and I as co-owners license stockmen, for ridiculously small fees, to graze their herds there subject to the regulations of the Forest Service. Moreover, grazing is a subsidiary use of the forests, which are dedicated by law primarily to the production of timber and the protection of the watersheds.

Timber production is much more important than grazing, especially in view of the growing timber famine, but watershed protection is more important still. The stock business of the West, its agriculture, its mining, its industry, and its community life all depend on the healthy condition of its watersheds.

The basic fact is that the national forests have been dangerously overgrazed. Early practices of the Forest Service were in part to blame. Scientific range management has developed only in the twentieth century: the Forest Service has had to learn from its own mistakes and in the beginning authorized more grazing than, as the outcome proved, the range could stand without deteriorating. More important, however, was the overstocking of the range during the first world war, when public demand for increased meat production forced the opening of the forests to much greater numbers of livestock than they had ever carried before. Widespread damage resulted, to the forest ranges, to the forests, to the vital watersheds they contain. Ever since then the Forest Service has been working to repair the damage and to reduce grazing to a safe amount. It has not yet succeeded and many forest areas are still being overgrazed, with continuing damage to the range, the forests, and the watersheds. In some places this damage has become critical, in a few it has come close to the edge of disaster.

The pressure group has consistently opposed regulation of grazing by the Forest Service but most of all it has objected to the reduction of the number of cattle and sheep permitted in the forests. (There are still more cattle in them than there were in 1906.) Meanwhile unregulated grazing on other public lands has damaged them far worse. By 1926 the forage value of eighty-four per cent of the unreserved public domain had been cut in half. By 1932 further depletion of these ranges, plus the anarchy of the stock business, forced stockgrowers themselves to demand government regulation. Under the Taylor Act most of the remaining public domain was organized and turned over to a new agency, the Grazing Service.

But what the stockgrowers wanted was protection from migratory operators who had no base property and could undercut them by moving herds from range to range, and some kind of umpiring that would keep them from cutting one another's throats. When the Grazing

Service began to discharge the further duties Congress had given it, repairing and restoring the damaged range, it was doomed. From 1941 on the pressure group made a sustained attack on it and by 1946 had destroyed it. Cuts in its appropriations reduced it to a skeleton force wholly subservient to the stockgrowers and it became a subsidiary agency of the Bureau of Land Management. Its grazing fees have been fixed at between a fifth and a third of those charged by the Forest Service, which in turn are always smaller, sometimes much smaller, than the fees charged on privately owned grazing land. Vast areas of its range are in dreadful shape today. This in turn has added steam to the demand for control of the grazing lands in the national forests.

It was during the final stages of the attack on the Grazing Service that plans for a similar attack on the Forest Service were matured. The Forest Service program for reducing the number of stock grazed in the forests was continuing. The need for it had become more urgent because in some places the deterioration of the range had become critical, because the wartime increase of population in the West necessitated a higher land-use policy, and because that increase also necessitated every possible measure that would develop, conserve, and protect the water supply which absolutely conditions Western life. The reductions in permitted grazing made by the Forest Service have been smaller than impartial public policy would require, they have been gradual, and except when an emergency situation called for drastic action they have been made with extreme consideration of the stockgrowers whose permits were being cut. They have been made only after discussion with the permit-holders, usually after consultation with specialists and the local advisory boards, and always with complete freedom of appeal through the administrative channels of the Service up to the top. All these facts are brought out by the printed record.

Necessarily, however, some reductions bore severely on individual operators, and no stockman who does not see the wisdom of protecting the future of his own grazing can rejoice in a reduction of his permit. The pressure group, in whose eyes no land that can be grazed has any other value, was angered and alarmed. Something had to be done about the Forest Service. If the advisory boards which consulted with the Service could be given administrative power, then stockgrowers themselves could control grazing in the forests. If grazing permits could be given the status of legal rights, then reductions could not be made. Better still would be to get the grazing areas out of the jurisdiction of the Forest Service and into that of the Grazing Service. A number of bills providing for such measures were introduced or prepared for introduction in Congress and the propaganda arm set up a vociferous advocacy of them or, alternatively, for such as could be effected by executive order. But best of all would be to turn all publicly owned grazing lands in the United States over to State ownership, as a step toward private sale, or to open them directly to private sale.

It was here that the pressure group attracted the support of interests far more powerful. But it was here too that trouble began. Too many stockgrowers and their local associations were opposed to such a program. Too many other interests would suffer from it—agriculture, mining, industry, power, villages and towns and cities, hunters and fishermen, dude ranchers. Too many conservation organizations and too many newspapermen found out what was being planned. Too great a national interest was at stake.

A tentative formulation of plans was made in August 1946 at a meeting in Salt Lake City of the Joint Committee on Public Lands of the American National Livestock Association and the National Woolgrowers Association. In *Harper's* for January 1947 I described those plans and at the same time and during the next few months other writers described them in other magazines and newspapers. There has never been any refutation of what we said about them. There never will be—stockgrowers who oppose the plans and conservation organizations have transcripts of the Joint Committee's meetings. And in the Denver *Post* for February 2, 1947, the Vice Chairman of the Joint Committee published an article which verified what we had said.

This premature publicity stopped the program in its tracks. Public opinion in the West was so instantly outraged, so many organizations began to protest, so many Western newspapers lined up in opposition that the program had to be—temporarily—abandoned. Bills implementing it had been prepared for introduction in the new Congress. They were never introduced—and various Congressmen hurried home to explain to angry constituents that it was all a mistake, that they had been cruelly misunderstood. There is no chance that, in the immediate future, any effort will be made to open the public lands to sale. The program has been laid away for future use; at present the issue is too hot for anyone to touch.

But, as the pressure-group press pointed out, there are various ways of skinning a cat. There was the immediate problem of halting the Forest Service cuts in grazing permits—it was too late to stop them for 1947 but how about 1948? There was the continuing problem of bringing the Service to see things as the pressure group wanted it to—by threat, by intimidation, by defamation. Stockgrowers' publications were filled with denunciations of the reduction-program as unnecessary, unjust, and arbitrary. Stock associations memorialized Congress, accusing the Forest Service of despotic and even illegal administrative policies, and demanding an investigation. The Legislature of Wyoming demanded an investigation and suggested that it be made by the Public Lands Committee of the House or the Senate. The Legislature also pointedly alluded to Forest Service appropriations, and this club—such a reduction of appropriations as had hamstrung the Grazing Service—began to be brandished in the trade journals with increasing frequency. Demands for the dismissal of forest rangers, forest supervisors, and regional foresters were made. A college professor who had discussed the proposed land grab in a radio broadcast was prevented from repeating his talk. The mail of Congressmen was filled with complaints against the Forest Service, so similar in phraseology that a common source was indicated.

Seldom has so much noise been made about so small a matter. Remember that all told the forest ranges supply only two per cent of the grazing for Western cattle and only seven per cent of that for Western sheep. Consider too that the proposed cuts for 1948 would reduce sheep-grazing in the forests by only two-tenths of one per cent and cattle-grazing in them by only three one-hundredths of one per cent. It was in order to prevent this minute reduction that the pressure group organized its campaign. It concentrated on a proposal that no reductions in grazing permits be made for three years and that during this "test period" an investigation be made to determine whether any reductions whatever were needed.

This is the pressure to which Congress and its committees yielded. On February 4, 1947, the House Committee on Public Lands resolved that its Subcommittee on Public Lands would hold public hearings on the grazing policies of the Forest Service. On April 17, 1947, the House of Representatives authorized such hearings with House Resolution 93.

Before the House Resolution was passed, the April issue of the *American Cattle Producer* published a "Notice to Forest Permittees," signed by the executive secretary of the American National Livestock Association. The same "Notice" was published by the *Record Stockman* and the *New Mexico Stockman* and, I believe, by other trade periodicals. It announced that hearings were to be held in the West and called for letters of complaint against the Forest Service, "in order to furnish this [the Congressional] committee with as much background material as possible." It listed seven kinds of complaint that would be most helpful to the committee. Its final paragraph thanked the prospective complainants for their help and remarked, "Generally speaking, it is the complaint of forest users that the Forest Service is judge, jury, and prosecuting attorney, all in one. In other words, it is a law unto itself." At the hearings so many witnesses faithfully parroted those words that they became embarrassing.

III

The House Committee on Public Lands, of which Congressman Richard J. Welch of California is chairman, consists of twenty-five members of Congress and the Delegates from Hawaii, Alaska, and Puerto Rico. Under the Reorganization Act it is charged with duties formerly distributed among six committees. Twenty-two of its members besides the three Delegates compose the Subcommittee on Public Lands, of which Congressman Frank A. Barrett of Wyoming is chairman. It was the Subcommittee that held the hearings. The number of its members who attended them varied; so far as I can make out from the record no more than nine were ever present at one time; ten signed the letter addressed to Secretary Anderson when they were over. Since the touring Congressmen were members of other subcommittees that had work to do in the West, some of the hearings did not touch on the Forest Service.

The Subcommittee had already scheduled hearings on Congressman Barrett's annual attempt to abolish the Jackson Hole National Monument. They were held in Washington April 14–19, 1947, and the printed record contains some illuminating items. Mr. J. Byron Wilson, chairman of the legislative committee of the National Woolgrowers Association and a registered lobbyist for the industry, appeared as a witness favoring the abolition of the Monument. The testimony of such a person about such an issue would seem farfetched and irrelevant if it were not obviously part of a pattern. The pressure group is interested in undermining all federal authority over any part of the public lands, and to abolish one national monument would create precedent for further inroads. The same reason explains the appearance of the U.S. Chamber of Commerce. The manager of its Natural Resources Department testified in person and a telegram from a member of its Natural Resources Committee was entered in the record. They were speaking officially for one of the larger interests which I have said feel an affinity for the pressure group's ultimate aims. At that time it was standing on a platform for distributing the public lands to private ownership more extreme than any other that has been acknowledged in public. A year later, however, in May 1948, it retreated from that extreme and revised its statement of public lands policy, which is now rather mild.

Congressman Barrett's bill for abolishing the Jackson Hole Monument would have transferred much of the land in it from the National Parks Service to the Forest Service. The record, therefore, strangely shows Mr. Wilson, the lobbyist, and Mr. J. Elmer Brock, the Vice-Chairman of the Joint Committee, praising the Forest Service for efficiency, co-operativeness, administrative skill, and expert knowledge. Other stockmen even praised its grazing policies. And with this praise Congressman Barrett found himself in generous agreement. Since he was harrying the Parks Service, the Forest Service seemed to him, by comparison, a superb organization. The same oddity was to be repeated later in the year. When Mr. Barrett staged his production in Wyoming, Colorado, and Utah, the Service was staffed with incompetents, petty tyrants, swivel-chair bureaucrats, and impractical theorists. But when the committee moved to Lake Crescent, Washington, where there was a proposal to detach a large tract of timber from the Olympic

National Park and turn it over to the Forest Service, for two happy
days the Service found itself admirable and expert again.

The committee held a preliminary hearing on Forest Service policy in
Washington on May 12, 1947. The only witnesses were officials of the
Service, who described the grazing policies and the multiple problems
they involve. Chairman Barrett, a lawyer by profession, had prepared
the pressure group's complaints with admirable thoroughness and put
them on the record like a lawyer's brief and pleadings. The tone for the
hearings that were to follow was set right there. Mr. Barrett's arraign-
ment was hardly a foundation from which a fact-finding inquiry could
be conducted. He was not going to be judicial; to use the language of
the "Notice to Forest Permittees," he was going to act as prosecuting
attorney on behalf of the pressure group and against the Forest Service. As such, he conducted this hearing very ably and with frequent
cinematic effects.

Mr. Barrett is obviously a very intelligent man. So are his fellow-
committeemen, though I confess that I cannot follow with full understanding the excursions of Mr. Lemke's mind—present at only a couple of hearings, he seemed to be principally interested in providing
booster advertising for the State of North Dakota. Both their impar-
tiality and their competence to make such an investigation as they were
about to embark on are, however, another matter. Chairman Barrett,
Congressman Robert F. Rockwell of Colorado who played the second
lead, and Congressman Wesley A. D'Ewart of Montana are all stockgrowers. The last two hold grazing permits on the national forests.
Congressman A. L. Miller of Nebraska, who understudied Mr. Barrett
and Mr. Rockwell, revealed at Lake Crescent that he could not recognize a burnt-over area in a forest. (He wondered if those blackened
snags might not be the "over-mature" timber that lumbermen were
so passionately eager to cut down for the common good.) Since no
one who knows anything at all about forests can fail to identify the
marks of fire, a faint doubt of his qualifications for judgment rises in
one's mind.

The record is upholstered with stately Congressional courtesy, committeemen's ornate praise of one another as "your distinguished Representative," and topical references to "this great State." One who reads

it comes to see that Congressman Peterson of Florida, who did not go West but attended the Washington hearings, wanted to bring out the facts. So did Congressman Crawford of Michigan, who attended in Washington and got back from an official trip to Alaska in time for some of the Western hearings. So especially did Congressman Fernandez of New Mexico, who frequently pinned down outrageous statements by witnesses, forced equivocation into the open, and drew out facts that except for him would have been buried under abuse. Mr. Fernandez, in fact, is the only member of the committee who seems to have been actively interested in giving the Forest Service a hearing. But the necessity of all Congressional committeemen to play ball on one another's home lots was dominant. This was Chairman Barrett's show and he must be allowed to stage it as he pleased. Mr. Rockwell supported him brilliantly. Dr. Miller (he is a Fellow of the College of Surgeons) backed them up well and, at Rawlins, went farther in attacking a witness than anyone else did anywhere. He was, however, obviously astonished to learn how small were the fees charged for grazing in the forests. His repeated elicitation from witnesses of the fact that they paid the Forest Service only about one-fourth of what grazing cost on the privately owned ranges of his home State was a discordant note.

The first hearing in the West was held at Glasgow, Montana, August 27, 1947. It was concerned with engineering projects and some public lands under the jurisdiction of the Soil Conservation Service; Forest Service matters were not mentioned. They were first taken up at Billings, Montana, on August 30. And here, if I read the script correctly, the performers went up in their lines. Mr. Barrett indulged in some of the blustering accusations of the Forest Service that he was to make much more prodigally later on, but the audience did not respond. For Montana was not answering the "Notice to Forest Permittees"; Montana was, on the whole, well satisfied with the Forest Service. A few officials of stock associations made complaints but they did not follow the outline of the "Notice" and seemed to be merely *pro forma*. A few individual stockmen expressed grievances, but these proved to be trivial and mostly irrelevant to the inquiry. Whereas a large number of individuals and associations, stockmen, chambers of commerce, veterans' organizations, civic and sportsmen's societies, labor

unions, and others had turned up to testify in favor of the Forest Service. The meeting had certainly not been planned as a vindication of the
Service but it certainly turned into one. Moreover, as many as twenty-
nine individuals (including the Governor of Montana) and organizations made it clear that they knew of plans to turn the grazing lands of
the forests over to other agencies, to the States, or to private sale. They
made it clear too that they were violently opposed. It was here that
Chairman Barrett and Senator Edward V. Robertson of Wyoming—
whose reason for sitting with a House committee and cross-examining
witnesses is not clear—began to assert that they had never favored any
such measures and in fact had never heard of any.

The assault on the Forest Service, then, made no headway at Billings.
It is easy to see why. The Service completed its adjustments of permitted stock to the carrying capacity of its Montana ranges twenty years
ago, and the stockmen are fully satisfied with them. Those ranges are
now sound and healthy—the Montana forests are the only ones of which
this is wholly true—and the resultant benefits to stockmen and public
alike are fully evident. No one would dream of suggesting that greater
numbers of stock be grazed on them. The Billings performance was a
bust.

On September 2, however, the company moved to Rawlins, Wyoming.
This is Mr. Barrett's home State and in a couple of Wyoming forests
the critical condition of watersheds had made some of the proposed
cuts in grazing permits very large. "The hearing as I understand it is for
the stockmen," a witness remarked. Though Mr. Barrett hastened to
cover that break by pointing out that they were for the general public,
the witness was telling the plain truth. The hall was packed with an up-
roarious audience of stockmen, who had obviously assembled on call.
They yelled, stamped, and applauded; the pressure group's witnesses
and the active committeemen, the Chairman and Messrs. Rockwell
and Miller, played up to them. Moreover, the oversight made at
Billings was corrected. Forest Service witnesses, witnesses who wanted
to testify in their behalf, and witnesses appearing for conservation societies were held to very short periods, mostly at the end of the day.
Most of their formal resolutions and statements were not read but only
entered in the record for later publication. At the end of the day Con-

gressman Miller spoke of the hearing as a "spanking" of the Forest Service and the word is mild. "I have sat through dreary hours," said Mr. Charles C. Moore, President of the Dude Ranchers' Association, "listening to repetition, testimony of personal problems, testimony filled with useless verbiage; of the approximate fifteen hours of testimony, less than one hour and one-half was accorded our side for discussion of matters supposed to be taken up by [the] committee." Mr. Moore made a formal protest and added, "Never in all my experience have I attended a meeting so one-sided and unfair, so full of bias."

Mr. Moore's judgment must stand. Comparatively few specific complaints against the Forest Service were made. Some of them were quite footless, others consisted of accusations for which no supporting evidence was offered. For practically all the others the Forest Service had factual and unanswerable rebuttals in its records of the cases, which show misrepresentation by the complainants or completely just and judicial handling by the Service. Most of these case histories, however, were not entered in the record till later: the audience did not hear them and the committee could not have seen them when it made its recommendations.

The committee was willing to listen to wholly irresponsible accusations. Hostile witnesses, for instance, charged the Service with the intention of eventually eliminating all grazing of livestock from the forests. This is an accusation circulated by the pressure group in order to arouse the fears of stockgrowers and it is entirely untrue. The Service has invested fifteen million dollars in range improvements (on behalf of the very men who were lying about it), extensive programs of range development are under way, and the demands of witnesses that these programs be speeded up sufficiently revealed that they knew they were lying. Equally vicious was the repeated statement that the Forest Service had destroyed its own ranges. Again, one witness said, "The forests of the West furnish the major portion of the summer pasture used by its stock," and this clear falsification (I have given the true figures above) is typical of much reckless testimony. Its purpose must have been either to inflame public opinion or to set up a drawing account of propaganda to be used later on.

The intention to discredit the Forest Service showed clearly in the testimony of officers of State and national stock associations. What they had to say was extremely generalized. The proposed reductions in grazing permits, they said, were unfair, arbitrary, and quite unnecessary. There was no need for reduction. The ranges were not in bad shape. Forest Service scientists did not know what they were talking about, they did not know how to manage ranges, their researches and experiments were silly and their reports wrong. Besides, only stockgrowers understood range conditions and no stockgrower would ever overgraze a single acre. Again, the Service was heavily overstaffed—the threat to get its appropriations cut down glints here. Again, it was not spending enough money for range improvements. (It is spending all it can get from Congress. And the state of mind from which these complaints issued is revealed in the bellyache by one witness that the Service was heinously squandering public money in building forest roads for fire protection.) Again, it was spending taxpayers' money for propaganda against stock interests. (This means that the Service, in its regular publications, has reported that some of its ranges are in bad shape and that there is opposition to its repairing them by reducing grazing. It is required by law to make such reports. In 1947 its total expenditure for education and information, including all bulletins and reports on all the manifold activities of forestry, was less than one-half of one per cent of its appropriation.) And, the accusation ran, the Service had incited attacks on the stockgrowing industry by foreign, that is to say Eastern, journalists. This also is entirely untrue; since it involves me I am discussing it in this month's "Easy Chair."

The printed record shows Congressmen Barrett, Rockwell, and Miller acting as open partisans and shows their more than occasional belligerence toward Forest Service officials and witnesses who wanted to testify in the interest of conservation. At the end of the evening Mr. J. Byron Wilson, the lobbyist, made his inevitable appearance and got consent to enter a statement for the record. It skillfully summarized all the accusations that the hearing had produced and it ended by calling for a Congressional investigation of the Forest Service. The Service, Mr. Wilson said, had grown so powerful that it was no longer accountable to Congress and an investigation would disclose that all the nonsense spouted about it at Rawlins was true. That demand for an investigation was not there idly or by chance: it was helping to lay some groundwork.

At Rawlins Chairman Barrett told the two highest Forest Service officials present that they were in for a tougher time at Grand Junction, Colorado, and he knew what he was talking about, he had advance information. A larger, more noisily contemptuous audience had been assembled there, and the "Notice to Forest Permittees" had been well implemented. A mimeographed broadside had been prepared and copies of it were distributed to everyone who entered the room. A quotation will be instructive.

> The Forest Service is a child of Congress, grown up without parental discipline or instruction, an arrogant, bigoted, tyrannical off-spring, the same as any off-spring reared in the same manner, void of respect of law or customs of our land or the rights or feelings of other people.
>
> We now demand the Congress to accept the responsibility of this outrageous off-spring and put the restraining hand of parenthood to guiding it in the straight and narrow way before it runs afoul of some sterner justice.

The reader will observe an interesting resemblance to Mr. Wilson's formal statement at Rawlins, though Mr. Wilson writes more suavely and grammatically. He will also observe the threat of mob violence in the second quoted sentence, another revelation of a state of mind. Let him remember that what the Forest Service is here accused of is action to protect the national forests from damage by improper grazing. Our forests and our children's.

The hearing at Grand Junction was better stacked than the one at Rawlins. Witnesses were required to sign cards and specify the subject they wanted to speak about. By a selective use of these cards, the testimony of conservationists, water users, city officials, and representatives of protesting organizations was kept to a minimum. (They were booed by the audience.) Almost all of them were limited to five minutes apiece, though there was as much time for complainants as they wanted. The Forest Service officials, who had been grouped together like prisoners, were not asked to make an answering statement until the evening session. Then Mr. Barrett announced, "I thought . . . we should give Mr. Watts and Mr. Dutton or any of their subordinates about fifteen minutes or more to answer any of the charges that were made here today."

So far as those charges were specific, they were practically all trivialities, distortions, or misrepresentations. The factual reports of the Forest Service disprove and dispose of them step by step—and reveal their reckless malice. But again those reports were entered in the record later on. They were not heard by the audience and could not have been consulted by the committee before it made its recommendations.

If the witnesses were out of bounds, so were the active committeemen. This is from the *Record Stockman,* which highly approves the behavior it is describing: "His [Chairman Barrett's] arms waved; he pointed an accusing finger at the Forest Service section of the huge, tense crowd. As he finished, his voice quaking with emotion, a large majority of the crowd rose to its feet, applauded, and hurrahed." This is from a report by the chairman of an Arizona conservation group: "Representative Barrett did all that he could to undermine the authority of the Forest Service, to belittle the scientific work that has been accomplished by some of the leading experts of our country, to discredit its employees from the Chief of the Forest Service . . . down to the Supervisor and Rangers." This is from a report by a representative of the Izaak Walton League: "Rep. Frank A. Barrett . . . launched into a shouting, fist-clenching outburst that was intemperate in language and at times reached screaming intensity." There are other eyewitnesses' descriptions of Mr. Barrett's passion and the record shows that Mr. Rockwell was not far behind him. It also shows that, almost at the end, a stockgrower from "the same [national forest] where Bob Rockwell runs cattle" testified that "we haven't much to complain about in our neighborhood and we are getting along all right with the Forest Service."

It was gaudy, gorgeous, and inflammatory. But it was a tactical mistake. Officials of cities whose water supply had been acutely endangered by overgrazing and especially a representative of the Colorado State Planning Commission got into the record factual descriptions that turned a bright light on the folly of the complainants. Other conservationists, among them cattlemen and sheepmen from the ranges under discussion, in the brief time alloted them controverted and rebutted much of the testimony that had been so noisily presented. A representative of the Farmers Union who had been gagged by the five-minute rule wired to Speaker Martin of the House that the committee's "firing squad hearings" were "a shocking exhibition" and "a reflection on the dignity and decency of the House of Representatives." And a large part of the Colorado press began to protest. The Denver *Post* spoke of "Stockman Barrett's Wild West Show." The Gunnison *Courier* used stronger language in editorials too long to be quoted here. The *Daily Sentinel* of Grand Junction, a town whose water supply was in danger, said in a blistering editorial that the committee was "weighted in favor of one side and presided over by a chairman, also a party to the controversy [he was not a party directly], missing no opportunity to denounce the other party in the dispute, which was given limited opportunity to present its case." And so on—the surge of public opinion was like that which had followed exposure of the land-grab scheme earlier in the year.

There were prompt reactions. The committee called off the hearing it had scheduled for Phoenix, presumably because conservation societies in Arizona were organizing to receive it. And when it moved to Salt Lake City, on September 8, things were different. The same kind of witnesses (sometimes the same witnesses, in fact) began the familiar act. But they ran into the mobilized opposition of a State which had been alarmed by repeated catastrophies resulting from overgrazing ranges, which understood that only by protecting its water supplies could it survive, and which knew that the one realistic hope of protecting them lay in the Forest Service and its co-operation with other government bureaus that direct conservation. Mayors of cities, representatives of many civic and labor and veterans organizations, stockmen, sportsmen, farmers, engineers, plain citizens forced their protests into the record. The pressure group had run into the hard fact of higher land-use and its spokesmen were stopped cold.

On September 20, after hearings elsewhere on other subjects, the committee was in Redding, California, dealing with the Forest Service again. The "Notice to Forest Permittees" was doing its stuff, and to a reader of the record the mob spirit makes the Redding hearing seem uglier, more reckless and sinister, than any other. But also the demonstration seems fantastic and it was certainly futile. Then, after hearings on unrelated subjects in California, the committee moved on October 4 to Ely, Nevada. Here something exploded in its face.

A member of the Joint Committee presented a long, well-argued, brilliantly-written summary of the theses and arguments on which the pressure group stands, with their single-minded concentration on grazing interests to the exclusion of all others and their plain distortion of the realities. He was arguing for transfer of the forest grazing lands to the emasculated Grazing Service (Bureau of Land Management) which, as I have said, is helpless to oppose the will of stockgrowers. Also he permitted himself a kind of talk common among his colleagues but theretofore sagaciously kept out of their testimony before the committee. The power of the government to regulate grazing, he said, "seems more nearly modeled on the Russian way of life" and though we are opposing Russian autocracy, in government regulation of the range we are building "that very same system." To protect the ranges, the forests, and the watersheds is communism.

But Nevada is a desert State and life there, even more straitly than elsewhere in the West, is a function of the water supply. So something like the breaking of a dam occurred. Beginning with the mining industry, the most important one in the State, and running through practically every other way of life, witness after witness repudiated as unsafe the proposed transfer of forest grazing lands, denounced proposals to sell the public lands, and backed the Forest Service to the hilt. As the flood rushed on, the Congressional attorneys for the prosecution were uncharacteristically silent. The last hearing turned into a rout, and a couple of days later the member of the Joint Committee who had testified was writing to Nevada newspapers, explaining that what he said had been horribly misinterpreted.

IV

The committee had visited only one of the forests whose condition it had undertaken to investigate. (That trip occupied only part of one day and the range visited was not one of those whose deterioration the Service wanted to offer in evidence.) It had not seen the reports of the Forest Service which replied to the complainants it had listened to. But, though it did not report to Congress under whose Resolution it was acting, it was willing to make recommendations. It made them in a letter to Clinton P. Anderson, the Secretary of Agriculture. That letter is dated October 8, 1947, four days after the Ely hearing, and it is signed by ten members of the committee. But by October 4 the committee had already begun to disperse and go home: the printed record and the local newspapers show that only five members were present at Ely. The letter must have been written in California before the hearings ended. What it said might just as well have been written in Washington in April.

The letter made six recommendations about Forest Service administration of grazing. Five of these recommendations were pure smoke screen—they dealt with practices effectively in operation already or with procedures which anyone would favor. The sixth recommendation, number two in the letter, was the payoff, the one for which the entire campaign had been conducted: "Effective immediately and extending for a three year 'test' period there shall be no reductions made in permits."

Conceivably pressure-group propaganda and the violent emotions encouraged at the hearings might have created a force which the Secretary would have found too great to resist. But the hearings had gone too far—their excesses, their partisanship, and the resulting misrepresentation were obvious—and so he was able to stand firm. In a letter to Congressman Barrett dated January 13, 1948, Mr. Anderson accepted the five immaterial recommendations but rejected the one on which everything pivoted. He accompanied his rejection with a detailed analysis that disposes of the charges so tiresomely repeated at the hearings. He demonstrated that the cuts made in grazing permits were not unnecessary or unduly large or arbitrarily imposed, that Forest Service administration is not capricious or biased, that its officials and representatives are not ignorant of the stock business but in the main know it through long experience, that its experts are not impractical theorists but scientists standing on the irrefutable findings of their science, that the Forest Service is doing justice to stockmen and protecting both their interests and those of the public. His letter makes mincemeat of the propaganda.

The Secretary's letter was just, courageous—and final. The hearings of the Subcommittee on Public Lands had failed of their immediate purpose. The three year "moratorium" on cuts in grazing permits had been killed.

But those who watch over the interests of a pressure group neither slumber nor sleep. Though the hearings failed of their immediate purpose, they got said and printed a great deal of stuff that may be useful for the long haul. The demands for a Congressional investigation of the Forest Service and other government bureaus that deal with the public lands, which were made repeatedly, were made with an eye to the future. They can be used in the effort to force the Forest Service to accept dictation from the pressure group: they add teeth to the threat to get its appropriations cut down. What is more important still, they are an open bid for the support of stronger and wealthier interests that would profit from any change in conservation policy, from any loosening of government regulation of the public lands, and especially from extinction of the public lands reserves.

Such threats, always dangerous, are especially so in an election year. In March 1948, a pressure-group spokesman testifying before a subcommittee of the House Appropriations Committee proposed just such an investigation—and Congressman Barrett, appearing before the same committee, backed him up. Congressman Engle, a member of Mr. Barrett's subcommittee, has called for "an impartial study"— and the phrase always means a study which will find that the ranges are not overgrazed. General Patrick J. Hurley, campaigning for the Republican Senatorial nomination in New Mexico, has pledged his "support to a thorough investigation" of what he calls the Forest Service's "unreasonable domineering bureaucratic management" of "grazing rights." (Complete adoption of the propaganda: there are no grazing *rights* in the forest: there are only leasehold permits.) Mr. Harold E. Stassen has adopted not only the pressure group's position but that of the landgrabbers at large and has called for "a major revision of public lands policy." No major revision of public lands policy is possible except one that would put an end to the public lands. And though Governor Dewey promptly attacked Mr. Stassen's position, he did so in words that made conservationists shudder and suggest that the public lands would by no means be safe in his hands.

There are other straws in the wind. In the May "Easy Chair" I called attention to a resolution by the New Mexico Woolgrowers Association which demanded a reduction of Forest Service appropriations in order to bring the Service to heel. Since then the same resolution has been adopted by the cattlemen's association of the same State and equivalent ones have been adopted by other State associations. Both of the national associations and various of the State associations have increased their publicity funds and begun a campaign "to neutralize unfavorable publicity against the cattle [and sheep] industry"—that is, to neutralize such articles as this one. Pamphlets, canned news stories, and press releases carrying the pressure-group message are now in full production. Two weeks before this was written an article clearly inspired by the pressure group and packed with obvious untruths appeared in a magazine of national circulation. (Mr. Kenneth A. Reid has already exposed the misrepresentations it contains, but his detailed analysis is not likely to be circulated on the same scale.) Various professional writers have been approached about presenting "the stockgrowers' side." (None I know has yet accepted.) An earlier agitation by the national associations to present that "side" is shaping up as a guided tour for editors, reporters, and feature writers through the Western stock country.

Even the land grab is stirring again, though, as I have said, there is at present no chance that it can get Congressional support. Since the committee hearings some of those who testified that they had never heard of it have come out in favor of part or all of it. At its annual convention in January 1948, the National Woolgrowers Association resolved that National Parks and Monuments (our wilderness and scenic reserves) ought to be opened to grazing and that "all lands not of timber value" (including watersheds) ought to be removed from the jurisdiction of the Forest Service. A month earlier the Secretary of the Wyoming Stockgrowers Association asked that those same lands be given "public domain status for ultimate State or private ownership," and he said the same thing more guardedly at the convention of the Izaak Walton League in February. In November 1947 the Farm Bureau Federation of Wyoming officially demanded that *all* the public lands except National Parks and Monuments eventually be turned over to private ownership. (There go the forests and, when someone remembers them, the graves of the Seventh Cavalry.) The pressure-group press alternates between declaring that no one has ever made such proposals and demanding that they be put into effect at once.

By itself, the pressure group cannot succeed in any of these attempts. In a fighting speech Secretary Anderson asked the New Mexico Cattle Growers Association, "If there is going to be a battle, who has the most votes—the livestock ranchers or a combination of conservationists, game protective associations, public power enthusiasts, and the water users? Who is going to come out second best?" This small minority of Western stockgrowers, with their refusal to take into account any interests but their own immediate ones, their ignorant and arrogant rejection of scientific knowledge, their noisy but so far inept propaganda, will always lose out as long as they do not get allies.

But there are two dangers. The attack on the Forest Service is only one part of an unceasing, many-sided effort to discredit all conservation bureaus of the government, to discredit conservation itself. It is a stubborn effort to mislead the public. Conceivably it could succeed. And it could end by producing combinations. Ever since the public lands were first withdrawn from private exploitation the natural resources they contain have been a challenge and a lodestar to interests that were frustrated when the reserves were made. Those interests are much more powerful now than they were then. The natural resources husbanded for the common good have enormously increased in value. The consumption of natural resources not publicly reserved has astronomically increased the lust to get at those that have been saved. If the interests that lust to get at them should form an effective combination they could bring the United States to the verge of catastrophe in a single generation.

The danger is not Western; it is national. Fifty per cent more saw timber is cut every year than is grown to replace it—what would happen to our future wood supply if the national forests should be turned over to private ownership? The widespread impairment of range lands is a naked fact and our tariffs amount to a subsidy to stockgrowers to destroy them—what would happen if government regulation of the publicly owned ranges should be ended? East of the Sierra and the Cascades, Western agriculture is absolutely dependent on irrigation—can the United States at large afford to let dams and irrigations silt up and cropland deteriorate because of unwise grazing and lumbering that destroy watersheds? Business, industry, population growth, and life itself in the West are absolutely dependent on the fullest possible production of water—can the United States carry eleven States bankrupted by floods, a falling water table, and the destruction of land, business, and wealth that results from them?

These overwhelmingly important questions are given a sharp irony by the fact that they must be asked at a moment when a new era in conservation is beginning all over the world. Awareness of the necessity of protecting natural resources is now more widespread than it has ever been before, and in the Untied States, the first nation that ever made conservation a public policy, the happiest omen is that this awareness has spread not only among the public but among scores of nationally important businesses and industries as well. But at the same time the acknowledged goal of other businesses and industries is to put an end to conservation forever. That is what gives national significance to a minute fraction of the cattle and sheep growers of the West who are hammering away at the program here described. We must keep an eye on them, inconsiderable as they are. But it is infinitely more important to make sure that no support of their program by anyone goes unobserved.

Note: After this article had been set up, on May 20, 1948, Congressman Barrett introduced House Resolution 604, which had not been reported out of the Rules Committee when *Harper's* went to press. It would create a committee of three Congressmen to investigate grazing matters on lands under the jurisdiction of the Department of Agriculture, the Department of the Interior, and the National Military Establishment, with authority to employ three "disinterested experts" to make a detailed study. This looks like more of the same and accords with the agitation described in this article.—*B.De.V.*

Statesmen on the Lam

(*Harper's Magazine,* July 1948)

I want to treat at greater length several topics merely glanced at in my article about the hearings before the Subcommittee on Public Lands. The first of them is what Senator Robertson of Wyoming, at the Billings hearing, called "the biased and prejudiced articles which have been appearing in weekly papers and monthly magazines." He and Congressman Barrett, at Billings and again at Rawlins, were referring to articles by Mr. Arthur H. Carhart, Mr. William S. Voight, Mr. Kenneth A. Reid, Mr. Lester Velie, and me. The articles of Mr. Reid and Mr. Voight have appeared mostly in publications of the Izaak Walton League. Mr. Carhart, for years a specialist in wild-life management, has written for various magazines. Mr. Velie is an editor of *Collier's* and in the summer of 1947 published there two articles that dealt primarily with the efforts of the pressure group I have described to get hold of the public grazing lands. His articles and the one I published in *Harper's* for January 1947 were the ones most often referred to at the hearings.

Both Senator Robertson and Congressman Barrett accused the Forest Service of "collaborating" in articles with the attempted land grab.

No, let's speak as cagily as a politician who is mending fences. They in-
sinuated that the Forest Service had done so. Senator Robertson "came
to the conclusion" that an Izaak Walton League pamphlet had been
worked out in collaboration with the Forest Service and had been
printed in the same shop as Agriculture and Interior Department
pamphlets, which could only mean the Government Printing Office.
(Whether he meant to imply that Forest Service funds had paid for it
is anyone's guess.) Congressman Barrett said, "I don't know whether
the Forest Service has collaborated with some of these writers in these
magazines or not. I have reason to believe it has; I'll say that much, I'm
not charging you with it but I really feel deep down in my heart that
you have."

The Forest Service has never asked me to write anything, has never
suggested that I write anything, has in no way collaborated with me in
anything I have written. It has volunteered no information to me. It
has given me no information except at my request and the information
it has given me is only of the kind which it is required by law to give
to anyone who asks for it. Senator Robertson's toes were pinched by
my having published in *Harper's* the number of sheep for which he had
grazing permits in a national forest. I knew that he held grazing permits, I had asked the Forest Service for the exact figures, and I had got
them. At Rawlins he asked Mr. Lyle Watts, the Chief of the Forest Service, "Information as to individual permits of permittees, is that given
out by the Forest Service to these writers?" Mr. Watts replied to the
Senator that when anyone wants to know how many stock anyone
runs on a forest under permit, the Forest Service would tell him.
"That," Mr. Robertson said, "would be Mr. DeVoto as well as Mr.
Velie." It would be Mr. DeVoto; by law it would be anyone who might
ask. The privileges of a Senator do not extend to keeping his grazing
permits secret.

More interesting are Senator Robertson's and Congressman Barrett's efforts to dissociate themselves from proposals to open the public lands to private purchase. At Rawlins Mr. Reynold A. Seaverson, the
President of the Wyoming Woolgrowers Association, read a long statement. At the end of it Senator Robertson said, "I do not see any recommendation at all that the lands comprised in the national parks and
monuments, the national forest lands, or the reclamation withdrawals

should be sold to individual stockmen. You make no recommendation such as that, do you?" Mr. Seaverson said no. Mr. Robertson: "You never have?" Mr. Seaverson said no. Senator Robertson: "Speaking as president of the woolgrowers, you would definitely say that such a statement made by Mr. DeVoto, or Mr. Velie, or any of the Izaak Walton leagues, or any dude ranches in this country, to the effect woolgrowers advocate such a purchase by private individuals is absolutely without foundation, would you not?" Mr. Seaverson: "Yes, Senator, without foundation whatsoever."

The impression created here is that Senator Robertson had never heard of any such proposals, that none had ever been made, and that Mr. Velie, other writers, and I had malignantly invented the notion in what Mr. Barrett called our "scurrilous articles." Well, on March 14, 1946, Mr. Robertson had introduced into the Senate his bill S. 1945, which I described in one of my scurrilous articles. This bill, if it had passed, would have granted to the States all the organized Taylor Act grazing lands, lands to be eliminated from various other public reserves, and "all lands eliminated as hereinafter provided from national forests, national parks or monuments . . ." It would have made mandatory the creation of State commissions and the elimination from national forests of any lands which those commissions should find "to be more valuable for grazing [in whose eyes?] or agriculture than for timber production." And it provided that all theses lands and all other lands which under its terms were to be granted to the States, "shall be subject to lease, sale, or other disposition as the legislature of such State may determine."

At Rawlins, Senator Robertson was strikingly ignorant of the provisions of his own bill. Moreover, in his official statement Mr. Seaverson had recommended that lands "suitable only for grazing" (who decides?) be eliminated from the forests. This, of course, is not a recommendation that they be sold, though such a recommendation usually accompanies that proposal. Conceivably neither Senator Robertson nor the witness had heard of the many proposals to open Taylor Act land and forest grazing land to sale that had appeared in the stockgrower's press, or of the twenty-nine protests against them made at Billings three days before, though the Senator was present there. Conceivably they had heard none of the repercussions of the article by the Vice Chairman of the Joint Committee in the Denver *Post* which said that "as a first step toward acquiring ownership of the land they use" the stockgrowers proposed that "the government be required to offer [the Taylor Act lands] for sale" and went on to admit that "stockmen hope" eventually to get into private ownership "some tracts now in national forests" and others "which never should have been included in national parks."

Conceivably. But the record shows that Senator Robertson was present at the opening of the Rawlins hearing at which he later questioned Mr. Seaverson. It seems odd that he did not hear the acting clerk of that hearing, at Mr. Barrett's direction, read a statement by the Governor of Wyoming, the Hon. Lester C. Hunt. Mr. Hunt's statement, so short that I think most people could keep it in mind, ended with several recommendations. The fourth one reads, "That the Federal Government either dispose of these forests *(a)* to private ownership, or *(b)* to the respective States in which they are located." For a few minutes, one would think, the Senator must have known about some of the proposals which his bill would have enacted, if only inadvertently, into law.

Congressman Barrett said at Glasgow, "So far as I know, no one in Congress ever advocated granting the forest or the timberlands to private ownership." At Rawlins he dissociated himself from such proposals and told a witness that Senator Robertson's bill, of which by then he *had* heard, was dead. Its spirit was not dead in November 1946, when a convention of the Wyoming Woolgrowers Association was discussing one of the bills which my articles mentions as having been in preparation when the land-grab scheme was publicized. The Casper, Wyoming, *Tribune-Herald* for November 14, 1946, reports Congressman Barrett's speech at that convention. It quotes him as saying that fifty-one per cent of the area of Wyoming belongs to the federal government and then going on, "We must work out a plan whereby the eleven public land States of the West can grow, develop, and promote their own economy on a free and equal basis. The problem is to work out a plan for returning these millions of acres to the States. If such a plan is evolved, I believe we can sell the plan to the whole Congress . . ."

Finally, it is worth noting that, after Mr. Velie's articles and mine had been thoroughly denounced by Mr. Barrett and Mr. Robertson at Rawlins, Mr. Charles C. Moore asked that they be entered in the record. Page 219 of the record at Rawlins, Mr. Barrett speaking: "We will consider it; there has been objection by the committee; Dr. Miller has objected." They were not entered in the record.

Observe that Mr. Barrett speaks of "returning" the public lands to the States. The pressure-group press habitually speaks of "returning" them to the States or to private ownership. This is high-quality dust for throwing in the eyes—or should I say wool for pulling over them? True, the public lands contain some microscopic tracts that were once State land: mostly they represent either even-up exchanges or purchases of land that had been forfeited to the States for non-payment of taxes. There are also microscopic tracts which were once privately owned but for which the government exchanged equivalent tracts, usually agricultural, from public reserves. There are other tracts, agricultural land abandoned as submarginal or cutover forest land, which the federal government bought from private owners for purposes of conservation. The total area of all these tracts makes only an infinitesimal fraction of the public lands. Except for that minute fraction it would not be possible to "return" the public lands to State or private ownership. They never belonged to the States or to individuals. They have been publicly owned ever since their acquisition from France, Spain, Mexico, and Great Britain.

By the acts of admission the Western States were granted various tracts of the public land within their borders, to support education and for other purposes: these are the State lands. By their constitutions the States renounced forever all claim to the remaining public lands. These lands, the public domain of the United States, however, remained open for entry by individuals under the Homestead Act, various grazing and timber and irrigation acts, the malodorous Stone and Timber Act, and others. But from time to time parts of the public domain were closed to private entry and as "reserves" dedicated to the common good and benefit of the United States: the national forests are one such reserve. They are exactly what the term says and what they have been from the beginning, public lands. When the propaganda talks about "returning" them to the States it is talking nonsense. When it talks about "resuming the historic land-ownership policy of the United States," it is talking about a policy from which the public reserves were excepted, exempted, and withdrawn. When it draws analogies between these lands and lands in the East to which the original States had a more or less undefined claim, which they relinquished to the federal government, and which were then opened to private entry—it is perverting historical fact. But all this is grist to the mill. The idea is to set up a specious claim that the Western States have been robbed of their heritage. The further idea is to demand the Western public lands if Hawaii and Alaska are granted parts of the public reserves when they are admitted as States. But the basic idea is to get the forests and grazing lands of the West that are now a common possession of the American people into private hands.

The state of mind behind this agitation is sometimes grotesque. The Vice Chairman of the Joint Committee on Public Lands of the two national stockgrowers associations is testifying in favor of abolishing the Jackson Hole National Monument—now composed of land always under federal ownership to which Mr. John D. Rockefeller, Jr., has been trying to add as a gift land which he has bought. "First of all," he says, "I deny that the federal government has any right to that land. It has no right by its treaties of acquisition. It has no right for the proposed retention of those lands, which are now outside its constitutional limitations of land ownership. . . . To me when you get a lot of federal bureaus operating and managing lands which are not the proper function of government provided in the Constitution, it is nothing more or less than a mild form of communism. And that malignant growth in the West is almost destroying the American form of government. . . . There is an arrangement [for?] taking our lands away from us, in violation of constitutional limitations and our act of admission as a State." Here the gentleman seems to be saying only that to reserve lands for national parks and monuments is communism. But in his article in the Denver *Post* two months earlier he had said flatly, "Federal ownership or control of land is a form of communism."

His constitutional argument is based on the clause in Section 8 of Article I of the Constitution, which confines to areas ten miles square the legislative authority of Congress over tracts granted by the States to the government for governmental use. Few constitutional ideas so absurd have been aired in public since 1787 but this sort of thing, if not accepted by his associates, is nevertheless useful to their purposes. The gentleman lives in Wyoming: one wonders what authority he accepts as guaranteeing his title to the land he owns there. And one is reminded of a suggestion made some years ago by a writer who had been studying the cattle-baron state of mind that germinates such arguments. Over its history, he said, under stockgrower control, Wyoming had failed to develop the mature responsibility for self-government that Statehood requires, and he saw no plausible evidence that it ever would develop it. He proposed that Wyoming be returned to Territorial status so that it could be governed responsibly.

Such curiosa, however, are harmless. A really dangerous irresponsibility is the refusal of such stockgrowers as the Joint Committee represents to admit that overgrazing damages the forage, the land, or the watersheds. The record of the hearing is spotted with assertions that the results of overgrazing were in fact not due to it at all. The heaped-up, irrefutable findings of many sciences and many scientists—in various government bureaus that deal with land, in State and private universities, in private foundations, in experiment stations, in similar institutions all over the world—are ignored, denied, or ridiculed. I have space to mention only one example, the common denial that natural processes of erosion are speeded up—and unnatural erosion caused—by the deterioration of plant cover which occurs when an area is grazed too heavily. No fact that science deals with is more firmly established, but the pressure-group propaganda—and as I showed here last year, that of the U.S. Chamber of Commerce—challenges and denies it.

Some members of the Subcommittee were willing to support that denial. At Rawlins Mr. Barrett said, ". . . . it seems to me that the Forest Service ought to make a little study of this thing [erosion—the service has been studying it intensively from the beginning] and be a little honest about it, and say here 'This thing has been going on for centuries; it was going on before there was a cow in Wyoming; that it was going on before there was ever a white man in Wyoming. . . .' Why blame it on the poor sheepherder and the little old cowboy that's try-

ing to make a living here on these hills?" There are places in Wyoming
where the poor sheepherder and the little old cowboy have accelerated
erosion several hundred thousand per cent and permanently impaired
the range, but science does not impress Mr. Barrett. And the jocose
Mr. Rockwell at Ely: "Geologists [scientists who apparently can be
trusted about the condition of the land millions of years ago but not
today] say the original height in my State of Colorado was 36,000 feet.
It has now gone down to 10,000 feet. I wonder what the Forest Service would have done to prevent that loss, had they been in service at
the time." An entire psychology is compressed in that arrogantly ignorant sneer. At Grand Junction Mr. Rockwell had listened to scientific evidence which proved that the water supply of that and other
Colorado towns had been endangered by erosion resulting from overgrazing. At Salt Lake City he had heard how erosion resulting from
overgrazing had brought an entire Utah county to the brink of catastrophe—and how scientific measures to arrest erosion and repair the
damage it had done had saved that county. But that was the talk of
long-haired scientists and only a practical stockgrower, such a man as
Mr. Rockwell, is qualified to judge the condition of a range.

Against such psychology as this only the force of the ballot can defend the public interest. Argument, demonstration, proof, considera-
tions of higher land use, of long-term values, or any values except the
immediate ones of the pressure group cannot alter it in the least. I
come back to Secretary Anderson, asking a secessionist group of cattlemen who, if it should come to a battle, had the most votes. It may
come to a battle—it could as early as the appointment of Republican
Secretaries of Agriculture and the Interior.

If the West cannot control the exceedingly small number of people
whose program would destroy it, the rest of the country will have to
control them for the West's sake and its own. Up to twenty Western
votes in Congress might be swung to support that program, and such
a bloc might be enough to hold the balance of power. But your Representative has a vote that counts as much as any other. Better make
sure that he does not cast it on this issue in ignorance of what is at
stake.

THREE
Desert, Water, and the West

*For if the watersheds go, and they
will go if cattlemen and sheepmen
are allowed to get rid of government
regulation of grazing, the West will
go too. . . . Much of the interior West
will become uninhabitable, far more
will be permanently depressed.*

"The West," 1947

The West

(*Harper's Magazine,* January 1947)

Since some of the statements made about watershed denudation in my article elsewhere in this issue may seem extravagant, I explain that they are not in the least hypothetical. They are based on contemporary and historical facts that are not open to question. Inhabited lands have been made uninhabitable, cultures have been impaired, and civilizations have declined because of the very practices that now threaten the interior West.

If Noah's flood occurred in Mesopotamia, as some have believed, overgrazing and overcutting were responsible for it. For the ancient civilization of Mesopotamia developed on a narrow belt of irrigable land along the two great rivers and perished of the blight that threatens the West today. The forests were cut down to provide the towns with wood and the ranges were depleted by overgrazing. The land fell sick and began to die. It could no longer retain the water on which the civilization depended or maintain its own fertility. Irrigation systems silted up. Floods destroyed the fields. Mud flows spread across villages and towns. Hillsides gullied and the soil blew away. Year by year, herds and flocks grew smaller, the standard of living fell, population declined.

The civilization had been wrung from the desert and to the desert it
eventually consigned itself.

More striking because nearer to us is what happened to the great central plateau of Spain. From the earliest times it was known as good
sheep and cattle country and the famous merino sheep were developed
there. During the thirteenth century, the owners of migratory flocks
organized associations strikingly like those of cattlemen and sheepmen
in the West today and began to demand privileges at the expense of
other interests in Spain. The master-association was chartered in 1273
as the Honrado Concejo de la Mesta. As in the American National
Livestock Association and the National Woolgrowers Association, the
bulk of the Mesta's members were small operators but leadership was
exercised by the big-shots. "The association had annually elected
officers, a disciplined organization, and regular dues. It hired lawyers to represent its interests at the royal court, at customs stations,
and at strategic points on its north-south routes [of seasonal migration, following the grass]. It . . . claimed and gradually won exemption
from the jurisdiction of local authorities and ordinary courts." (Garrett
Mattingly.)

The Mesta was an effective pressure group and the repeated protests
of agricultural Spain against the privileges granted it were quite unavailing. The crown found the Mesta a reliable source of tax revenue
and such a source became indispensable as the imperial expansion
moved across the Americas. So the crown granted it privileges and
immunities—very much like those now sought by Western stockgrowers—that in turn helped to destroy the empire. It received "the right
to pasture en route in all unfenced fields and in fallows, fenced or not"
and the "right of pasture in all fields in which crops were not actually
standing. Its herders had the habit of stripping young trees to supplement grazing and of burning off woodland in the fall so as to have
more spring pasture. Both these practices became legal."

As early as the time of Charles V this privileged class had done irrevocable damage. "The expanding economy increased the demand for
foodstuffs and much increased their price, but agriculture was unable
to expand." By the end of his reign, "agriculture was definitely declining throughout Castile," irrigation systems necessary in this semiarid

land were growing ineffective, and agricultural land was deteriorating. Philip II clearly understood that the sheep had fundamentally impaired the national economy—and before the end of his reign the great flocks themselves were beginning to decrease. The inevitable had happened: overgrazing had cut down forage and the land would not support so many sheep. "Much former pasture no longer yielded grass. . . . By 1600 Mesta herds were down to less than two million head [a fifty per cent reduction in less than fifty years] and central Castile was becoming the desert which it has largely remained ever since."

Spanish agriculture has never recovered from the depression forced on it by that time and Dr. Julius Klein concludes that deforestation, attributable to the Mesta, was a principal cause. Dr. Mattingly calls the economic collapse of Spain in the seventeenth century "one of the most spectacular events in modern history" and holds the destructiveness of the Mesta's practices to have been a major factor in it. Ten per cent of the soil of Spain is classified today as worthless and thirty-five per cent more as poor.

In the words of L. Martin Echeverria, "destruction of timber and soil cover has turned much of Spain into a man-made desert." Destruction of timber and soil cover made the seat of Mesopotamian civilization a desert. They can make the modern West a desert. They will do so—within this century—if cattlemen, sheepmen, and logging interests have their way. If the watersheds now held by the government are turned over, even in part, to private control.

As my article says, the process of destruction can be vividly seen in Utah. The situation there is the more poignant in that no better farmers than the Mormon people ever lived—and that their virtues as a society have contributed to bring on the crisis which now confronts that society. The Mormon desire to hold the family together has tended to divide and subdivide the family lands, force them to support always increasing populations, and so graze beyond the safe limit, and so in the end impair the land and threaten its people.

The richest, most valuable, and most intensively cultivated land in Utah lies in a narrow belt at the western foot of the Wasatch Mountains in the valley of Great Salt Lake. Its location is typical of rich agricultural land throughout the intermountain West, which in general lies on the floors and along the lower slopes of valleys and is arable solely because it can be irrigated by diverting over it the water of streams that come down canyons in the mountainsides above the valleys. On the narrow belt of rich land in Great Salt Lake Valley the annual rainfall is about fifteen inches—that is, five less than the twenty inches that make it possible to farm without irrigation. Forty miles west of the Wasatch, the rainfall declines to between four and seven inches a year; that is, the land is absolute desert. But—and this is the master fact of agriculture not only here but throughout the interior West—on the mountain watersheds it averages between forty and fifty inches. Agriculture is possible only because that copious rainfall can be used for irrigation. Without it the arid West could have only a dry-farming and grazing society, with the low social level and absence of town and city life that such a society means. Maintenance of healthy watersheds is absolutely indispensable to the West.

The results of overgrazing the Wasatch watersheds began to be felt almost fifty years ago, when the population was only a fraction of what it is today. But both overgrazing and its effects are cumulative and the great damage has been done in the past thirty years, most spectacularly in the past twenty. The distance between Salt Lake City and Ogden, where the most valuable farmland is (mostly in Davis County), is about thirty-five miles. In the past twenty-five years fifteen Wasatch canyons in that thirty-five miles have poured disastrous floods over the farmland at their mouths. Most of the mountain area from which those floods came is now included in a national forest, and the Forest Service and the Soil Conservation Service as well as other government agencies (including the CCC [Civilian Conservation Corps]) have long been trying to restore the land whose depletion was responsible for them. But the government got on the job too late to prevent the floods of the 1920's, 1930's, and 1940's—and others that are still to come, though they will grow fewer and less disastrous as the work of repair goes on. The sole cause of those floods was the denudation of the watersheds while they remained in private hands. Fire and cutting of timber had a part in that denudation but the most important cause was the destruction of plant cover by overgrazing.

Such a flood is one of the most appalling spectacles in nature, especially when it takes the form of a mud flow—the large-scale removal of saturated earth from the slopes and its deposition on the benches and valley floor, always in fields that had been richly productive and sometimes in the streets and yards of towns. In the course of a few minutes geological changes are produced that would require many thousands of years of natural processes. Any buildings that happen to be in the way are damaged, ruined, or destroyed. Fences, roads, railroads are obliterated. Boulders weighing up to two hundred tons or more are carried out on the plain. Gravel and worthless kinds of dirt are deposited on the fields, whose topsoil and mineral constituents are leached away. The land begins to die. Up on the mountain sides small gullies become deep chasms, whose edges will be undercut and further torn away by every succeeding rain. Canyon streams which were stabilized a geological epoch ago gouge new, unstable channels. The natural processes of erosion are intensified many thousand fold. Soil washes away, hillsides gully, the process of deterioration widens with every rain, the vicious cycle accelerates.

The economic effects are obvious. The range becomes less productive; it will feed fewer sheep and cattle; the exhaustion of the best remaining portions is hastened. Stock owners sink into debt, go bankrupt, give up. The yield of farmland declines: ruined land will produce no crops at all, impaired land produces constantly smaller crops. Real estate values drop steadily; the cost of maintaining irrigation systems and the cost of fertilizing land rise even more sharply. The standard of living declines. People begin to move away and find their land unsalable. People who were intending to move in decide not to do so. Relief rolls increase. Communities begin to die.

A government scientist reports that in Davis Country, Utah, during a single ten-year period, the damage done by such floods amounted to "about $75 per acre for the entire watershed," an amount which when "apportioned to the denuded areas from which the flood waters come . . . aggregated approximately $1,245 per watershed acre." These estimates apply to the places directly responsible in the area of immediate crisis. But I must repeat that in dollar value and in potential danger, the small area of catastrophic floods are much less important than the steady degradation of watersheds as a whole. The process of deterioration goes on all the time: streams, irrigation systems, farmlands, ranges suffer a wasting fever which, if it is allowed to run its course, can end in only one way.

It is being allowed to run its course throughout the arid West, except for exceedingly minute areas, wherever cattle and sheep graze lands that are not subject to government regulation. The primary watersheds of the West are nearly all in government hands and are therefore subject to control, though a good many of them had been seriously impaired before the government took them over. The object of the open conspiracy that my article describes is to get rid of government control in the areas where it is now applied. To prevent the government from saving the watersheds. To shovel the West into its rivers. To make the interior West Mesopotamia or the plateau of Castile.

Why does this gigantic acceleration of erosion occur? "Of all the factors which influence run-off and erosion the plant and soil mantle are the most vital." (In Davis County the town of Centerville acquired about half the watershed of a canyon directly east of town, restricted grazing on it, and succeeded in getting agreements from owners of the remaining half to restrict grazing on their lands to the safe amount. Every storm that produced disastrous floods in the neighboring canyons, one of them only about three miles away, passed safely and undestructively down Centerville Canyon.) Properly grazed, a range will maintain itself in excellent condition; proper grazing is healthy for it. But as soon as overgrazing begins, both forage and soil begin to deteriorate. Plants and grasses less capable of holding back run-off begin to take the place of the original cover; weeds succeed them, the cover thins generally; bare spots appear. Poor soil produces poor cover; poor cover produces poor soil. All the processes of erosion accelerate by the square. Every rain, every wind, every year increases the deterioration.

If measures are taken in time, the range can be brought back completely and usually at small expense. The more they are delayed, the more expensive restoration becomes, the longer it takes, the less complete it can be. Sometimes it is enough merely to close the range for a period. Sometimes engineering works that put an all but intolerable financial burden on landowners have to be undertaken. Sometimes, as on the Escalante watershed in southern Utah, communities have to be moved away. Sometimes only small success can be hoped for at best; sometimes the utmost that can be done is to protect the lower lands from further damage, leaving the upper ones permanently impaired.

The effects of watershed erosion may be felt hundreds or even thousands of miles from the areas where the damage is done. Children may drown near Kansas City this year because a cattle baron had too many steers along the Big Horn before 1890. A great river such as the Snake has to be protected throughout its course and up to the sources of its smallest tributaries—farms, ranches, towns and cities in western Idaho, with all their water and power and irrigating systems, can be affected by what happens on the slopes of the Teton and Gros Ventre Mountains, and on all the hillsides from there on south and west.

The historian finds no convincing evidence that the cattle business was ever run intelligently enough to survive unassisted even in its great days, and is completely skeptical that it ever will be. Right now, with the sheep business co-operating, it is trying to make the cattle business impossible in the West within a generation. That, however, is not the greatest danger. For if the watersheds go, and they will go if cattlemen and sheepmen are allowed to get rid of government regulation of grazing, the West will go too—farms, ranches, towns, cities, irrigating systems, power plants, business in general. Much of the interior West will become uninhabitable, far more will be permanently depressed. The United States cannot afford to let that happen—you cannot afford to.

While you are thinking about it, remember also that one of the pressures now urging cattlemen to destroy the range comes from the fact that they have, by their own official figures, at least fifteen million more cattle to graze than they ever had before. Those are the cattle which they have withheld from sale for the greater part of four years—from sale to you and sometimes during the war from sale to the Army and Navy in which their sons were fighting. According to the Western press, action like this, when taken by a labor union, is a sitdown strike, inspired by Russia and encouraged by the New Deal. But when the sunburnt horseman does it, the Western press sees it as the protest of free men against interference with private enterprise by the bureaucrats and wildeyed theorists of Washington.

Flood in the Desert

(Harper's Magazine, August 1952)

In the mountain West last winter's snowfall was one of the heaviest of which there is any record. It was the heaviest on record in the Sierra Nevada, which always gets much snow, as the whole country learned when a great streamliner was marooned for three days in Donner Pass. When I visited the Pass early in May most of the snow was gone, though in sheltered places you could find drifts up to twenty feet deep. The runoff, however, had been gradual; the rivers of the western slope seemed unlikely to flood. The floods I kept hearing about while I was in California were to the eastward. They were in Utah, and that did not make sense.

For the typical Utah flood occurs not in the spring but after midsummer, and it is produced not by melting snow but by a cloudburst. In the past thirty years many such floods have taken the form of mud-rock flows. A cloudburst does not last long but at its greatest intensity the rain may fall at the rate of three, four, even six inches an hour. When such a weight of water strikes an area on a mountainside that has been denuded of vegetation it may sweep an enormous mass of soil into the flooding creek of a canyon. A torrent of mud rushes out of the canyon,

154

taking with it gravel and rocks and boulders that may weigh two hundred tons or more. It damages or destroys whatever buildings, roads, and orchards may be in its path, and spreads over villages and fields, sometimes to a depth of many feet. In the late nineteen-twenties such flows threatened to ruin the richest farming region in Utah, Davis County, which lies at the western foot of the Wasatch Mountains. I once described in the Easy Chair the project, directed by the Forest Service and manned chiefly by CCC workers, which rehabilitated the watersheds, saved Davis County, and made it extremely unlikely, in fact almost impossible, that such floods will occur there again. Knowing how seriously impaired many Utah watersheds are, I assumed that their bad condition was responsible for the floods I kept reading about. Indeed for some years conservationists have been predicting serious floods for Salt Lake City, where the newspapers said the worst of them now were.

When I got to Utah, however, I found that my assumption had been wrong. Most of the rivers of the Wasatch front were in flood. The three largest Utah cities, Salt Lake City, Ogden, and Provo, had suffered considerable damage; so had many smaller communities. Sizable creeks were rushing down some of the streets of Salt Lake City, whose appalled citizens were building sandbag barricades like those I had seen three weeks earlier at Council Bluffs. On the flat land along the rivers thousands of acres had been inundated. But the Forest Service scientists assured me that the impairment of the watersheds was not responsible for the floods. True, most of the silt they carried had been deposited in the rivers by previous summer cloudbursts, which were also responsible for the deeply gouged riverbeds that made excellent storage receptacles for it. But the floods occurred because of the unprecedented snowfall of last winter and because a period of unseasonable summer heat interspersed with heavy rains melted the snow with unprecedented speed. That combination would have produced floods regardless of the condition of the watersheds. There can be no dissent from the finding of the Forest Service experts, and yet there remains a phenomenon which it does not cover. Some of the canyons above Salt Lake City where trouble had been predicted were in flood. Just north of the city Davis County begins and I drove across it, across the region which twenty-odd years ago was experiencing those catastrophic mudrock flows. The Davis County creeks are precisely like those at Salt Lake City and they come down from the same mountains, which presumably had a fairly uniform snowfall throughout; the only difference is that their watersheds have been protected for twenty years. Every one of them was now well within its banks and was flowing beautifully clear water, not the chocolate-colored stuff that was depositing silt in Salt Lake City basements.

Davis County ends where the Weber River comes out of Weber Canyon into the pleasant little valley of Uinta. And the Weber was incredible, at least to one who remembered it as a small and shallow stream only a dozen yards wide in summer. It was a quarter of a mile wide, had cut a new channel in Uinta valley, was flowing dark brown water with the velocity of a rocket. It had washed out many long stretches of highway; it was undercutting the Union Pacific roadbed; upstream towns and villages were furiously building levees against it. And eight miles north of it, the Ogden River was pouring a similar and only slightly smaller flood over roads and summer houses and the flat land below the city.

The Davis County creeks, whose watersheds had been rehabilitated, were not in flood; other Wasatch creeks just north and south of them were. So I went on to the Logan River, which flows through one of the most beautiful canyons in the Wasatch before coming out on the benchland where the fourth largest city in Utah stands. There was no flood here; nothing had been damaged; no one was sandbagging streets or houses. The Logan was well within its banks; its water was clear; it was the healthiest stream I had seen in Utah. Now it is true that this watershed being in great part limestone country is somewhat more stable geologically than those to the south, but there is something else that I cannot ignore. Long ago the Logan watershed was very seriously damaged by excessive timber-cutting and by what is the curse of the entire West, prolonged overgrazing by stock, but the people of the region took action in time. At their insistence the Cache National Forest was established to repair and protect it. This was about 1906, so that the watershed has had nearly fifty years of proper management. It has restored itself, producing an ever-increasing yield of timber and ample forage for the stock that graze it—and producing no floods or waste of water. Add to this the one canyon in Davis County that made no trouble during the disastrous years. The people there also recognized the danger in time, prohibited grazing on the denuded parts, properly regulated the grazing elsewhere, and thus protected the watershed till it restored itself. That creek was safe and stable following cloudbursts that produced serious floods in creeks no more than three miles away.

In the next few days I traversed much of Utah by plane and automobile. The experience dramatized what I already knew by heart: the rigorous conditions of life, the inexorable problems, and the pressing dangers of Utah, which are typical of the whole mountain West, though sometimes more extreme. It is a beautiful country and it is a desert. Of its 85,000 square miles only 3 per cent is arable or, in any but the most limited sense, habitable. Basically it is a farming and stock-growing economy, but farming and stock-growing are possible only where there is water. They can never develop much past their present level; allow for the greatest conceivable advance in scientific agriculture and in the reclamation of now unirrigated land, and still there can be but little gain. If Utah is to have any considerable increase in population (already it is exporting much of its annual crop of college graduates), or any sizable increase in wealth, or any general rise in its standard of living, they must come from new industries. And industry is absolutely limited by the amount of available water and absolutely dependent on the production of water. And the ability of this region to produce water has been badly impaired by the denudation of its watersheds.

What happens in Utah, in all the arid West, depends on elevations of 8,000 feet and more. The minimum annual rainfall necessary to produce crops without irrigation is generalized at twenty inches. At the foot of the Wasatch, where the magnificent fields and orchards are, the rainfall is fifteen inches, five less than the minimum. Fifty miles farther west it falls off to four or five inches, to absolute desert, and the average across the state is about seven inches. But on the peaks it averages between forty and fifty inches. Winter snows above 8,000 feet make possible the crops of Utah (of all the West), the towns and cities, and all industry present and to come. Mr. Reed Bailey of the Forest Service has found the right phrase for the mountains: they are humid islands in a desert.

The plane I took from Portland to Salt Lake City landed in a dust storm; another one was making the sun a sickly pale-green disk the afternoon

I left Utah. Popular belief attributes these dust storms to the atomic explosions in Nevada, but it is wrong; they were occurring when I was a child in Utah. In some more nearly flat parts of the West they are usually due to improper methods of cultivation, such as failure to plow on the contours, and especially to the cultivation of soil so unstable that it should never have been plowed but used only as grazing range. But in Utah they are due primarily to unwise and excessive grazing of the mountain, foothill, and desert range. Wherever I went it was the same story, and a hideously visible one. Most of the range in the West has been or is being overgrazed; only on ranges administered by the Forest Service is effective rehabilitation being done, and it is not being done on all of them, and on some of them it is not being done fast enough. The dust that hides the sun in Salt Lake Valley comes from ranges, most of them in the desert, where the plant cover has been exhausted.

But dust storms are the least of it. The same dislodged soil is the silt that gives the flooding streams their chocolate color. It increasingly chokes the irrigation systems that are the arteries of Utah. It is steadily filling up the reservoirs that store the water on which wealth and even life depend, and just as steadily it is rendering the big dams and the little ones less useful. (Practically all the dams in the West but especially the most famous ones. Year by year such mammoths as Boulder Dam pile up the sediment that makes their reservoirs shallower, and engineers must plan other, probably less efficient, certainly more expensive dams to replace them.) And as the soil that should stay in place becomes dust storms and silt and sediment, water that should sink into the ground where it would be available for use runs off in floods. There is always less water for city and rural life, less water for the industries that might transform the state.

You see it unmistakably from a plane: mountainsides bare from unwise logging, from the burning of brush for a variety of mistaken reasons, from forest fires and brush fires that got out of control, from grazing on slopes that should not have been grazed at all, from excessive grazing where a moderate amount would have been safe. Almost at the tips of peaks, gullies have formed and are joining in a web; great bare patches carry the scars of landslides. Brooks, creeks, and rivers that should be as clear as Logan River are tan or brown; they carry long, dark stripes into the still water of reservoirs that only gradually become green and then blue. You can see it on the ground. Forage plants are "pedestaled," the soil has washed or blown from their root systems; Russian thistle and similarly worthless weeds are everywhere (the dreaded halogeton has not yet invaded the parts of Utah I saw, but it will); sheep have fed as high as they could reach on the desert juniper. Bare patches are spreading; so are the gullies that carry away soil with the run-off. And figures rise in one's mind: with more than twice as many people as it had fifty years ago, the state is able to raise fewer cattle and sheep than it did then.

This is true of all the arid West but the process has gone farther in Utah than in most other states and is more ominous there. And there is poignancy in the fact that the very virtues of the people, of the tremendously successful social experiment of Mormonism, have helped to accelerate the process. Probably no one but the farseeing genius Brigham Young could have built a society in Utah, and he could not have built one except with the industrious, obedient, co-operative Mormon people. Relinquishing the region's great mineral wealth to the Gentiles, he founded his society on an agricultural base, to maintain the vigor of family life, of rural communities, of mutually helpful enterprise. Practically all the arable and irrigable land in Utah, and the water, came into Mormon hands. But farms or ranches adequate for single families, and ranges adequate for small communities of ranchers, were not adequate for the families of the sons that grew up round them and for the communities thus enlarged. So in order to bolster the patriarchal family, pressure went on the land, and the long process of degrading it originated in the most estimable motives. Now the unforeseeable has come about: in order to progress further, Utah must industrialize—but cannot unless it repairs the injured land, saves the water it now loses, and finds ways of utilizing to the utmost the land's potential ability to produce water. And as in Utah, so to some degree in all the West.

In the Dixie National Forest I saw the biggest range-reseeding project in the world, 40,000 acres where in only four years an exhausted land has been brought back almost to maximum productivity, erosion has been halted, the soil anchored in place, the stock business stabilized. Far too few people have learned its lesson and the cost of reseeding is high, but the time is at hand when we must all master the lesson and will count the cost trivial. Even more impressive, to me, was the Forest Service's Desert Experimental Range. The entire staff here for research, experiment, and management has usually been a director, a part-time assistant, and occasionally some part-time laborers—but the results are staggering at once to the eye and to the imagination. Put it simply: in a seriously impaired desert range some small plots and some large plots have been fenced off, and bands of sheep have been grazed on them to the extent proved safe by experiment. These plots, that is, have been grazed properly, in the right numbers and herded in the right ways. In most places, proper grazing has turned out to be two-thirds of that to which the eroded range had been subjected. And the fenced plots have restored themselves unassisted; the range outside them, continuing to be overgrazed, has continued to deteriorate.

For a few feet inside the fence the noxious and unpalatable plants still grow; then the healthy, useful growth chokes them out. The "upward succession," the progress from less to more desirable plants, goes on smoothly. Gullies, checked and filled by new growth, are disappearing. The land is producing a maximum crop of forage. And the Station has found that it will improve as fast under proper grazing as it will when not grazed at all. Whereas outside the fence, weeds choke off forage plants, gullies and bare patches multiply, and the soil is washed away to settle eventually in storage reservoirs or on dinner tables in Salt Lake City. And the stockmen who use the regulated plots, though they graze a third fewer sheep, make more money than they did before. At a smaller overhead they get more wool and meat and they lose far fewer lambs.

Here the land has been healed by no more than wisdom. This is desert range and in the West there are forty million acres like it, grazed now by half a million cattle and between four and five million sheep—and deteriorating with terrifying rapidity. That vast area is now producing between a third and a half of its potential usable forage; it can produce no more because it has been so viciously abused. With proper grazing practices it could be restored to full productivity; the profits of those who use it would be doubled and, what counts more, the erosion that is steadily reducing the West's water supply could be stopped. Stockmen who use the fenced allotments at the Desert Experimental Range have learned the lesson it makes clear. But Utah and the West in general have not, and I was shocked to learn there that other bureaus of the government which are concerned with grazing have manifested no interest in it.

It has taken a long time to work out the principles of the scientific management of timber land and range land, of watersheds. But enough is known now so that the steady destruction of the West's principal resource could be halted and reversed; the rest must wait on public realization, acceptance, and support. Meanwhile the West clamors for the industry that would emancipate and enrich it—and the water runs off in floods, the water table falls, the reservoirs silt up, and dust clouds shut out the sun. A flight down the principal valley of the Wasatch is a symbol of a million square miles. At your left hand are the peaks, the givers of life and wealth; below you is the narrow strip of fecund land, the orchards and fields and towns; and always crowding close at your right hand is the desert. Utah is caught between millstones, between public education and the arrest of its promise; between, it may be, public education and disaster. So is the future of the whole West.

Our Hundred Year Plan

(*Harper's Magazine*, August 1950)

I doubt if anyone ever got to Oregon by traveling the Missouri River downstream, though the *New York Times* thinks I did. I had hoped to pick up this month where I left off last month and to tell you about a couple of Westerners and a couple of tenderfeet afloat on the Big Muddy. Including, for instance, the happiness of one tenderfoot, a General Staff officer of the U.S. Army, when he saw his first wild buffalo, a Black Angus which Mr. A. B. Guthrie, Jr., pointed out to him in a cottonwood grove. But our historical research came to the attention of various newspapers, which got so many things about it wrong that in fairness to our hosts I must correct the record. If I had been that bad at seventeen Frank Francis or Darrell Greenwell would have fired me from the Ogden *Evening Standard,* circulation 2,618 in those days. P.S. to the *Times:* if our trip was at the taxpayers' expense, the Bureau of Internal Revenue had better look into a large deduction I am going to claim on my next income tax return.

Our hosts were the Army Engineers. Mr. Guthrie had the skepticism of any newspaperman, plus that of any emigré Westerner who keeps an eye on conservation. ("You talk about the West the way a man would talk about a woman he'd divorced," he complained to me though I did not observe in his conversation any marked resemblance of the West to Joan of Arc or Kathleen ni Houlihan.) But the blue spot was on me. For some time whenever the Engineers and I have had dealings we have locked our watches and wallets in the safe, and the last piece I wrote before becoming their guest put the slug on them, hard I hope. They knew precisely where I stood about their conservation activities, and they made no effort to seduce me. From General Pick on down their attitude toward Mr. Guthrie and me, reporters on tour, was: We'll show you what we've got, we'll show you anything you want to see, we think our stuff is good but if you decide it isn't that will be just our tough luck. They did not add, we'll show you a good time too but they showed us one, as good a time as I've ever had.

If there was propaganda in this, maybe it succeeded. For on the last day of the trip, when we attended a meeting of the Missouri Basin Inter-Agency Committee and listened to reports and speeches, I reversed the one-two order of my villains. I decided that in regard to the ultimate objectives for which many billions of dollars are going to be spent in the West, the Bureau of Reclamation is more socially irresponsible than the Engineers.

The Engineers picked us up at Great Falls, whence I last reported to you, and flew us to the Three Forks, where the Missouri begins. They then took us the entire length of the river, by boat, by plane, and in one short stretch by automobile. One experience they gave us was, for me and a history I am working on, absolutely beyond price, three days in a small open boat on the upper Missouri. They showed us their dams, reservoirs, levees, flood walls, and all the skills, equipment, and paraphernalia that they involve. They showed us their plans. They arranged a big flood in the James River and showed us that; they had another flood in reserve, in the Little Nemaha, but we didn't have time for it. They detailed Engineer officers and high-ranking civilian officials to explain things to us and answer questions. We asked questions for ten days and they answered them freely, fully, and satisfactorily. Except for one kind of question, ultimate objectives and ultimate values. They did not try to answer that kind.

Where does it come out? The Engineers are an elite and their *esprit de corps* is amazing. Their enthusiasm, team play, and dedication to the job are all-out, and I have seldom seen such subordination of the individual career to the envisioned end. The jobs they do, they do superbly, with a mastery of engineering, a skill and ingenuity that—since they fairly represent the military services at work—make it clear why the United States was irresistible in the war. Moreover, the jobs they do are inspiring. Of course all large-scale construction is inspiring—it shows the human intelligence mastering the environment and the human will dominating the contrary and hostile will of nature—but dams and flood-control works are especially so. In my time I have reported some enormous operations, but I have seen nothing else so impressive as what the Engineers are doing on the lower Missouri. I feel sure they are going to make the Missouri the kind of river they set out to, from Omaha on down. From Kansas City on they have already done so. And, considering what the Missouri is and how futile mankind's attempts to control it have been ever since it wrecked its first bullboat or drowned out its first Indian village, that achievement stuns the imagination.

(Let's praise other skills too. The company that spent a day with the Inter-Agency Committee could not possibly have been selected with more accurate calculation of political values. The barge that steamed down the celebrated nine-foot channel past the Committee's boat, filled with I forget how many freight-train loads of wheat, was timing and stage-management that brought down the house. No quarterback noticing a defensive half's tendency to close in could have called a spot pass more expertly than speechmakers on the *Sergeant Floyd* pointed out to the crowd of politicians, newspapermen, and business leaders that the Engineers had a complete plan for control of the Nemaha watershed and that the loss, ten days earlier, of twenty-six lives and millions of dollars would have been prevented if Congress had appropriated the money to carry them out.)

I'll go further. Given things as they are—and that's how we are given them—I think that the Engineers have made not only a successful solution of the problem of flood-control on the lower Missouri but the best one possible. They have converted the Missouri's bends into frictionless drawing-board curves, they have made the river an instrument to control itself and co-operate with the human race, they have just about drawn its fangs from Kansas City on. They have forestalled and prevented hundreds of millions of dollars of damage to industry and agriculture and have made possible developments that will amount to many millions more. There are not going to be any more catastrophic floods in that section of the river. Except, of course, the theoretical granddaddy of all floods which, so the Pick-Sloan spokesmen tell the downriver folks every day, may strike at any moment from tomorrow on till they have been able to build their last dam on the last affluent of the last tributary of the lower Missouri.

Yes—but. They have done this with regard to flood-control so nearly exclusively that other values, and especially the other conservation values, go howling down the wind. I have not got space to analyze the Pick-Sloan Plan for the development of the Missouri River Basin, which is going to cost so many billions of dollars that neither the Engineers nor the Bureau of Reclamation—the Hatfields and McCoys who have stopped shooting each other so that together they can shoot the moon—cares to publish an estimate of the ultimate sum. I hold with the opposition: I consider it a reckless extrapolation of engineering mysticism. Nobody has made an effective answer to such criticisms of it as are embodied in, for instance, the Hoover Commission's "Task Force Report on Natural Resources" or the Public Affairs Institute's "The Big Missouri: Hope of Our West." Nobody in either agency has tried very hard to answer them; they know they are not called on to.

Get me right. I do not believe we are going to have a Missouri Valley Authority. Though the man whose thinking about the West I respect most bet me at Great Falls that there will be one within four years, I don't think one is possible. If it were, I would have only one argument in its favor. The reasons why I oppose any more river valley authorities are too complex to be stated here but they are fundamental—and still, if an MVA were possible, I would favor it because it would put an end to the composite of certain waste, probable damage, and possible disaster whose name is the Pick-Sloan Plan.

But what I want to talk about is not the Pick-Sloan Plan but the vast dream of Western development of which it is a part, and a state of mind associated with it that could produce a national disaster. It is only one item on a list of proposed Western developments certain to be carried out, if not to completion, at least so far as the Treasury of the United States can bank for them. There are, for instance, the Colorado River Development Program, the Columbia River Development Program, the Central Arizona Project, and the Central Utah Project. Further projects can—and will—be added to each of these the way you add rooms to a pre-fabricated house. Others are now only gleams in the engineering eye, but gleams that could add billions to billions for a total that could hardly be expressed in one line of type. Let us not forget that, a couple of years back, the Bureau of Reclamation proposed to take the Columbia River (which flows more water than any other in the United States except the Mississippi) where it emerges from the Cascade Mountains and conduct it to California—more than two hundred miles to the state line and then two hundred miles filled with mountains beyond that. If you think that the Bureau was fooling, or if you think that such a job could be done for a dollar-forty-nine, you're wrong.

All this is aimed at the industrial development of the West. I have written about that a good many times in *Harper's;* I trust I have written about it in terms of what seems possible. Integrated industrial development of the West—I'm talking about the West east of the Sierra and Cascades—is a national interest, a national problem, and a great and shining national promise. (Mr. Morris E. Garnsey, an economist at the University of Colorado, has recently published a book called *America's New Frontier.* The most important book about the West since Joseph Kinsey Howard's *Montana: High, Wide, and Handsome,* it will tell you what industrial progress means to the West and therefore to the nation.) But no one knows how much industrial development in the West is possible and while we spend billions for it very few people are trying to find out. We know that limits are absolutely fixed by the topography and distances of the West, by its capacity to sustain population, by its soils and climate, by the amount of water, and by the facts of life. We do not know what those limits are. But they are a hell of a long way this side of what the various planning boards and chamber of commerce promoters have in mind, and what the Engineers and the Bureau of Reclamation talk about to justify work that will cost more money than there is any present sign the United States will be able to afford. Work which, I repeat, may be in great part wasted and may produce disaster.

For the ultimate vision that is supposed to justify the Projects I have mentioned and all others still to come, though I have never yet found anyone who could state it in concrete words or even in figures—this hypothetical end not only implies an industrial development in the West of a natural and evolutionary kind, it implies a concentration of industry there, including a shift from other parts of the country, that is conceivable only in an opium dream. It implies a population much denser than the West can feed and fifty times as much water as the West will ever have. It implies changes in the economic and social alignment of the United States which would stand the nation on its head but which, of course, would be stopped at the furlong post by the other sections, since they would be paying for their own decay. Of the great and never concretely expressed vision, some part is certainly moonshine. I believe that a very large part is moonshine but I can't guess how large for I know no way of dividing infinity into fractions. I do not believe, for instance, that there will ever be heavy industry up the Missouri above, say, Omaha. (Yes, and if your heavily subsidized ninefoot channel brings ore from Venezuela to Omaha, what will happen to Geneva and other places where the native Western ore is to be worked?) I don't believe that any Western state will ever be industrialized in the way Ohio is now, or Pennsylvania. I don't believe that there can be concentrations of industry anywhere except in certain parts of Colorado, Utah, Montana, and possibly South Dakota. I don't believe there will be diffused industry of much importance anywhere else in the West.

But the boys are playing it with the joker and the deuces wild. (Twelve billion dollars in water development bills currently before Congress, as just one item.) The vision is for the appointed time, two hundred years hence at a guess, but the construction is for tomorrow and next year, up to the appropriations that can be logrolled through. The projects are supposed to be integrated, but if they ever are they don't stay put; parts of them which are supposed to dovetail with the rest are abandoned in favor of unexpected opportunity or local pressure, and a partially integrated system is a partially wasted one. Locally this does not matter, for at slight cost to itself the locality gets dams, ditches, and power plants, and a shot in the arm from big construction payrolls running through five years. It does not matter to the two big construction agencies, either, for they can go on doing their stuff. But the West may get out of it a fatal impairment of the natural resources that are supposed to keep it and us flourishing to the end of time. The United States may get out of it a loss running to scores of billions of dollars for irrigation systems watering non-irrigable land, heavily sub-sidized but practically unused navigation channels, non-utilizable and perhaps outmoded electric power, and dams that are miracles of engi-neering genius but quietly silt up while performing perhaps a quarter of the functions for which they were supposed to be built.

We don't know. There is no way of subjecting the beautiful dream or the all too real construction to criticism made in the national interest. Criticism outside the Bureau of Reclamation and the Corps of Engi-neers cannot be amplified above a whisper. Criticism within those agen-cies cannot be trusted. The Bureau does not operate outside the West, and if the Engineers think of ultimate objectives, ultimate values, or the national interest I found no evidence in two weeks of search. Gen-eral Pick was the only one who tried to answer my final questions. He believes that the United States should be vigorous, healthy, and pow-erful, and that we have got to have jobs for our increasing population. Who doesn't? and we are all against sin too. But when asked how much of the Pick-Sloan Plan could be carried out, how much of it was economically and socially justifiable, or what its bearing on the future of the West or of the United States was, he simply said that perhaps we couldn't do it all but we ought to do as much of it as we can. Maybe, but also maybe not. It is possible that doing as much as we can will turn out to be disastrous. The point is, nobody is bothering to inves-tigate that possibility.

General Pick is Chief of Engineers. Among his subordinates I found no one who was thinking in national terms, or in fact thinking beyond the job at hand. The routine answer to a question of value or of the na-tional interest was, "We aren't concerned with that; we merely do what Congress tells us to." As a former reporter for the *Evening Standard*, I find the second half of that sophisticated and the first half all too tragically in good faith. At the end of my talk with the most brilliant officer I met—I feel sure he is an engineer of genius and know he is a magnificent administrator selflessly dedicating his gifts to the job he is called on to do—he summed up by saying, "Don't you think that is a hell of a philosophical question to ask a poor engineer?"

Well, it isn't. The time has come when we have got to make engineers take up philosophy or else lay them by the heels. You can build a multiple-purpose dam all the way across Death Valley, and I do not doubt that if you do you will solve construction problems so brilliantly that engineers in heaven will weep with delight. I have no doubt, either, that the Bureau of Reclamation or the Corps of Engineers would build the dam at a gleam in any eye. But we should spend hundreds of millions of dollars to subsidize construction miracles without getting a teaspoonful of water, a square yard of arable land, or a kilowatt of power. The admiration in heaven would not compensate the people of the United States.

We have here an urgent example of what President Conant of Harvard has been talking about, the helplessness of the public to bring expert criticism to bear on what experts say. The engineering projects in the West amount to an American Five Year Plan, Fifty Year Plan, and Hundred Year Plan rolled up together. They are going to be carried through as far as the credit of the United States will permit. The Western bloc in Congress will see to it that they are, and Senator Douglas's superb and wholly futile attack on the last pork bill shows what the technique is. What President Truman said about these projects on his Western tour amounted to just this: I bought the West two years ago and I'm here to assure you there is enough money so that you'll be happy to stay bought. There is no party line in these matters, the only answer a Republican candidate would bother to make out West would be a promise to pay still more. Meanwhile the Five-Fifty-Hundred Year Plan calls for by far the largest expenditure the United States has ever made for internal improvements, by far the largest it has ever made for anything except war and defense. Ninety per cent of its objectives, at this stage, are entirely hypothetical. An undetermined part of them are also fantasy, guess, mirage, dream, vision, hope; some part of them will fail; some part of them may turn out to be fairly large-scale disasters.

These parts are undetermined but they may be a large fraction of the whole, and they may cost us the loss of many billions of dollars. There ought to be some way to get them criticized and appraised beforehand.

I don't know what the answer is. One proposal made by a task force of the Hoover Commission was to retire the Army Engineers from civilian construction. Another one, aimed at getting hobbles and a halter on the Bureau of Reclamation, was to abolish the Department of the Interior. They were idle suggestions. Another was to create an independent board which would have plenary power to pass on engineering projects in the national interest. That made more sense, though I do not know how you could assure that such a board would be either competent or unbiased, or that competent criticism would be brought before it. In any event, it won't happen.

But I offer a suggestion to the *New York Times* or *Herald Tribune,* asking it, however, to look at a map and find out where Oregon is and which way the rivers flow. Take a date, say June 1, 1950. Find out what, at that date, the fully matured plans of the two agencies for the West were, what further projects were being planned, what others were in the stage of intent, wish, or dream. Find out what the estimated costs of these amount to.

If you can. No one knows now; I doubt if either agency knows within a 50 per cent margin of error. But find out what you can and publish the results. If you accomplish nothing else, at least a wave of astonishment will travel across the United States.

And Fractions Drive Me Mad

(*Harper's Magazine*, September 1954)

We are all able to help the kids with their arithmetic problems through the Fourth Grade and well into the Fifth. What, therefore, are we to think when the principal engineering agency of the government, the Bureau of Reclamation, makes mistakes in simple arithmetic? When the Bureau repeats such mistakes, crusades on the basis of them, induces the President and Congress to act on them, and refuses (with, as one witness said, "its slide-rule stuck") to acknowledge them? The mistakes in question were made in the plans for a multiple-purpose project which would cost a mere $176 million if construction costs hadn't risen since the estimates were made. The project, however, is part of a big one that will eventually cost a good many billions of dollars. The episode of the stuck slide-rule should interest not only conservationists but all taxpayers, Easterners, Westerners, Congress, and most especially officials of the Department of the Interior who must be guided by the Bureau's mathematics.

Last December Secretary McKay approved for authorization by Congress a unit, called Echo Park Dam, of the Bureau's tremendous Colorado River Storage Project. This is the dam to be built in Dinosaur

National Monument which will breach the basic national parks policy and insure destruction of the national park system. Conservationists had successfully opposed the construction of the dam till Mr. McKay approved it. One of their basic arguments was that the destruction of Dinosaur Monument was unnecessary because the results which the dam was intended to achieve could be achieved just as effectively, and at less expense, by construction outside the Monument. The evidence and the public opinion it aroused led Mr. McKay's predecessor to refuse approval of the dam and direct the Bureau of Reclamation to make a study of alternative sites. What the Bureau made instead was some mistakes in addition.

Of the unit of measurement called an acre-foot you need know only that it represents the amount of water that would cover the area of one acre one foot deep. To meet the storm of protest which greeted his approval of Echo Park Dam, Secretary McKay issued a statement. He based his case for the dam on comparative evaporation losses. None of the proposed substitutes for Echo Park was acceptable, he said, because their reservoirs would lose far greater amounts of water by evaporation. In comparison with Echo Park, he said, the net loss would be "approximately 100,000 to 200,000 acre-feet per year." These are the Bureau's figures, and an approximation that can't be figured more closely than that provides a broad-minded margin of error. For, as Mr. McKay noted, even the smaller figure represents the water-supply of a city of half a million people.

In January the House Subcommittee on Irrigation and Reclamation held public hearings on the project. In the meantime competent critics had challenged the Bureau's figures, as they had been doing at intervals for four years. Under Secretary Tudor, however, again rested the case for Echo Park Dam on the alleged difference in evaporation loss. Speaking for the Sierra Club, Mr. David R. Brower once more pointed out some staggering errors in the official figures. One of the rejected alternatives "does not evaporate 165,000 acre-feet more than Echo Dam Park as [Mr. Tudor] testified but 2,610 acre-feet *less*, whole storing some 700,000 acre-feet more." The Bureau had made mistakes in addition and subtraction. And its figures contained "an error in multiplication or division or both" which represented the evaporation loss of the proposed alternative as 51,000 acre feet (six months' water supply for Mr. McKay's hypothetical city) greater than it actually would be. Also, instead of subtracting from the evaporation loss of the proposed substitute that of Echo Park Dam, which of course would not be built if the substitute were, the Bureau had actually added it in. Here was a loss of 86,000 additional acre-feet which would not occur, though the Bureau had said it would. Add 51 and 86. Of Mr. McKay's "approximately 100,000 to 200,000 acre-feet per year," 137,000 were the Bureau's bad ciphering. Nor was that all.

Before the record of the hearings was printed, someone altered a key statement of Mr. Tudor's and one of his statistical tables, in order to meet Mr. Brower's criticism. Presently the Bureau informed Mr. Tudor that its figures did seem to be off a little, and in March he wrote to the chairman of the Subcommittee, bringing the alleged net loss by evaporation down almost 50 per cent, to 70,000 acre-feet a year. Critics went on pointing out what must be oversights, faulty slide-rules, or someone's inability to pass the semester exams for the Fourth Grade. Finally, in April the Bureau published some data which said in effect, Well, is our face red! So Mr. Tudor wrote to the Subcommittee again, saying that his amended figure of 70,000 acre-feet was out by 45,000—an error of 60 per cent—and that the net loss by evaporation seemed to be 25,000 acre-feet per year. He added that he wouldn't blame the Subcommittee if it should doubt the reliability of this figure too. He believed it was sound, he said, but had ordered a check of all the figures, just in case. Damn good idea, for a lot of them have been challenged, but why not make that proposed study of alternative sites?

These admitted errors stood unchanged when the Committee on Interior and Insular Affairs reported favorably on the Colorado Storage Project, including Echo Park Dam. As I write it is uncertain whether this session of Congress will get round to authorizing the Project. If it does, Dinosaur Monument will have been ruined and the national parks system undermined on the basis of errors in arithmetic too gross to be permitted a schoolboy. Only the Bureau's own figures were involved and not only engineers but humble conservationists caught the errors. So some questions. Had the Bureau ever checked its figures till testimony at the hearings forced it to? If not, why not? Was it aware that the figures were in error when it gave them to Mr. McKay and Mr. Tudor? While Mr. Tudor was testifying, the Regional Director who had jurisdiction over the project was at his side. Was it not his business to know about the errors and his duty to acknowledge them? Is it not somebody's duty now to hold up the entire project till we all, including the Bureau, know where we are?

I am not now talking about the negligent ease with which the Department of the Interior, whose duties include protecting the national parks, breached the policy that has withstood all attacks by private interests. Quite apart from that, the episode of the non-existent evaporation loss has serious national implications.

President Truman appointed a very able Water Policy Commission to study the complex, chaotic problems of our water supply. Its authoritative report was published in 1950. We are still without a water policy four years later, primarily because the Bureau of the Budget has prevented any legislation that would provide the beginning of one. In desperation President Eisenhower has now set up another commission, consisting of the Secretaries of Defense, Agriculture, and the Interior. Its job is to break through the barrier and get some legislation started.

On the way to policy legislation, it should appoint a board to examine the Bureau of Reclamation's plans for the development of the Colorado River. There should be other experts as well as engineers on the board; none of its members should be in the employ of the government and none should have any connection with the power industry. It should be directed to make a complete study, at whatever expense may be necessary, and to propose such amendments, changes, additions, or deletions as it may decide are desirable. But its first job should be to publicize the existing plans so that they may be subjected to appraisal by the public.

The vast water and power systems which the Bureau of Reclamation has built in the West are among the most notable achievements of mankind. The amazing development of the West during the last generation would have been impossible without them. The Bureau will be the principal force in the development of the remaining water resources of the West, and it is the only possible organization for the development of the Colorado. But also in regard to the Colorado it has up to now operated almost without criticism. Even in the states that are to benefit from its plans few people have any clear idea what they are; elsewhere the public has almost no idea and does not know the stakes. This is an unhealthy situation. The future of the West, and therefore of the United States, depends on adopting the best possible solutions of problems of a greater order of magnitude than any we have previously dealt with. There can be no perfect solutions but there can be no assurance that we are getting the best ones attainable without the constant examination that makes public opinion authoritative. It is not the Bureau's function to make decisions of policy. It has nevertheless made them in regard to the Colorado and, as Echo Park Dam shows, Congress will tend to act on its recommendations unless informed public opinion is brought to bear on them. Precisely because the Bureau's plans have not been subjected to public criticism, they must be.

The Colorado River is not the Columbia. The Columbia will always have more water than use can be found for. Comparatively speaking, its flow is stable, its basin is coherent and unified, and plans for maximum efficient development are, so to speak, easily made. Such plans, in fact, exist and are in part the work of the Bureau of Reclamation. And here there has been constant publicity and criticism: the Bureau has had to bear the highly skeptical scrutiny of the utility companies and the Corps of Engineers. No serious flaw could have gone undetected very long.

The Colorado flows about a tenth as much water as the Columbia. It is a desert river and flows through a desert, through the most arid portion of the country, and mostly in canyons appallingly deep, difficult of access, and a long way from agriculture, industry, and cities. All the states it flows through are desperately pressed for water, and to those that have the worst water deficit an interstate compact allots half its flow. Or rather half of an arbitrary and probably optimistic estimate of its mean annual flow. That the West must use as much of the Colorado as proves possible cannot be questioned. Nor can it be questioned that the federal government, which means the Bureau of Reclamation, will have to develop the Colorado. Neither the states nor private business can develop it; they are not interested in trying; if they did try, the result, because of the kind of river the Colorado is, would be anarchy. Failure to realize that only federal development is conceivable is a flaw in the otherwise brilliant articles that Mr. Raymond Moley has lately been publishing, articles which should notify the West that the long indifference of the East is ending.

But that the plans of the Bureau of Reclamation are the best that could be made *is* open to question. They have been changed often and, it would seem, capriciously. Some changes have been made because of what to an outsider has looked like expediency or political opportunity. No doubt we could have predicted the formal judgment by the Corps of Engineers that the entire Colorado River Storage Project is an unsatisfactory solution to the problem. But conceivably the Engineers are right. Congress and the public have no way of knowing, and won't have unless such an appraisal as I suggest is made.

Nor can there be any doubt that a large part of the cost of developing the Colorado will be borne by the government, the general taxpayer. This is not only a social and economic necessity; it is also proper. The West is the nation's storehouse of unused natural resources. An expanding Western economy is essential to national prosperity. Federal funds must play as basic a part in it as they did in transforming the South from "the nation's number one economic problem."

But if the ends for which the necessarily astronomical sums will be spent are a national concern, so are the ways in which they are spent. What the West and the Bureau of Reclamation disregard is that the problems are not local but national, that the rest of the country is involved in them and will have a voice. What kinds of development of the Colorado? By what stages? How far in advance and how fast? These tremendous works modify human adjustments to the terms which nature has set for Western society.

It is the nation as a whole, not the West and the Bureau, which must determine which modifications are desirable—and, among these, which are more desirable than others which they will forever preclude.

Take, as representing one species of determination, the Central Arizona Project, which no one can now suppose will ever be built as planned. It would have committed us to spending one and a quarter billion dollars (or maybe twice as much) to maintain cultivation on some 150,000 acres of land that had only insecurely been brought under irrigation to begin with. The land itself could have paid *no* part of this sum; it could barely have paid the annual operating costs of the project. The capital investment was to be repaid by the sale of power—at a ratio to total costs justified by no existing public power project. The public would have been paying interest charges for upward of seventy years and to a total twice as great as the capital sum. The Bureau blithely planned the expenditure of such sums for such inconsiderable results. On what justification?

A different order of finality can be observed in the diversion of water from the Western Slope of Colorado to the Eastern Slope. The great untapped mineral resources of the state are in the western half, the present phenomenal increase in wealth and population on the other. There must come a point where the development of one section must be slowed down if the other is to go on developing, and another point where the development of one or the other must be halted for keeps. The Upper Colorado River Compact gives Colorado its share of the water to do with as it may choose, but the hard and inescapable fact is that the United States will moderate between the slopes. The Bureau claims that its plans take account of all possible future water uses on the Western Slope. But neither Colorado nor the United States can accept the claim untested.

The enduring drama of the West is provided by its aridity; lack of water sets an absolute limitation to its development. There can be no changing that limitation, but this side of it the ratios and proportions are adjustable. Immediately ahead of us are decisions about the final, irreversible establishment of proportions. They are difficult decisions, they will be painful, and God help the United States if they are not realistic and in the outcome right.

Let's suppose that it is possible, granted willingness to pay the bill, to add 200,000 acres to the irrigated farmland of Utah. Would we be justified in reclaiming the full amount? Suppose a trial balance shows that reclaiming half that area would be economically sound but that the money for the other half would be best employed restoring the productivity of half a million acres in the South—and let Utah deal as it best can with the rest of its share of Colorado River water. What then?

Clearly the problem is national and demands the utmost information procurable.

Suppose it comes to choosing between a hundred thousand more Californians and the same number of Arizonans for the fabulous new industries of the Southwest. (One of the unsettled questions of the Colorado Compact may work out in just such terms.) No solution is possible except by the United States—none by either state, or by the West, or by the anarchy of chance or the heaviest battalions would be tolerable. But that means the government, Congress, an informed and educated public—and at least one of the questions which the public must answer is whether Californians or Arizonans are the better buy. There is only so much water in the Colorado River but, though there is more money than water, there is only so much money too.

From here on out we cannot afford to decide anything wrong. Up to now there was a margin that allowed for waste and made mistakes assimilable. But we have reached the order of magnitude that makes wrong decisions catastrophic. The mechanism of decision is political. This does not mean at all that the decisions can be partisan: it means that Congress will make them. Fortunately in matters such as this, Congress always knows a little more than the public at large, for the conflicting interests educate it; but it can never know much more and, without the public base, the education it gets from the interests can be unsound. This means that the people of the entire United States have got to learn a lot about the Colorado River, the great river of the American desert, and have got to learn it fast. One would have assumed that the most authoritative teacher was the Bureau of Reclamation. But its arithmetic is bad and we must have a board of review.

FOUR
Protection of the National Parks

Congress did not provide money to rehabilitate the parks at the end of the war, it has not provided money to meet the enormously increased demand. So much of the priceless heritage which the Service must safeguard for the United States is beginning to go to hell.

"Let's Close the National Parks," 1953

National Park Service

(*Harper's Magazine,* March 1949)

Last September a forest fire started on the side of a peak in a remote part of Yosemite National Park. Before it was put out it had burned more than ten thousand acres of timber (in the direction of the Hetch Hetchy Reservoir, which helps to supply San Francisco with drinking water) and had cost the United States $90,000 for fire-fighting alone. The scar of that fire will disfigure Rancheria Mountain, in one of our most famous scenic areas, for many years. Ugliness is an intangible, so its cost cannot be appraised, but the manager of a privately-owned scenic resort would understand that forest fires depreciate his capital assets. There is no way of appraising tangible but indirect costs of the Rancheria Fire, either, but they amount to a good deal more than the cost of fire-fighting. As taxpayers you and I have to pay for damage done to property of which as citizens we are co-owners.

Why did this fire do so much damage? Because it took twenty-four hours, instead of two minutes, to get word to Park Headquarters that fire had broken out. Why did it take so long? Because it had been impossible to keep Park Service telephone lines in distant areas in good condition and the one that led to this area had been forced out of operation. How could such deterioration occur in one of the most publicized places in the United States? Well, the National Park Service simply did not have enough money to maintain all of the Yosemite telephone system in working order.

Olympic National Park contains eleven public camp grounds. Minimum public health standards cannot be maintained at any of them. Nowhere in the Park are facilities for water-supply or garbage-disposal adequate. Some toilets have decayed and collapsed. Many individual camp sites are no longer usable because tables and fireplaces have deteriorated beyond repair. Some bridges in the Park road system have had to be condemned; some still in use are dangerous. All the roads are degenerating. Some of them are regularly flooded because revetments, culverts, and drainage ditches cannot be kept in repair. Some roads have had to be closed; long stretches of others are being undermined. The Park Service cannot get money to take care of them.

Death Valley National Monument has an area of nearly two million acres. The permanent force which the Park Service is able to assign to it consists of a chief ranger, three rangers, and a naturalist. They cannot even man the checking stations at the three main entrances (where visitors register so that they can be kept track of in a desert that is sometimes dangerous) because they must patrol the main roads, clean up camp grounds, and serve as janitors for toilets. The water lines— important in a desert—have deteriorated so badly that they may have to be shut off. The Park Service has about seventy buildings in the area, some of them shacks originally erected in the understanding that they were to be temporary. The maintenance staff consists of one man and there are practically no funds to buy materials for repair. Three hundred miles of highway built more than fifteen years ago have been so neglected that they cannot be repaired, they must be reconstructed. There are no funds for reconstruction.

At Grand Teton National Park a visitor must arrive at a public camp ground before 2 P.M. or there will be no room for him to camp. The Park has at last got all its trails open for the first time since 1941 but cannot afford to put them in first-class condition. The Tetons attract mountain climbers and they are not all experts, so that half a dozen times a season one of them must be brought down from some precarious place on a stretcher. The Park is so understaffed that when this happens from fifty to seventy-five per cent of the whole ranger force has to abandon everything else in order to do the rescue job.

At the Statue of Liberty, a National Monument, most of Bedloe's Island is closed to the public because the walks cannot be put in proper condition. Many of the half-million people who visit it every year wonder aloud why there is no historical and interpretative museum; one has long been planned but there are no funds to build it. Beginning in March there is a season when moisture condenses on the inside walls and the water drips on the visitors. A heating system would obviate this unpleasantness, would make the place comfortable in cold weather as it assuredly is not now, would protect the health of the Park Service personnel, and would prevent deterioration of the symbol that means the United States to hundreds of millions of people. A heating system cannot be installed: no funds.

Three years ago, administration of the Lake Textoma Recreational Area was turned over to the National Park Service. There were practically no visitors then; last year there were two and a half million. And last year the Service could hire only three men for sanitation and clean-up work. It has no administration building; most of its office furniture has been borrowed from other government agencies. It brought forty-five trucks and automobiles to the area; eighty per cent of them are more than eight years old and the maintenance crew consists of two men, who must also take care of roadmaking equipment. The rangers who patrol the lake have one motor boat, a ten-year-old, thirty-one-foot cabin cruiser that can travel twelve miles an hour. When someone seems to be in a hurry about drowning, the rangers borrow a private boat, if one happens to be at hand.

These are just specimens. The National Park Service administers 180 areas all told: national parks, national monuments, historical parks and sites, military parks, recreational areas, parkways. From many parts of this large system similar reports have been made to me. Lack of adequate funds is causing one of our great public possessions to deteriorate at an alarming rate—while the demands put on it by the public are rapidly increasing. Many requirements of the public cannot be satisfied. Measures necessary to safeguard their health and comfort cannot be taken. Much irritation has to be inflicted on them. Many camp grounds are overcrowded and new ones cannot be built. Enough guides cannot be hired; enough maps and interpretative pamphlets cannot be printed; enough lectures cannot be given. There are not enough museums. Many people come away from parks without seeing what they wanted to because enough guided tours cannot be provided.

Meanwhile much of the physical plant is wearing out: telephone systems, sewage systems, power systems, warehouses, living quarters. Construction machinery and even fire-fighting equipment are deteriorating for lack of proper buildings to keep them in. Nearly everywhere roads are going to pieces. Some have had to be closed. Some trails for hikers, riders, and mountain climbers have also had to be closed, either because they could not be maintained in a safe condition or because they could not be patrolled.

No government bureau is more efficient, more dedicated, more hard-working, or public-spirited than the Park Service. The National Park system, an American invention, is the admiration of other governments, many of which send representatives here to study it. The National Parks and the areas integrated with them by the Service were set apart for the preservation of priceless scenic beauties, natural spectacles, and historic and prehistoric sites. But the appropriations for the Service are simply not large enough to enable it to do the full job that Congress and the people have charged it with. Meanwhile the eventual, the once avoidable, bill for deterioration goes on pyramiding. Meanwhile also irreparable damage has been done.

Take another consequence of the lack of funds. Morning Glory Pool was once one of the most beautiful places in Yellowstone Park but it finally revolted against the debris thrown in it by tourists, blew its crater, cleaned itself out, and is now just any spring, its beauty much diminished. The mere presence of a ranger is a deterrent to such vandalism as that which destroyed Morning Glory Pool but a ranger who cannot be hired deters nobody. So a large case of exhibits at the foot of Bright Angel Trail, in the Grand Canyon, was destroyed last year when somebody broke the cover, a sheet of plate glass so large that it had had to be carried down the eight miles of trail by manpower since it could not be packed on mules. Grand Canyon also lost a heavy oak cross in the "Shrine of the Ages," where religious services are held. The super-intendent reports his inability to maintain mounted binoculars at ob-servation points. So does the superintendent of Vicksburg National Military Park. The plate glass over a big panoramic picture-diagram in Rocky Mountain National Park was twice broken and each time the exhibit was ruined by subsequent rains; cabins high on the side of Long's Peak where first-aid equipment is stored are regularly broken into and the contents scattered. At Zion Canyon merrymakers climbed to a ledge and rolled boulders down on the toilets, destroying them. At Scotts Bluff National Monument the observation station, with its bronze markers and orientation map, has been destroyed repeatedly. At the birthplace of George Washington an ancestral brass candlestick was stolen. At Gettysburg a sword was pried out of a statue and stolen and in eight years souvenir-hunters have carried away 403 parts of cannon.

Souvenir-hunters operate wherever they are not watched, chipping off pieces of stalagmite at Mammoth and other caves, chipping rock or wood from other famous sites, pocketing small objects in historic buildings, wrenching off hardware, digging up bulbs, and stealing signs. Directional signs are also favorite targets for people who like to throw stones, and those that are made of wood are popular for fuel. So are picnic tables. And, of course, everywhere people write and carve their names. Various "pioneer registers," rock faces where historic figures recorded their passing or where Indians left their signatures in pic-tographs, have been defaced by tourists who carved their own names over the original ones. There are names and initials in masonry, plaster walls (of famous Spanish missions, for instance), and original wood-work that can never be restored. Lipstick, which is almost irremovable, has recorded the peripatetic love of Joe and Polly nearly everywhere, from the Statue of Liberty to the cone of Old Faithful. A common job of Park rangers, who should be serving the public, is removing obsceni-ties from the walls of toilets. An evangelical sect painted its warnings of the wrath to come along Going-to-the-Sun highway in Glacier Na-tional Park.

Vandalism is largely a crowd phenomenon. If there were enough rangers to patrol the most crowded, most spectacular, and most famous places, and enough others to catch and prosecute a few offenders, most of it would never occur. But the Park Service has not got funds to hire them.

I cannot treat here the privately-owned areas inside Parks or on the approaches to them or to historic sites, holdings that must be bought for the sake of protection and decent dignity. Many are hideous or vulgar, some are slums, none are subject to any kind of regulation. Certain areas of the actual battlefield of Gettysburg are beginning to resemble Coney Island; a real-estate development locally called "Slab-town" is encroaching on that of Yorktown. Two years ago the Director of the Park Service estimated that all the private holdings inside the National Parks could be bought for twenty million dollars. Last year Congress made the first appropriation toward that highly desirable end: two hundred thousand dollars. At that rate the Parks will be complete in a century, if nobody raises his price. We may also remember that the Park Service's plans for development—construction of new roads and trails, opening up of important areas now inaccessible, relocation of buildings, construction of new camp grounds and other accommodations for the rising number of visitors, increase of recreational and educational facilities—these plans, developed by experts over many years, move exceeding slow and in many places are at a standstill.

In short, the National Park Service is failing to perform some of the functions assigned to it and is able to perform but few of them as well as it wants to. Great expense caused by unwise economy measures is piling up and will eventually have to be met. A good many areas that are among the favorite vacation places of the American people have become shabby or worse, and some of the wilderness, scenery, and natural spectacles in which the public takes the greatest pride are threatened with disfigurement and even destruction. Almost the entire National Park system is already overstrained by the steadily increasing number of people who use it. The situation is shocking: it is becoming critical.

How did it come about? In two ways: the National Park system is an inadvertent victim of the war, and the postwar attendance has been greater than the prewar set-up, even if it had been fully restored, could have handled. During the war only a skeleton force was maintained, and shortages in material and labor made proper upkeep impossible.

Since the war the Service has never been able to get back to full strength and has never been able to catch up with the job. (Not to mention the new Parks that have been created and the new historic sites and recreational areas that have been turned over to it.)

Service personnel, attendance, and congressional appropriations were in a fair equilibrium in the late 1930's, but by 1941, the last prewar season, the Service was already stretched to the utmost, trying to spread appropriations wider than they could be made to go. In 1941 it had 5,104 permanent employees and 21 million people visited the Parks. Last year, 1948, it had 2,393 permanent employes [*sic*], less than half as many, and visitors numbered 30 million, an increase of forty per cent. The cost of hired labor, material, supplies, and machinery has risen just as much for the Service as it has for the country at large.

For the current fiscal year the Park Service appropriation is 13 million dollars, of which less than five million is for roads, trails, and physical improvements. The Director has estimated that to rehabilitate the Parks and equip them to meet the increased demand would require $145,000,000 for building and rebuilding roads and another $115,000,000 for other needed developments. (The latter figure is considerably less all told than the increase—not the total sum—in appropriations granted in a single year to the Army Engineers for nonmilitary projects.)

Unlike some government bureaus, the Park Service has no enemies, so far as I know, in either Congress or the Bureau of the Budget. The disastrous situation has arisen through sheer disregard—concentration first on the war and then on defense measures has diverted everybody's attention elsewhere. Congress does not sufficiently realize what has been happening, the Service does not and cannot set up such a bullroaring as the Bureau of Reclamation does when someone threatens to reduce its appropriations, and anyone who wants a reputation for guarding the Treasury can always demand why anything must be done about Old Faithful while the promised twelve-foot channel for barges in Goose Creek remains undredged.

Nevertheless the situation does exist, it is disastrous, and it must be met. Elementary business principles require us to protect a large national investment. The satisfaction of the millions who use the Parks must be assured. And the declared will of Congress and the people, that the areas administered by the Park Service be kept inviolate for succeeding generations, must be carried out. The Park Service must have a lot more money than it has been getting. And it must begin to get it at once.

Shall We Let Them Ruin
Our National Parks?

(*The Saturday Evening Post,* July 1950)

*Do you want these wild splendors kept intact for your kids to
see? Then watch out for the Army Engineers and the Bureau
of Reclamation—because right where the scenery is, that's
where they want to build dams.*

No one has asked the American people whether they want their sover-
eign rights, and those of their descendants, in their own publicly reserved beauty spots wiped out. Thirty-two million of them visited the
National Parks in 1949. More will visit them this year. The attendance
will keep on increasing as long as they are worth visiting, but a good
many of them will not be worth visiting if the engineers are let loose
on them.

The entire National Park System comprises an area less then three
quarters of 1 per cent of the area of the United States. It contains
only sites that are universally acknowledged to be supreme in beauty,
grandeur and spectacle. They were set aside to the sole end that they
should be preserved as they are, that there should always be places
where Americans could have the inestimable experience of untouched
wilderness, unspoiled natural beauty and unmarred natural spectacle.
That end is now in danger of being subverted by engineering construction. No one can doubt that the public, if told all the facts and allowed

to express its will, would vote to preserve the parks from any alteration now or in the future. But the public is not being told all the facts; it is not being given a chance to express its will.

Most people who have seen the Grand Canyon consider it our supreme natural spectacle. What would it look like if the Colorado River at the bottom of the gorge, the river that carved the gorge, were to be made a dry stream bed?

Down near the Arizona-Utah boundary is Rainbow Bridge, the most famous and most beautiful of all the natural bridges, a high, superbly symmetrical arch of stone, long ago set aside as a National Monument. The water of a storage reservoir may undermine it and bring it down. Should we permit that to happen?

After the Green River flows out of Wyoming to cross parts of Northwestern Colorado and Northeastern Utah, it roars and riots through a series of deep, narrow canyons, one of which is named Lodore. If a dam were to transform the tempestuous Green in Lodore Canyon into a lake 500 feet deep, would you drive 2000 miles to sail a dinghy there?

These and other areas of unmatched beauty or sublimity, which were made National Parks or National Monuments so that they could be preserved untouched forever, are in danger of being ruined by engineering projects. Should we let them be ruined?

The National Park Service is a bureau of the Department of the Interior, where, in appropriations, it is overshadowed by the Bureau of Reclamation, which builds dams. Though the Park Service has other duties, its primary job is to administer the National Parks and Monuments. The act of Congress which created it directed it "to conserve the scenery and the natural and historic objects and the wildlife therein, and to provide for the enjoyment of the same in such manner and by such means as will leave them unimpaired for the enjoyment of future generations."

These words are perfectly clear and they enact into law a policy that goes all the way back to the establishment of Yellowstone National Park in 1872. In fact, it goes back further, to a handful of citizens of Montana who first explored the Yellowstone country and who, though they might have homesteaded all its marvels for themselves, decided spontaneously that it must belong to all the people of the United States.

The Act of Dedication of this, the first national park any nation ever set aside, established Yellowstone Park "as a public park or pleasuring ground for the benefit and enjoyment of the people," and directed the Secretary of the Interior to preserve "from injury or spoliation . . . all timber, mineral deposits, natural curiosities or wonders" and to retain them "in their natural condition."

The legally enacted policy cannot be misconstrued: the parks and monuments are to be preserved as they are naturally, without deface- ment. It has been maintained so far, though not without hard effort. Because some of these areas contain valuable minerals, timber, water resources and water power, there have been many attempts to get the law changed so that they could be exploited. These attempts, which would ruin the parks if they succeeded, have heretofore usually been made by private groups intent on getting hold of public resources for their own profit.

In the last few years, however, a curious development has brought the National Park System under attack by two public agencies. Each of them has about a third of a billion dollars of public funds to spend every year, and so can exert incomparably more pressure than any cor- poration that ever cast a covetous eye on the wilderness beauties which were set aside for posterity to enjoy. One of these agencies is the Bu- reau of Reclamation, the other the Corps of (Army) Engineers. Their campaign of attrition raises fundamental questions about our grand- children's heritage of wilderness scenery. It also involves serious issues in regard to the power of Federal agencies to subvert public policy. How the campaign works and what hinges on it can be clearly seen in the current effort of the Bureau of Reclamation to get authorization, which is now not legally possible, to make over Lodore Canyon in Colorado.

The canyon was named and first traversed by the adventurous one- armed geologist, John Wesley Powell, on his exploration of the Green and Colorado rivers. It was on June 8, 1869, that he took his boats into this deep and narrow gorge. Confined between sandstone walls that are alternately overhanging and set back in terraces, the Green here be- comes an unimaginably violent chaos of rapids, falls, whirlpools, sucks and chutes. This twenty-mile stretch is one of the most hazardous — and most spectacular — parts of the so-far-untamed Green River.

HERE IS ONE OF OUR GREAT SCENIC AREAS

Before entering Lodore Canyon, the Green flows tranquilly through a mountain meadow called Brown's Park. At the lower end of the canyon it emerges into another beautiful, high-walled valley which Powell named Echo Park. Massive rock formations rise from the floor of Echo Park, and here the Yampa River flows into the Green from the east, having just emerged from a narrow, twisting canyon wholly unlike Lodore, but equally overpowering. The Green then flows westward through two more canyons. The setting of these four canyons is a landscape of brilliantly colored, fantastically eroded mesas, buttes, mountains, gulches and high basins. A panorama of fantasy, overwhelming to the imagination, this high rock desert has certain resemblances to the Bryce Canyon and Zion Canyon country and to Cedar Breaks, all in Utah, and to the setbacks and vistas of the Grand Canyon, which is in Arizona. But as each of these tremendous spectacles is, it is unique, of its own individual character and quality. It is one of the great scenic areas of the United States.

In 1938, Lodore Canyon, Yampa Canyon, Echo Park, the two subsidiary canyons and their rock-desert setting—327 square miles all told—were made a National Monument and transferred from the public domain to the National Park System. About a third of it is in Utah, two thirds in Colorado. If the area had been called, say, Green River National Monument, its nature and importance would have been self-evident in the name. But a National Monument already existed at its western edge, a small tract of eighty acres which had been set aside to protect the greatest known deposit of Mesozoic fossils, especially dinosaurs. The new reservation was added to this and the whole received the name of the original small part, Dinosaur National Monument. As a result, during the effort to keep a magnificent scenic wilderness from being defaced, many people have supposed that only the quarry where dinosaur fossils are excavated is at stake, though, as a matter of fact, the quarry has never been endangered.

When the monument was established, most of Brown's Park was left outside the boundaries. This exclusion was made because, years earlier, the Reclamation Service—now the Bureau of Reclamation—had declared Brown's Park a possible site for a reclamation project—that is, for a reservoir from which water could be pumped to irrigate a small area in Eastern Utah. The Bureau of Reclamation has by now abandoned whatever intention it may have had of so using Brown's Park. But it has undertaken to construct a hydroelectric-power development in Dinosaur National Monument. Both the laws which govern power projects and those which protect the National Park System forbid the construction of power dams in National Parks and National Monuments. There are, however, various ways of skinning a cat if you are good with a skinning knife. No one has ever said that the Bureau of Reclamation isn't.

In 1943, the First Assistant Secretary of the Interior made a "reclamation withdrawal" covering most of Dinosaur National Monument—that is, he officially declared it an area which could be used for reclamation projects. The "withdrawal" was almost certainly unauthorizable and therefore of no force. Furthermore, it was so smothered in administrative routine that, though it would destroy the monument, the National Park Service did not learn of it when it was made. On the basis of this questionable and semicovert withdrawal for reclamation—for irrigation—the bureau then began to plan a power development, which is prohibited. It proposed to build two dams with attendant power plants, one at Echo Park, the other at Split Mountain, farther down Green River. The estimated cost of the project is $207,000,000.

The dams cannot be built as the law now stands. They can be built if the law is changed—if pressure sufficiently powerful can be brought to bear on the Secretary of the Interior so that he will be forced to recommend their construction, and then on Congress, so that it will amend the acts which now apply. The Bureau of Reclamation has enormous sums to spend in local communities for direct and indirect local benefits; it generates political pressure as expertly as it does electric power. As soon as its plans for Dinosaur Monument were published, an agitation to breach the fundamental policy of the National Park System was set up in Utah and three neighboring states. It would be naïve to suppose that the bureau had no part in organizing this agitation; it was already well organized when the plans were made public.

The National Park Service first heard of the project as a daydream of the Bureau of Reclamation in connection with a vast plan for the transformation of the West called the Colorado River Project. The Green River is, of course, part of the Colorado River system. It was, so to speak, a theoretical, just-possible expedient to be tentatively considered in case equivalent results could be secured nowhere else in the Colorado River basin—and to be considered then only after exhaustive study and only after consultation with the National Park Service.

In spite of this understanding, *and without consulting the Park Service or obtaining clearance from the Secretary of the Interior,* the bureau laid the Dinosaur Monument project before the bodies that administer the interstate agreement which apportions water from the Colorado River. In February of this year those bodies recommended the immediate construction of Echo Park Dam. This would require legislation from Congress to authorize construction that is now prohibited in the monument—and the heat was on. Especially, the heat was on the Secretary of the Interior, one of whose duties is to protect the public interests—your interests—in the National Park System. The Western bloc worked smoothly. When Secretary Chapman ordered a public hearing, four Western senators and five Western congressmen appeared to add their testimony to that of embattled mayors and chambers of commerce that the nation would be well served by the abandonment of the policy which has protected the National Parks.

THEY SAY IT'S NECESSARY FOR IRRIGATION

The hearing disclosed that not only heat had been generated but much fog, or smoke screen, as well. The Echo Park and Split Mountain project is solely a power development, but it received much support it otherwise might not have got because it has been represented in the West, where irrigation is a sacred word, as an irrigation project. Again, the people of Utah have come, or have been led, to believe that water which the state has been allotted from the Colorado can be got to a still theoretical and prodigiously expensive reclamation project in Central Utah only from the reservoirs which the Bureau of Reclamation has planned in Dinosaur Monument. Actually, the bureau's own plans show that this water is to be taken from another project, farther up Green River and outside the monument. Utah and neighboring states have come, or have been led, to believe that these dams are indispensable for storage water allotted them from the Colorado. Actually, the bureau plans to provide most of this storage at another dam far to the south of the monument, and the rest of it—if any more is needed for the allocations — could be provided at other sites outside the monument.

Finally, Utah believes that the sites of these dams are the only ones where power for its still-theoretical project could be generated, whereas there are many feasible sites outside Dinosaur Monument. And at the public hearing, Gen. U.S. Grant, III, himself an engineer, showed that the use of one of these other sites would reduce the cost of the project by a third. Nevertheless, the various appeals mentioned above have been blended to make a really formidable confusion.

No Western state would receive any benefit from the construction of these dams inside the monument that could not be insured by alternative construction outside it. What about the people of the United States as a whole, whose property the monument is? On behalf of sectional and even local interests, the general public will have to pay the non-recoverable cost, always a large fraction of the total cost, of a $207,000,000 project. In return it will suffer the permanent ruin of an area of great natural beauty.

For it will be permanently ruined. If you cut down a forest, Nature will probably grow another one in the course of a few centuries, but if you change a river, a mountain or a canyon, you can never change it back again. The downriver dam in Dinosaur Monument would defile the mountain-park country along and below it and substitute a placid reservoir for the turbulent river above it. The other one, Echo Park Dam, would back water so far that throughout the whole extent of Lodore Canyon the Green River, the tempestuous, pulse-stirring river of John Wesley Powell, would become a mere millpond. The same would happen to Yampa Canyon.

Throughout both canyons the deep artificial lakes would engulf magnificent scenery, would reduce by from a fifth to a third the height of the precipitous walls, and would fearfully degrade the great vistas. Echo Park and its magnificent rock formations would be submerged. Dinosaur National Monument as a scenic spectacle would cease to exist.

A specious argument which has been used in connection with this assault on Dinosaur Monument is also a steadily increasing danger to other parts of the National Park System. We long ago passed the point where reclaimed Western land could repay the cost of the projects that reclaimed it, as it was originally intended to do. If it costs several hundred dollars an acre to make land worth fifty dollars an acre, the rest of the cost must be charged to something besides reclamation. If the project includes the production of electricity, the sale of power will take care of part of the remainder. If it includes flood protection—and, nowadays, try to find any dam on any babbling brook that is not supposed to—whatever fraction of the remainder can be allocated to flood control can be written off altogether, since the whole country benefits from reduction of flood losses. But honest cost accountability ends right there; no additional economic justification can be found. Hence, the Bureau of Reclamation has begun to publicize a shimmering but carefully unanalyzed value which it calls "recreation."

If the bureau can successfully allege that its projects create facilities for recreation, then it can charge to them as much of the uneconomic cost as it is able to get away with. Nobody doubts that the American people need facilities for recreation and will need more of them as our population increases. But what kind, where, at what cost, and who shall pay for them? Should we write off $10,000,000 of the cost of an irrigation project because it will provide bass fishing for one North Dakota county? Should Philadelphia and Birmingham be taxed to provide sailboating for Las Vegas?

If it is able to force the Echo Park project through, the Bureau of Reclamation will build some fine highways along the reservoirs. Anyone who travels the 2000 miles from New York City—or 1200 from Galveston or 1000 from Seattle—will no doubt enjoy driving along those roads. He can also do still-water fishing where, before the bureau took benevolent thought of him, he could do only white-water fishing, and he can go boating or sailing on the reservoirs that have obliterated the scenery.

But the New Yorker can go motoring along the Palisades, boating in Central Park, sailing at Larchmont and fishing at many places within an hour of George Washington Bridge. No one will ever drive 2000 miles to row a boat; no one will ever seek recreation in a National Park except the kind for which the "pleasuring ground" was created—the unique experience of awe and wonder that an untouched wilderness spectacle provides. The only reason why anyone would ever go to Dinosaur National Monument is to see what the Bureau of Reclamation proposes to destroy.

Similarly the Army Engineers are proclaiming the "recreational value" of a flood-control dam which they propose to build in Kentucky and which would ruin much of Mammoth Cave. It would also deface a beautiful valley which is now a paradise for sportsmen, and would inundate some of the richest farmland in the state. It has not been proved necessary or even desirable, and local communities supposed to benefit from it have denounced it. Its value for flood control is insignificant; Tom Wallace, the editor emeritus of The Louisville Times, finds that "it would affect by only a mere fraction of an inch the flood crest at the lowland city of Paducah." But the point here is that it would drown out part of Mammoth Cave National Park and would back water into Mammoth Cave itself, one of the most famous natural wonders in the United States.

For over a century, the underground rivers, some of which—with the equally celebrated "sink holes"—would be affected by the dam, have been the most popular feature of the cave. The most important of them all is Echo River, the one down which visitors are taken by boat through several miles of domes, chambers and corridors shaped by the amazing architecture of water leaching limestone and decorated with a fantastic sculpture of stalagmites and stalactites. The proposed dam will make Echo River unusable whenever it is retaining flood waters, and when they recede the whole route will be hideously plastered with mud and debris.

It will also kill the eyeless fish and other blind species of the cave, which are famous as curiosities and as scientific evidence of the adaptation of life forms to their environment. The silt carried by flood waters will destroy them and many species of underground plants as well. Yet the state of Kentucky raised $3,000,000 to acquire Mammoth Cave, dedicate it to the general public and give it to the United States so that the National Park Service could preserve it unimpaired.

The blind fish highlight another aspect of the National Park System that is in peril As wilderness that is preserved intact, the parks and monuments are laboratories for the field study of natural processes. The balances of Nature, the web of life, the interrelationships of species, massive problems of ecology—presently it will not be possible to study such matters anywhere else. They are also invaluable for the study of hydrology, geology, and even meteorology. American science cannot afford to lose the facilities for large-scale study of untouched nature that the National Park System provides. And to alter the natural conditions at all is, for the purposes of science, to ruin everything.

Thus there is the mysterious matter of Glacier View Dam, which would flood some 20,000 acres in the western part of Glacier National Park. In its plan for development of the Columbia River watershed, the Corps of Engineers proposed to build a flood-control dam at Glacier Point, on the North Fork of the Flathead River in Montana. Well-tutored local interests supported it—and, as usual, were expertly organized before the public at large heard of it—but national conservation organizations backed the Park Service and the Department of the Interior in protesting it. Eventually the Engineers agreed to abandon the project. A joint memorandum signed on April 11, 1949, by the Secretary of the Interior and the Secretary of the Army recommended to the President that Glacier View Dam be eliminated from the master plan. That appeared to settle the question.

But four months later Congressman Mike Mansfield, of Montana, introduced a bill in the House of Representatives directing the Corps of Engineers to proceed immediately with the construction of Glacier View Dam. Congressman Mansfield was representing the interest of local communities in the local expenditure of many millions of dollars, of which Montana would be called upon to pay only a small fraction of one per cent. Can anyone suppose that the Corps of Engineers, thrown for a loss on the first try, has not had a hand in the renewed agitation? If passed, this bill will be a precedent-making alteration of the basic law that protects the National Parks.

Glacier View Dam would destroy wilderness scenery of great beauty, obliterate mountain streams and lakes, and submerge 8000 acres of virgin forest. In doing so, it would eliminate more than half the winter range of the white-tailed deer—and extinguish the species in the park—and a third of the winter range of its elk and mule deer, besides killing half the moose in that part of the park and a considerable population of beavers, muskrats and other species.

The irrevocable loss of wildlife, however, is less important than the fact that the disturbance of the balance of nature would be felt nearly everywhere in the park. The relationships of species with one another and with the environment would be changed, the flora of the park and the interrelationships of its species would be changed, even the topography would be changed. In short, Glacier National Park would cease to be the invaluable field laboratory it now is for the study of natural processes. Yet the act of Congress that took jurisdiction over it provided "for the preservation from injury or spoliation of all timber . . . and for the protection of the animals and birds in the park from capture or destruction." This was in addition to the basic law which the public believes to be binding in itself, the law which directs the National Park Service to conserve scenery and wildlife "by such means as will leave them unimpaired."

Thus, whether or not Congressman Mansfield was running interference for the Army Engineers, one of their projects has been revived after they had committed themselves to abandon it. Here is the gimmick that enables one bureau of the Government to circumvent another one, to undermine national policy and to work contrary to the public interest in the National Parks. Even when controversies have been formally settled and projects abandoned apparently for good, the park system—and the public trust—is always under the threat that engineers may revive their discarded plans at any time.

Take, for example, one of the most amazing and most recklessly expensive schemes ever dreamed up. It is in the discard now and will not threaten the Grand Canyon so long as Oscar Chapman is Secretary of the Interior. But secretaries change, administrations change and formal commitments by the Bureau of Reclamation change, while the itch of engineers to perform costly miracles goes on forever—and so do the aspirations of the state of Arizona.

The lower part of Grand Canyon National Park and the full extent of Grand Canyon National Monument at its western edge will be somewhat, though not materially, changed by Bridge Canyon Dam, which the Bureau of Reclamation expects to build across the Colorado River. This dam, which the pending legislation which will authorize its limits to the minimum height that the bureau proposed, will back water clear through the monument and some distance into the park. At the time of maximum high water, which corresponds with the peak of the tourist season, the reservoir will extend into the main gorge of the Grand Canyon and the famous Havasu Canyon that leads off it. To that extent, primitive conditions will not be preserved.

The Bureau of Reclamation at first proposed to build Bridge Canyon Dam to a much greater height, and so to make a longer stretch of the Colorado in the main gorge a millpond instead of the irresistibly powerful river it now is. The National Park Service, however, succeeded in getting it limited to the proposed minimum height. But originally the Grand Canyon was threatened by a much more catastrophic change, and that threat, though it was turned back and is now quiescent, is certain to be revived. Doubtless, when it is, the familiar gimmick will be used. Local interests will pressure an Arizona congressman into introducing a bill which will amount to an end run round the Park Service and the general public.

For the Bridge Canyon Dam just mentioned is a $265,000,000 unit of a project which is designed to give Central Arizona its allotted water from the Colorado River, a project whose total cost is to be well over $1,000,000,000. At one time it was proposed to divert water from Marble Canyon Dam—which is to be built outside the park to the east—by way of a forty-four-mile tunnel through solid rock to Kanab Creek, at its western boundary, whence it would reach the reservoir to be created by the Bridge Canyon Dam. The purpose of this stupefying proposal was to use the drop to generate power for other, equally staggering parts of the project. It would have come close to drying up the Colorado River, which created the Grand Canyon and is the climax of its magnificence, and making it a dry stream bed for the full length of the main gorge.

Secretary Chapman's predecessor, Julius A. Krug, and Assistant Secretary Warne thumbed it down. They declared the Kanab Diversion Tunnel unnecessary and unjustified, not only now but for as far as they could see ahead. Secretary Chapman is certain to stand on their decision, but we have not heard the last of the Kanab Tunnel. It will be revived and violently agitated.

Being only forty-four miles long, the Kanab Tunnel was comparatively small potatoes. The engineers have dreamed up an even more fantastic way of getting water through solid rock from Marble Canyon to Bridge Canyon. As one of three possible solutions of making one part of the Central Arizona project generate power to pump water to other parts, they proposed a tunnel 143 miles long. This will not happen, either . . . now. But you never can tell about tomorrow. If the people of the United States want their Grand Canyon to remain as it is, they had better keep an eye on it.

But keeping informed about such attacks on the National Parks is extremely difficult. The engineering projects mentioned here are plans for the development of the mountain West. There are others like them, notably the Pick-Sloan Plan for the Missouri River. The vision is to create 3,000,000 acres of new agricultural land and to develop 8,000,000 horsepower of hydroelectric energy. These plans may be vital for the future of the West, and the future of the West is vitally important to the United States. But the people have no adequate idea of how sound the plans may be, how far some of them may fail, how much money may be wasted. Engineers of unimpeachable professional standing have asserted that large parts of them are mistakenly conceived or even potentially disastrous. But the public has no chance to judge.

Nor has the national interest any effective representation against purely sectional interests as represented by the Bureau of Reclamation and the Western activities of the Army Engineers. How desirable is it to reclaim agricultural land at a time when agricultural surpluses cost us hundreds of millions of dollars a year and agricultural methods become steadily more productive? To reclaim desert land in the West when for a small fraction of the cost we could restore exhausted land in the South? To build power plants for an assumed industrial development in the West that cannot come for many years and may never come? To build now for the production of electric power fifty years hence, when atomic energy may make it obsolete in twenty-five? The Bureau of Reclamation and the Corps of Engineers feel no obligation to discuss such questions on behalf of the public.

It is, in fact, almost impossible to bring effective criticism to bear on the projects of these two agencies. As far as the individual citizen is concerned, the data are kept secret. They are not publicized outside the West and only the favorable ones are publicized there. By the time a project is laid before Congress it has already been decided upon, the local interests have been organized and the Western senators and representatives—one of the most powerful blocs in Congress—have been lined up. Within the West there is severe infighting for the allocation of projects, but when it comes to getting projects to be allocated, there are neither state nor party lines: there is only a solid West. The Bureau

of Reclamation and the Army Engineers have a vested institutional
interest in the West, the interest not only of continuing to function but
of expanding and growing more powerful. They have vast sums of
money to spend. Their preliminary planners, field agents and entire
official hierarchy readily lay down the shovel and the hoe, and pick up
the microphone at any hint that their plans may be interfered with or
even inquired into. Both are able to summon to their support an organized political pressure that only nationwide public opinion could
defeat.

That is the larger picture into which the assault on the National
Parks fits. Unquestionably, the national interest requires the parks and
monuments to be preserved unmarred, as they were intended to be.

No emergency serious enough to justify invading the National Park
System arose during either World War. No emergency is in sight now.
But with as much time for planning as might be required, with promising and perhaps better alternatives only cursorily investigated, the
Bureau of Reclamation is able to threaten Dinosaur National Monument with destruction. And probably the bureau's hand was not idle
in a California agitation that has succeeded in introducing into Congress a bill to investigate all the possible power sites in Kings Canyon
National Park. This park preserves the most magnificent mountain
country in California outside Yosemite Park. Its boundaries were drawn
so as to exclude areas which ought to have been included, but which
were left out precisely because they were valuable power sites. The Engineers threaten Mammoth Cave with a dam which even Kentucky
does not want. They threaten Glacier Park with a dam which they formally agreed not to build.

If any of these attempts should succeed, the law which protects the
parks will be circumvented and there will be no protecting any of them
from similar impairment thereafter. The parks do not belong to any
bureau, any group of planners or engineers, any state or section. They
belong to all of us. Do we want them? Will our grandchildren want
them?

Let's Close the National Parks

(*Harper's Magazine*, October 1953)

The chief official of a national park is called the Superintendent. He is a dedicated man. He is also a patient, frustrated, and sorely harassed man. Sit in his office for an hour some morning and listen to what is said to him by the traveling public and by his administrative assistant, the Chief Ranger.

Some of his visitors are polite; some aren't; all have grievances. A middle-aged couple with a Cadillac make a formal protest: it is annoying that they must wait three-quarters of an hour to get a table at Lookout Point Lodge, but when it comes to queuing up in order to use the toilets at the Point—well, really! A woman in travel-stained denim is angry because Indian Creek Camp Ground is intolerably dusty. Clouds of dust hang over it, dust sifts into the sleeping bags at night, dust settles on the food and the children and the foliage, she has breathed dust throughout her two-weeks stay. Another woman reports that the toilet at Inspiration Cliff Camp Ground has been clogged since early last evening and that one of the tables there went to pieces at breakfast time. A man pounds the desk and shouts that he hit a chuck-hole on Rimrock Drive and broke a spring; the Drive, he says,

is a car-killer and will soon be a man-killer. Another enraged tourist
reports that a guardrail collapsed when his little girl leaned against it
and that she nearly fell into the gorge. The representative of a nature
society sums up his observations. He has hardly seen a ranger since he
reached the park. (One reason is that most of the rangers are up in
the high country fighting a forest fire.) Tourists have picked all the
bear grass at Eyrie Overlook and the observer doubts if the species will
come back there. Fifty-one names have been freshly carved in the vicinity of Cirque Falls, some of them actually on the famous Nine Centuries Tree itself. All but one of the camp grounds look like slums; in
the observer's opinion, the reason why they look that way is that they
are slums.

Such complaints must be distinguished from the irrational ones
voiced to the Superintendent by tourists who are cantankerous, crack-
brained, tired, or merely bewildered. They must be so distinguished
because they are factual and true. (The Superintendent, not having a
plumber, will send a ranger to clean out the toilet but replacing the
guardrail will leave him too little money to buy lumber for a new table.
He squeezed $1,200 from his budget to enlarge Indian Creek Camp
Ground and so reduce the dust there but Brawling River undercut fifty
feet of main road and the emergency repairs cost $1,350.) He answers
all complaints courteously, as a representative of the National Park Service and the United States Government, but he has no effective answer.
He is withheld from saying what would count, "Build a fire under your
Congressman." He cannot go on and explain that the Service is suffering from financial anemia, that it is the impoverished stepchild of Congress, and that the lack of money has now brought our national park
system to the verge of crisis. He cannot say this and neither can his su-
periors in the Washington office, but it is true.

Between visitors the Chief Ranger has been developing this theme.
He got together a crew yesterday and put them to work on the decay-
ing bridge inside the north entrance; it can be shored up for the rest of
this season but next year it will be beyond help and the north entrance
will have to be closed. He also went over Beaver Creek Trail again yesterday and he is scared; unless some work can be done on it at once it
must be closed as unsafe. Costs on last week's rescue job are now in.
Fourteen men worked three shifts a day for two days to bring that

climber with a broken hip down from Deception Peak. A doctor had to be summoned from eighty miles away and an ambulance from a hundred and seventy-five miles. The episode cost just over a thousand dollars, which will have to come out of the budget, and this means one summer ranger less next year. (In 1936 the park had two more summer rangers than it has this year—and only one-twelfth as many visitors.) Furthermore, Ranger Doakes, an expert alpinist, has demanded overtime pay for that rescue—sacrilege in the Service, but the Chief Ranger cannot blame him. The recent increase in rents hit Ranger Doakes hard. He got only a 137 per cent increase, which was less than some others, but it brought his rent to 23.5 per cent of his annual salary.

Let's leave the Chief Ranger's remaining woes unprinted and look at this latest device for reducing pay by compelling personnel to subsidize the National Park Service budget. The most valuable asset the Service has ever had is the morale of its employees. I have said that the Superintendent is a dedicated man; all his permanent staff and all the temporary rangers and ranger-naturalists are dedicated men, too—they are all lovers and all fanatics or they would have quit long since. Ever since it was organized the Service has been able to do its difficult, complex, and highly expert job with great distinction because it could count on this ardor and devotion. The forty-hour week means nothing in a national park. Personnel have always worked sixteen hours a day and seven days a week whenever such labor was necessary. Superintendent, rangers, engineers, summer staff, fire lookouts—they all drop their specialties to join a garbage-disposal crew or a rescue party, to sweep up tourist litter, to clean a defouled spring, to do anything else that has to be done but can't be paid for. They are the most courteous and the most patient men in the United States and maybe once a week several of them get a full night's sleep. If you undermine their morale, you will destroy the Service. Well, the latest increase in rents has begun to undermine it.

By decree of the Bureau of the Budget the rents of government housing must be equalized with those of comparable housing in the same locality. In the end this amounts to some sleight of hand in the bookkeeping of the U.S. Treasury but it is probably sound in theory. Sound, that is, for a lot of government housing—but not for that which, to a varying degree, shields NPS employees from the weather. In the first place, the locality with which rents must be equalized is the nearest resort town outside the park, where rents are two or three times as high as in the nearest non-parasitical town. In the second place, there is practically no comparable housing. These are not the massive dwellings of a military installation, the imposing and luxurious ones that the Bureau of Reclamation erects, or the comfortable cabins of the Forest Service that were built by the CCC. Apart from a few such cabins by the CCC and a few new structures which the Service has been able to pay for from the pin-money that passes as its appropriation, they are either antiques or shacks. The best of them are usually inadequate— one-bedroom houses for couples with two or more small children, two-bedroom houses for couples with two or more adolescent children. Many of the rest of them belong in the Hoovervilles of 1931—CCC barracks built of tar-paper in 1934 and intended to last no more than five years, old warehouses and cook shacks built of slabs, curious structures hammered together from whatever salvaged lumber might be at hand. I have seen adobe huts in damp climates that were melting away from the rain, other quarters that were race-courses for rats, still others that would produce an egg shortage if you kept chickens in them.

Park Service employes are allowed an "isolation deduction" of from five to forty per cent, intended to compensate them for being forced to live at a galling and expensive distance from the services of civilization. Even so, the already high rents have been cruelly increased by the last directive from the Bureau of the Budget. On a list I have at hand of seventeen dwellings in Grand Teton National Park, the lowest increase (*after* the isolation deduction) is one hundred per cent, the highest two hundred per cent, the average one hundred and fifty-plus.

At this park there is an associated ingenuity. The park pays Teton County, Wyoming, $26,000 a year in lieu of taxes; it produces God knows how much for the state in gasoline and sales taxes; the business brought in by its visitors is all the keeps the town of Jackson solvent or even alive. But a hangover from the controversy over Jackson Hole National Monument, a controversy created for profit by local politicians and the gamblers and land speculators allied with them, has enabled the town of Jackson to pressure the state administration. By decree of the state Attorney General, park personnel are not residents of Wyoming, though any itinerant Okie who paused there would be, and must therefore pay for the transportation and tuition of their children who attend public schools. They total $158 per pupil. It makes quite an item in the family finance of an underpaid public servant who has now had his rent increased, the rent of a leaky and rat-ridden crate which he cannot select but must take as assigned—and in which he gets no equity though he pays a fifth of his salary or more.

This last summer I visited some fifteen NPS areas. It was a commonplace to meet a park employee who had had to bring a son or daughter back from college, as a result of the rent increase. It was even commoner to find one who had decided that the kids could not go to college when they finished high school. In many places, wives of park personnel are working for the private firms licensed to operate businesses in the parks, and this is a highly undesirable practice. The chief clerk of one of the most important parks works weekends in a grocery store in order to stay fed while retaining the job he loves. I could add to these specimens indefinitely but let it go with the end-product: the most valuable asset of the National Park Service is beginning to erode away.

So are the parks and national monuments themselves. The deterioration of roads and plant that began with the war years, when proper maintenance was impossible, has been accelerated by the enormous increase in visitors, by the shrinkage of staffs, and by miserly appropriations that have prevented both repair and expansion of facilities. The Service is like a favorite figure of American legendry, the widow who scrapes and patches and ekes out, who by desperate expedients succeeds in bringing up her children to be a credit to our culture. (The boys work the graveyard shift in the mills; the girls' underwear is made of flour sacking.) Its general efficiency, the astonishingly good condition of its areas, its success at improvising and patching up is just short of miraculous. But it stops there, short of the necessary miracle. Congress did not provide money to rehabilitate the parks at the end of the war, it has not provided money to meet the enormously increased demand. So much of the priceless heritage which the Service must safeguard for the United States is beginning to go to hell.

Like a number of other small areas in the system, the Black Canyon of the Gunnison has *no* NPS personnel assigned to it. On one rim of this spectacular gorge there are a few inadequate guard rails, on the other and more precipitous rim there are none. When I visited it, one of the two registers for visitors and all the descriptive pamphlets had been stolen. The ranger force at Mesa Verde National Park is the same size it was in 1932; seven times as many people visited it in 1952; the figures for June 1953 were up 38 per cent from last year's. The park can man the entrance station for only one shift; automobiles which arrive in late afternoon cannot be charged the modest entrance fee. It cannot assign a ranger exclusively to fire-duty at headquarters, though it is in an arid region where destructive fire is a constant danger; the head-quarters ranger must keep the fire-alert system operating while he attends to a dozen other jobs. All park facilities are strained to the utmost. Stretches of the main road keep sinking and must be repaired at excessive cost because there is not money enough to relocate them where the underlying strata are more stable. There is not even money enough to replace broken guard-rail posts along the edge of the canyon. Colorado and New Mexico are about to construct a new highway past the park to the famous Four Corners. On the day it is completed visitors to Mesa Verde will double in number and the park will be unable to take care of them. It will be paralyzed.

Last year Senator Hunt of Wyoming made a pleasure trip to Yellowstone Park, at least a trip that was intended to be pleasurable. He was so shocked by the condition of the roads that he wrote a letter of protest to President Truman. (It got buried under the election campaign.) And yet, considering the handicaps, Yellowstone has done magnificently with its roads; those of many other parks are in worse condition. (Of the *main* road system in the park 15 per cent is of pre-1920 standard, 42 per cent of pre-1930 standard, and only 27 per cent of 1930–1940 standard. Exactly three miles of new road have been constructed since 1945 and those three complete a project that was begun before the war.) This is the oldest, most popular, and most important national park. In 1932, when 200,000 people visited it, its uniformed staff was large enough to perform just over 6,000 man-hours of work per week; last year, with one and one-third million visitors, the shrunken staff performed just over 4,000 man-hours per week. Like nearly every other popular park, it has reached the limit of performance and begun to slide downhill. There are not enough rangers to protect either the scenic areas from the depredations of tourists or the tourists from the consequences of their own carelessness—or to gather up the litter or to collect all the entrance fees that should be paid. Water and garbage and sewage systems are beginning to break down under the load put on them; already some sewage is being discharged in Yellowstone Lake. The park's high plateaus covered with lodgepole pine are natural fire-traps which some day will be burned out because the budget will not permit adequate fire-protection.

I have touched on only a few of Yellowstone's critical problems. What I have said is true also of all the most popular areas administered by the Service and in some degree of almost all the less accessible areas. There are true slum districts in Yellowstone, Rocky Mountain, Yosemite, Mesa Verde, various other parks. The National Park Service does a far better job on its starvation rations than it could reasonably be expected to do, but it falls increasingly short of what it must do. It is charged with the preservation, protection, maintenance, development, and administration of 28 national parks, 5 national historical parks, 85 national monuments, 56 areas of various other classifications, and 785 National Capital parks. Their importance to the American present and future is simple incalculable; they are inestimably valuable. But Congress made no proper provision for rehabilitating the areas at the end of the war or for preparing them for the enormous increase in use—more than thirty million people visited them last year. It could have provided for renovation and expansion at about a fourth or a fifth of what the job would cost now—but it didn't. It requires the Service to operate a big plant on a hot-dog-stand budget.

The crisis is now in sight. Homeopathic measures will no longer suffice; thirty cents here and a dollar-seventy-five there will no longer keep the national park system in operation. I estimate that an appropriation of two hundred and fifty million dollars, backed by another one to provide the enlarged staff of experts required to expend it properly in no more than five years, would restore the parks to what they were in 1940 and provide proper facilities and equipment to take care of the crowds and problems of 1953. After that we could take action on behalf of the expanding future—and save from destruction the most majestic scenery in the Untied States, and the most important field areas of archeology, history, and biological science.

No such sums will be appropriated. Therefore only once course seems possible. The national park system must be temporarily reduced to a size for which Congress is willing to pay. Let us, as a beginning, close Yellowstone, Yosemite, Rocky Mountain, and Grand Canyon National Parks—close and seal them, assign the Army to patrol them, and so hold them secure till they can be reopened. They have the largest staffs in the system but neither those staffs nor the budgets allotted them are large enough to maintain the areas at a proper level of safety, attractiveness, comfort, or efficiency. They are unable to do the job in full and so it had better not be attempted at all. If these staffs—and their respective budgets—were distributed among other areas, perhaps the Service could meet the demands now put on it. If not, additional areas could be temporarily closed and sealed, held in trust for a more enlightened future—say Zion, Big Bend, Great Smoky, Shenandoah, Everglades, and Gettysburg. Meanwhile letters from constituents unable to visit Old Faithful, Half Dome, the Great White Throne, and Bright Angel Trail would bring a nationally disgraceful situation to the really serious attention of the Congress which is responsible for it.

Intramural Giveaway
(*Harper's Magazine,* March 1954)

When I included in last month's Easy Chair some notes on Dinosaur National Monument, I did not intend to discuss the subject again. Though I mentioned the fact that the Monument had been threatened by a proposal of the Bureau of Reclamation to build two dams in it, I assumed that the proposal was dead or at least would be quiescent for a long time. Shortly after *Harper's* went to press, however, the Secretary of the Interior recommended the construction of one of them, the one called Echo Park Dam. Bills authorizing it have already been introduced in Congress. If one is passed, we need not worry any more about getting appropriations to rehabilitate and maintain the national parks. For it will be the beginning of the end and presently there won't be national parks worth worrying about.

The passage of the bill would in effect repeal the provisions of the Federal Power Act which prohibit dams in the national parks and the clause in the proclamation establishing Dinosaur Monument which forbids them there. It would breach the principle which has protected the parks from exploitation ever since the creation of the National Park Service in 1916, indeed since the first park, Yellowstone, was established in 1872. Thereafter no determined effort to get hold of the natural resources which the parks contain could be stopped. Mr. McKay's approval of Echo Park Dam precipitates a crisis. If Congress should follow his recommendation, the national park system as we know it, as it was intended to be, will be open to destruction.

All this because of a dam which probably need not be built. The purpose which it is intended to serve, together with the other dam (Split Mountain) which the Bureau of Reclamation has also proposed to build in the Monument, could probably be served as well or better by alternative dams outside the Monument. I have to say "probably" for no one really knows, including the Bureau of Reclamation and the Secretary of the Interior. No detailed study of the alternatives has been made. When the Bureau tried to get the dams authorized in 1950, General Ulysses S. Grant III, formerly of the Corps of Engineers, made a survey of alternative sites. He found that the alternatives would do just as well and that at one of them a dam could be built at considerably less expense than the Bureau's plan called for. (The present estimate for Echo Park Dam is $176,000,000; eventual costs always exceed the Bureau's estimates.) General Grant's criticism has never been answered. So far as anyone knows, the Bureau has not studied the alternatives he proposed. So far as anyone knows, in fact, it has made only a field reconnaissance of any sites except its chosen ones. In December 1952 Mr. McKay's predecessor, Secretary Chapman, recommended that the whole project be reopened and that a thorough study of possible alternatives be made. The Bureau's attitude, however, has always been that it intends to build those dams, regardless. Apparently Mr. McKay concurs.

In the October–December issue of the *National Parks Magazine,* Mr. McKay undertook to state the Administration's policy about the national parks. He announced that he would defend them to the utmost. But also he became the first Secretary of the Interior to put himself on record as conceding that something other than a dire national emergency might some day justify invading them. He went on to say, "I intend to permit no encroachment upon the national park system without careful and thorough study. If there is to be any encroachment upon the parks, it must be proven unmistakably that it will produce for the nation values that outweigh greatly those which are to be changed or destroyed."

The Secretary has always had the authority to order a "careful and thorough study" of Echo Park Dam in relation to the suggested alternatives. One would think that his predecessor's recommendations required him to order it. But the study has not been made; instead Mr. McKay has now authorized the destruction of the values of Dinosaur Monument, without specifying the values for the nation that outweigh them. But the Utah delegation in Congress gets its fences nicely repaired, the pleasant town of Vernal will get several years of boom spending, and the local speculators in real estate will cash in on the flier they took when the dams were first proposed.

Last month I mentioned two bills that have been introduced by Congressman Leroy Johnson of California. They would make Dinosaur National Monument a national park and would change its name, which is much to be desired. For the name has kept the public from understanding what is at stake. In 1915 the famous quarry in Utah from which so many fossil skeletons of dinosaurs have been taken was made a national monument, so that it could be preserved and protected. Properly enough, this eighty-acre reservation was called Dinosaur National Monument. It was a mistake, however, to retain that name when two hundred thousand acres were added to the reservation in 1938, to preserve and protect some of the most majestic scenery in the United States. That scenery, the canyons of the Green and Yampa Rivers, is what the dams would ruin.

The Yampa flows into the Green at the foot of a spectacular cliff called Steamboat Rock. Echo Park is just below the junction; the name was given to this area by John Wesley Powell, on his original descent of the Green and the Colorado. On its way to the junction, the Yampa flows through one of the most beautiful canyons in the West, the Green, through an even more spectacular canyon which Powell named Lodore. These are characteristic sunken canyons of the high-plateau country, like the Grand Canyon. Below them the augmented Green River flows through two more magnificent chasms, Whirlpool Canyon and Split Mountain Canyon (where the Bureau proposes to build its second dam.) Dinosaur National Monument consists of these four canyons. It was enlarged to its present size for the sole purpose of preserving them in their primitive state.

Since I have mentioned the Grand Canyon, I must make clear that Dinosaur Monument is not a lesser copy of it. They are not comparable except that each is unique. Dinosaur is the supreme example of one particular kind of natural spectacle. The pyramids and setbacks of the eroded rock desert come to climax here, and in Lodore Canyon rapids of the Green River create some of the wildest water in the Colorado River system. The Green is less turbulent below the junction and so is the Yampa as it flows through its long, looping canyon, but they are sufficiently exhilarating when run. Skilled boatmen run them quite safely, however, and that under their guidance the trip is feasible for tourists Mr. Eggert's documentary film, which I mentioned last month, fully demonstrates. No comparable boat trip is possible anywhere else, in or out of the national park system. The Monument is beautiful when seen from the rim or the bottom of its canyons, but by far the best way to see it is from a boat.

There is nothing to replace Dinosaur Monument if it is ruined, and the proposed dams would ruin it. Echo Park Dam, whose construction the Secretary has now recommended, would make placid mill ponds of Lodore Canyon and Yampa Canyon. Split Mountain Dam, which belongs to a later phase of the project, would reduce Whirlpool and Split Mountain Canyons to the same mediocrity. At Steamboat Rock there would be five hundred feet of water; the vertical cliffs of the Green and the Egyptian setbacks of Yampa Canyon would be reduced to nonentity. As a spectacle the Monument would cease to exist. The Bureau of Reclamation points out quite truly, however, that the reservoirs would be fine places to go sailing, and therefore the usual percentage of the cost is to be written off for "recreation" and hence nonreimbursable, charged to the public.

The two proposed dams, Echo Park and Split Mountain, are units in the grandiose plans to develop the water resources of the Colorado River system. Specifically, they are part of the Colorado River Storage Project. Now development of the Colorado is absolutely necessary to the growth and prosperity of the West, whose future depends on the most effective utilization of every water source it has. The vast engineering works which the Bureau of Reclamation has planned for the Colorado kindle the imagination. It is certain that they or other works planned to the same end will eventually be constructed—or rather it is certain that as much Colorado water as is possible will be made available to the states of the upper and lower basins. It is also true that some of the Bureau's plans are pure engineering mysticism, that they have not been subjected to impersonal and authoritative criticism, and that the United States at large does not realize what a tremendous expenditure of money they will require.

Those plans urgently need criticism. The public and the government have no way of knowing whether or not they are the best solution of the problem involved. The Bureau has changed them so often and so capriciously as to suggest that the engineering necessities of the Colorado depend on whatever the Bureau can get away with. The civilian branch of the Corps of Engineers has expressed pointed distrust of the Bureau's plans. Perhaps this could be dismissed as the tactics of a rival organization, since the Bureau and the Engineers fight each other (at public expense) everywhere except on the upper Missouri, where they co-operate in the Pick-Sloan Plan—but the distrust is on record nevertheless and it should be aired and investigated. And that the states can have violently different opinions about the development of the Colorado is evident in the blood feud between California and Arizona over the Central Arizona Project.

It is certain that the federal government is going to spend vast sums of money to develop the Colorado. No matter how economy-minded the Administration may be, and no matter how devoted to its still undefined principles of "partnership" and "local control," it will not risk losing the West—and failure to support reclamation development on an enormous scale would lose the West. As regards dams there are no party lines. One might perhaps guess that the problem of a Republican Administration is to find a formula which allots to private business the profitable activities associated with reclamation and makes the government responsible for the unprofitable ones. (One way would be to let private companies generate electric power at a multiple-purpose project and have the public pick up the check for flood control, recreation, navigation, the interest component of irrigation systems, and the firming of power at downstream dams.) If so, then possibly Secretary McKay's recommendation of Echo Park Dam (together with two other dams farther down the Colorado authorized at the same time) is intended to assure the West that the Administration is orthodox and will stand on the gospel. The Idaho Power Company sees a profit at Hell's Canyon, so the Administration will abandon the plan to use the site for a federal project. Nobody sees a profit in construction in this long stretch of the Colorado, so the government will build the dams.

This suggestion, of course, may be doing Mr. McKay a hideous injustice. It may be simply that he is backing the most powerful bureau in his Department against one too weak to make itself felt, and that the happy political timing is inadvert. It nevertheless remains true that the whole plan for the development of the Colorado River should be subjected to searching review and criticism by a board of qualified engineers who are not connected with the Bureau of Reclamation. Such an inquiry would seem a natural for an Administration that has spent a year reviewing practically everything. It would cost money and it would take time. But it might prevent mistakes that could be catastrophic to the West. Every conservationist in the country, and I dare say every engineer and hydrologist outside the Bureau, would greet the appointment of such a commission with relief and enthusiasm.

Quite apart from such an inquiry, however, possible alternatives to Echo Park and Split Mountain Dams should be fully and minutely investigated. Congress should demand such a study as a preliminary to taking up Mr. McKay's recommendation of Echo Park. Certain facts are open to everyone's view. The Federal Power Act and the basic law of the national parks forbid the construction of dams inside the Monument. The Proclamation which enlarged the Monument forbids it. Congress is asked to amend these laws and reverse a policy which has never been violated—and a qualified engineer who has studied the alternatives says that the dam is not necessary for the purpose intended, that dams which will not violate the policy can be built outside the Monument. It is hard to see how Congress can ignore facts of such gravity. It ought also to be deterred by the nationwide opposition that was expressed when the dams were proposed in 1950.

It has never been clear why the two dams were suddenly brought forward at that time. Apparently the Department of Defense was considering some hush-hush development, perhaps atomic, in the West and wanted assurance that plenty of power would be available. Apparently too the Bureau of Reclamation, in spite of the fact that Echo Park Dam is primarily for water storage, not power, promptly dusted off its plans and undertook to guarantee the power. The combined pressure, plus perhaps some desire at a higher level to assist Senator Elbert Thomas' campaign for re-election, was so great that Secretary Chapman instructed the Bureau to draft a recommendation for Echo Park and Split Mountain Dams. That, however, was as far as it got. Whatever the Department of Defense was contemplating, it changed its mind—or changed the location of its project. And public opinion opposed the invasion of the Monument with remarkable vehemence and unanimity. Mr. Chapman never did recommend the dams. Instead, he pigeonholed the project and eventually, as I have said, he proposed a study of alternatives. "Careful and thorough study" was Mr. McKay's phrase.

Meanwhile, however, the state of Utah rejoiced in the belief that construction of these dams would mean the early completion of its great Central Utah Project. Like every Western state, Utah desperately needs water, and two interstate compacts guarantee it a stated percentage of the only important source left, the Colorado River. Those facts, however, have no bearing on the present question, since the alternative dams would serve the Project quite as well as Echo Park and Split Mountain. What is even more striking, the water which the state is actually to get for the Central Utah Project is to come not from the Echo Park Dam but from another unit, Flaming Gorge Dam, which is to be built farther up the Green River and well outside the Monument. Mr. McKay's recent recommendations did not include Flaming Gorge Dam, and since that is the key to the entire project his recommending Echo Park Dam at this time makes no visible sense on any ground. Except, of course, that for some years construction payrolls will gladden the town of Vernal, where an oil boom is tapering off and where people who bought land in 1950 can now take their profit. Pork appears to be an acceptable substitute for water.

It is customary for people who have irons in the fire to dismiss as "sentimental" reminders that some beautiful scenery, some untouched nature, some wilderness areas have to be preserved intact for future generations, in a nation whose steadily increasing population cuts down the available areas every year. To oppose a dam whose need has not been demonstrated is hardly sentimental, however, and it remains true that once a natural area has been despoiled it can never be restored. In this case not only the canyons of the Yampa and the Green are at stake: breaking the prohibition that up to now has never been broken would put all the national parks in peril. The basic principle of the national park system is that the areas contained in it are to be maintained inviolate, which means exactly what it says. So far they have been protected from exploitation, by private parties, of the natural resources they contain; many raids of them have been attempted but all have been turned back. It remains exploitation when a federal bureau does the exploiting; it has merely become Administrative policy. Suppose that the Maine Power Company of Idaho now proposes to file on any possible power site in any national park asserting that as national value kilowatts outrank vistas. On what ground can the Secretary of the Interior, the supposed protector of the parks, oppose the raid? By his own act he has endangered all the parks that contain power sites, usable water, timber, or minerals.

Presumably even the National Park Service cannot try to defend its holdings. Formerly a career service, it has had its "policy-making" officials—director, assistant director, chief law officer, director's secretary—classified under Schedule C and so denied Civil Service status. One wonders why. Or does one?

FIVE
The Western Land Grab, 1950s

> You had better watch this, now and
> from now on. The land grabbers are
> on the loose again and they can be
> stopped only as they were before, by
> the effective marshaling of public
> opinion.
>
> "Two-Gun Desmond Is Back," 1951

Two-Gun Desmond Is Back

(*Harper's Magazine*, March 1951)

The humble sheep-walker has come down from the rocks and the bronzed horseman rides again. They are after the National Forests in thirteen Western states; they have been for years. They tried to steal them in 1947, together with all other public lands that could grow a little grass, but they got stopped. They decided that they had been trying to get away with too much at a time, so now they will settle temporarily for control of the forests, with some additional tricky stuff thrown in. Understanding that the methods they thought up for themselves in 1947 were too crude, they have hired some brains to brush a little suavity and finesse over the steal. You have got to know about it because it is your property they want to alienate.

As I said in *Harper's* at the time, if the 1947 effort had succeeded it would have been the biggest land grab in American history. All the public lands that could be grazed at all were to undergo forced sale to stockmen. Those that were being grazed at the time were to be sold to the stockmen who were using them, sold at a rigged estimate of the grazing value alone without regard to other uses or values, and the happy beneficiaries of their own thrift were to have up to forty-five years to pay the gratuity. Any public land that wasn't being grazed but had some grass on it was to be sold on the same terms to the queue of stockmen lined up for it, and presumably anybody who could graze a cow in Yosemite Valley or on the lawn in front of headquarters at the Custer Battlefield could bid it in. The plan had the simplicity of the pastoral mind. But it was barefaced fraud and the pastoral mind did not get away with it. It endangered so many Western and national interests, private as well as public, that as soon as the light was turned on it public opinion killed it. The bills that had been written were never even introduced into Congress; as one of the congressmen who had been detailed to smooth the way remarked out loud, once the public found out about them they became too hot to handle.

But, again as I pointed out in *Harper's,* there are many ways to skin a cat. The boys got out a different skinning knife and went to work on the Forest Service. The idea was to bring it into disrepute, undermine public confidence in it by every imaginable kind of accusation and propaganda, cut down its authority, and get out of its hands the power to regulate the grazing of stock in the National Forests. The last has always been a major objective, not the ultimate objective but one that is a prerequisite for everything else in the plan. The Forest Service is the federal agency charged with administration of the National Forests on behalf of the public. Grazing is only a minor, subsidiary, and contingent use of the forests, and the Service has to regulate it in accordance with a safe and equitable balance of all other uses. To regulate it, especially, to prevent stockmen from overgrazing the forest ranges, impairing or even destroying them, and gravely endangering other and more important forest values.

Precisely that is what the stockmen want to prevent. They want to get the power to regulate grazing taken away from the Forest Service and turned over to the stockmen who use the forest ranges. Everybody who has even looked into the matter knows what that would mean.

Let's be clear about something else: this is not the Western stock business as a whole. About nine-tenths of the Western cattle business and about three-fourths of the Western sheep business never touch the National Forests at all. The pressure campaign is conducted by a joint committee, now called the Grazing Committee, of the two big trade organizations, the American National Livestock Association and the National Wool Growers Association, working with various state organizations and a variegated assortment of other helpers. A good many of the small local stock associations and a good many Western stockgrowers as individuals oppose the campaign but they seem unable to make their opposition count. Don't ask me why the bulk of their Western colleagues simply stand by and let things slide; I have never understood why. One does not suspect them of undue saintliness and yet with amazing disregard of self they unprotestingly accept the handicap of the preferential treatment which their competitors who use the forest ranges get from the Forest Service and the public.

As taxpayers they help subsidize that preferential treatment—and so do you. For every dollar a stockman pays to graze his stock on National Forest land, one who leases privately owned grazing land pays at least three dollars, sometimes as much as six dollars. The public, including you, pays the difference; it subsidizes the user of forest ranges by writing off two-thirds of this grazing fee. It then spends part of what it does get improving the range for him.

You and the lessee of privately owned grazing, however, take a worse beating than that. A lot of publicly owned land, the remnants of the Public Domain, was organized into grazing districts under what is known as the Taylor Act, districts which are administered by the Bureau of Land Management, Department of the Interior. (The Forest Service is a bureau of the Department of Agriculture.) For reasons and by methods which I have several times explained here, the local stockmen soon got effective control of the Taylor Act lands. So where a holder of a Forest Service permit pays a dollar for grazing, and where the lessee of private land pays at least three dollars, the Taylor Act licensee pays at most twenty-five cents. (Currently there is a move on—it probably originates in Moscow—to raise this to about twenty-nine cents.) The subsidy here is eleven-twelfths. You are paying it. The legislation which the Grazing Committee has worked up proposes a study of grazing fees on forest ranges with a view to revision. Guess what "revision" means.

As co-owner of both the Taylor Act lands and the National Forests, you might require Congress to see to it that your licensees get their hands out of your pocket and pay the market rate for grazing, and I

don't say that wouldn't be a good idea. Or if your heart bleeds for the
sunburned supplicant for your bounty—how long since you could
afford a sirloin?—you might at least require him to bid competitively
for the privilege of using your ranges. When someone wants to cut
timber in your forests he has to enter a sealed bid against all others
who want to bid and can make the required guarantees. Not the cowboy and the shepherd, types who are always bellyaching about bureaucratic tyranny.

The National Forests are the property of the American people. By far
their greatest value, Western and national, is the preservation and protection of watersheds. The West is arid country; not only its solvency
but its very survival depend on its water supply. On the safeguarding
of that water supply and the utmost possible production of water the
expansion of industry in the West depends, and the expansion of Western industry may be a matter of life and death to the United States if
full-scale war comes. Any future expansion of Western agriculture also
depends on water production. Vital parts of every important watershed in the West are in National Forests—and stock-grazing is a threat
to a watershed the moment it becomes overgrazing. Many watersheds
have been damaged by overgrazing, and the efforts of the Forest Service to reduce and repair the damage—in large part by reducing the
number of stock grazed in areas that have deteriorated—have always
met with truculent opposition by the stockmen. A prime objective of
this campaign, as of all its predecessors, is to end the power of the Forest Service to reduce the number of stock in overgrazed areas. To prevent a public agency, that is, from administering the public land for
the public benefit.
    There is no legal right to graze public land. The stockmen have long
been trying to create such a right by legislation, to make it adverse to
all other forest uses, and to vest it in the present holders of grazing permits—thus handing themselves a fine capital gain at public expense.
Grazing on the public lands is a privilege and the man who holds a
grazing permit is a licensee. In the forests, moreover, grazing is a
subsidiary use, subsidiary not only to water production but to other
uses which are worth more to the public and to the balance of properly managed land units as a whole. The forests are after all forests, not

primarily grazing areas. They contain the only federally owned merchantable timber, federal reforestation is conducted on them, and they are the basis of the national forestry program. And they have many other uses. In the Western forests to which the proposed legislation is to apply there were just under 17,000 grazing permits last year. There were about 35,000 "special use" permits, ranging from private summer camps through commercial recreation enterprises and on up to prospecting and mining. There were 15,000 revenue-producing timber sales. And more than 16 million people used these same forests for recreation. The proposed legislation undertakes to subordinate all such uses to stock-grazing and then to take the regulation of grazing away from the Forest Service.

I have space to mention only some of the proposals; I will return to the subject some months from now. Most of them are familiar and all of them are aimed at the constant objectives of the stock associations. They undertake to give local boards, composed of the stockmen who use the ranges they are to pass on, the administrative power that is now vested in the Forest Service, ultimately that of the Secretary of Agriculture. The regulation of grazing, that is, would be vested not in the representatives of the public but in the grazers. On their consent all other uses of grazing areas would depend. Any kind of emergency action in the public interest would be impossible. If drought, fire, flash floods, a bad winter, or one of the sudden lapses from productivity to which overgrazed land is subject should threaten the water supply of a Western town or irrigation district, no action could be taken unless the local board of licensed grazers should, as the proposed bill puts it, "concur."

Even if the board should concur, no holder of a permit could be required to make any changes in less than five years, by the end of which irreparable damage might be done to the range, to the public interests, and to other private interests.

The proposed bill provides that no holder of a grazing permit can have it canceled, or the number of stock it licenses him to graze reduced, if he has borrowed money on it. Nothing is specified about these immunity-producing loans except that they be "bona fide." If I lease a store building from you, that is, I can force you to extend the lease indefinitely and on the original terms so long as I can get someone to lend me money on it. No amount or percentage specified; just legal tender.

It also provides that if land for which a grazing permit has been issued is turned to some other and higher use, or if the number of stock it licenses is reduced, then the holder of the permit shall be "compensated" to the extent of the "damage" he may suffer. Damage not to private property, that is, but to the subsidy he gets from the public. If you want to change the terms of the lease I hold for your store building when renewal time comes, you must pay me damages. Nice going. No miner, prospector, water-user, timber-cutter, or dude-wrangler—no other user of the forests supposes he is entitled to a bonus.

These are some of the proposals the stockmen intend to make for getting administration of the National Forests into their own hands and cutting themselves a melon. There are others, including a tricky one that would change the basis of investment in home property by which many grazing regulations are now scaled. They add up to the old game with a new backfield formation. But the proposed legislation contains a more dangerous threat to the National Forests, the public lands in general, and the national stake in conservation. It is worded to take advantage of any possible change in public-land administration and it seems to favor unification of land-management policy. That is a very pious idea—or would be if the plain intent of the whole game were not to bring the regulation of grazing in the National Forests under the Taylor Act, and if this wording were not aimed to bring it under the Taylor Act if the executive departments of the government are reorganized.

The possibility that precisely this might be tried has kept a lot of conservationists from favoring the establishment of a Department of Natural Resources, as a task force and a minority report of the Hoover Commission proposed to do. We foresaw as all too easily possible what the stock associations are in fact now trying to bring about: the degradation, rather than the improvement, of public-lands management. Unification of grazing land under one bureau would indeed be desirable—if certain fundamental principles were applied to it and if certain fundamental values were safeguarded. One absolute consideration is this: the National Forests are multiple-use lands and grazing in them will always be a subsidiary use, whereas the Taylor Act lands are primarily grazing lands and have only minor value for other purposes. For reasons repeatedly explained here it will not do to bring grazing on forest lands under the provisions of the Taylor Act. And it will not do to concentrate the management of public grazing land under the Bureau of Land Management as it is now set up. The former is what the present stock-association campaign is trying to do immediately, and the latter is what the phrasing of its proposed legislation is designed to insure.

You had better watch this, now and from now on. The land grabbers are on the loose again and they can be stopped only as they were before, by the effective marshaling of public opinion. Your property is in danger of being alienated, your interests and those of your children are threatened, and your money is to be used to subsidize a small percentage of the Western stock business while it makes further inroads on the public wealth. If the proposed legislation has not been introduced in Congress by the time this column is printed, it soon will be. The only question is whether the boys will try to do it by a series of first downs or with a touchdown pass that puts everything in one bill. You had better make sure that your Representatives and Senators understand quite clearly what is going on and where you stand. Then if you don't belong to one of the conservation societies, join one and keep in touch.

Another thing. The land grabbers have a habit of talking loudly and indiscreetly. Loud talk in a hotel lobby in Salt Lake City, one summer evening in 1946, was what enabled a reporter to dig out the record of a secret meeting of the Joint Committee, publish the carefully guarded plans for the land grab, and so touch off the public outcry that stopped it. Right now the stock associations are claiming out West that this time they have got the Department of the Interior on their side. They are saying that the Bureau of Land Management and the Bureau of Reclamation favor their proposed legislation.

This cannot possibly be true but the cowboys can gain a lot of ground merely by claiming that it is. For people remember occasions in the past when parts of Interior have lusted to get back jurisdiction over the lands that were withdrawn from it when the Forest Service was created. The plausibility thus traded on ought to draw a flat declaration from Director Clawson and Commissioner Straus that they do not favor the legislation and that no one under their authority will be permitted to assist it.

For there could be no better way to divide the forces of conservation than to let that old issue be revived even in appearance, and no better way of assuring the victory of anti-conservation forces than to increase or create rivalry among the federal bureaus that are charged with conservation. The public needs a solid front, absolute co-operation among those bureaus, and the bureaus need the united support of all conservationists. The brains the cowboys have hired are trying to serve their clients by the old and formidable game of dividing the opposition. We have all got to be on guard, to walk the bounds and keep our eyes peeled, and that goes for your representatives in Congress.

An Old Steal Refurbished

(*Harper's Magazine*, October 1952)

One of the planks in the Republican platform is intended to impair your investments and real-estate holdings out West. The hands that got it inserted in the platform were the hands of General Pat Hurley but the voice is the voice of a stockgrowers' committee who neither slumber nor sleep. It provides a fulcrum from which to exert leverage if the Republicans win in November, so that certain stockmen who hold grazing permits in the national forests can further enrich themselves at public expense. It is the latest move in the attack on the Forest Service which I have been describing here at intervals for the past five years. It commits the Republican party to a curtailment of public authority over an invaluable natural resource. It also makes the party conspicuously vulnerable, and one wonders why the rest of the platform drafters, highly practical men all, allowed General Hurley to stick them with so loud a smell. As the campaign goes on General Eisenhower is going to find himself in trouble unless he repudiates it.

The public lands are just what the phrase says they are, the lands owned in common by the people of the United States. As one of the co-owners, you share in the income they produce and you are taxed for their protection and administration. You are also taxed to subsidize the Western stockmen who graze cattle and sheep on them. That is, those stockmen pay a much smaller fee than the grazing is worth, a much smaller fee than Western stockmen who graze privately owned lands have to pay, and taxes make up the difference.

Ever since the Forest Service was organized—it is the oldest of the agencies that administer public grazing lands—there has been an unremitting effort to get that subsidy increased. It has taken many forms. It has tried to prevent the government from charging anything for the use of the public lands. It has tried to prevent the government from regulating their use. It has tried to give stockmen who use the lands the sole authority to regulate grazing and to set fees. (In a notable victory it succeeded in doing just that for the lands administered by the Grazing Service, now the Bureau of Land Management, of the Interior Department.) It has tried to alienate the public lands entirely and to turn them over to the stockmen who use them, at negligible cost or no cost at all. It has tried various modifications and combinations of all these approaches. And it makes another all-out try in the public-lands plank that has been carpentered into this year's Republican platform.

The public-lands plank begins resoundingly, "We favor restoration of the traditional Republican lands policy. . . ." Well, what is the traditional Republican policy?

Is it the policy of Theodore Roosevelt? He made conservation a basic policy of the federal government. It was he who established the Forest Service and saved for the public millions of acres of timberland and grazing land, entire watersheds, and hundreds of power sites— saved them against the furious opposition of just such stockmen as those who wrote the current plank. He gave the West—and the nation—the Newlands Act and reclamation, the Inland Waterways Commission, the once honorable Rivers and Harbors Act, a basis for a public waterpower policy, the authority under which public control of waterpower was eventually exercised, and much else there is no space to list here.

His was a great conservation policy and there were associated with him such honored Republicans as Gifford Pinchot, Henry Stimson, the great Secretary of Agriculture James Wilson, James R. Garfield, W. J. McGee, and many others. But though this is a great Republican tradition, there is no occasion to restore it, for it is still in force. It has been the fixed policy of the federal government, in spite of continuous efforts, mostly Republican, to hamstring or destroy it. Later administrations, including that of another great conservationist, Franklin Roosevelt, have only built on it.

But there is another traditional Republican public-lands policy. In Theodore Roosevelt's time it was exemplified by the Western Senators and Representatives who fought him, fought the creation of public-land reserves, fought the establishment of national forests, and in particular fought the unholy theorem that the public could charge stockmen a fee for grazing stock on public lands. Grazing fees were evil, they were unconstitutional, stockgrowers had a God-given right to use the public lands free of charge. That cry rose all across the West with the assessment of the first grazing fee, it has never quite died out, and there is a clear echo of it in the public-lands plank now. Again, there was the public-lands policy of Secretary Richard A. Ballinger, which was to hand over the public coal lands to well-heeled private operators and to give other favorites a very free hand with the national forests. There was also the policy of Secretary Albert B. Fall, which was to turn over the public oil lands to private operators on a similar basis but somewhat less suavely.

And let us recall the public lands policy of Herbert Hoover and his Secretary Wilbur, the memory of which has got lost under more catastrophic Hooverisms. When the midterm election of 1930 swept them to oblivion, they were preparing to fulfill the stockgrowers' oldest and most desirous dream. They were undertaking to turn over the remaining public domain of the United States to the individual states it was located in, so that it could be sold for chickenfeed to the grazers who were using it—provided that buying it for chickenfeed should cost them less than leasing it on terms they themselves might set. Finally, there is ex-Congressman Frank Barrett of Wyoming, now running for the Senate, who tried to do the same thing and who lent a hand to others who were trying to put the national forests as well up for sale. Mr. Barrett lost out on the big one but he succeeded in establishing for the Bureau of Land Management the great, patriotic, and most Republican principle that when grazing fees are set the value of the grazing must by no means be taken into account.

Which traditional Republican policy is the plank talking about? A lot of us would like to know. A lot of us especially in the East, whose public-lands function seems to be to prevent the West, every little while, from committing suicide. It is clear to us that a handful of bronzed horsemen, Two-Gun Desmond and his gang, have slipped one over on General Eisenhower.

Let's quote that first sentence in full: "We favor restoration of the traditional Republican lands policy, which provided opportunity for ownership by citizens to promote the highest land use." (When Desmond starts shooting, "highest land use" always means grazing.) It shows that in the neolithic minds of the stockmen's committee the great land grab is not dead even now. They still hope that, somehow, the stockmen who now pay ten cents for a dollar's worth of grazing in the national forests will be allowed to buy the ranges they use for, say, two cents on the dollar. Everyone else knows that they never will be allowed to, including Mr. Barrett, who burned his fingers badly when the land grab was tried. Neither the West nor the East will stand for it; no administration could put it over. Not even if providence should make Pat Hurley President with Two-Gun Desmond for his Vice President.

But the presence of that sentence in the public-lands plank will cost General Eisenhower a lot of votes unless he denounces it. Remember, this has been tried. In the only Republican Congress since the first Roosevelt landslide, the boys got ready to spring their land grab. Twenty-four hours after word of it got out, the trains and planes were full of Republican Congressmen hurrying West to explain to their constituents that it was all a vile rumor, that they had been cruelly misrepresented. One of them got licked at the next election, another one and a Senator fell in love with private life and decided not to run again, and every last one of the others started singing a different tune, loudly. The survivors can be interviewed at any time.

The preamble, then, is nonsense: nobody is going to provide "opportunity for ownership by citizens" of the Forest Service ranges. The plank goes on to call for "an impartial study of tax-free federal lands."

(In Desmond's jargon "impartial" means advocating what stockmen want.) Many studies of the federal lands are available now but this is familiar stockmen tactics, which have been well described as "attack, investigate, postpone"—ends that could all be accomplished by a new and properly loaded study. Following this item, the plank gets down to business with a pledge: "In the management of public lands and forests we pledge the elimination of arbitrary bureaucratic practices. To this end we favor legislation to define the rights and privileges of graz-ers and other co-operators and users, to provide the protection of in-dependent judicial review against administrative invasions of those rights and privileges, and to protect the public against corrupt or monopolistic exploitation and bureaucratic favoritism."

This meshes with the program which the stockmen have been try-ing for years to get adopted. It is especially tied in with the campaign of the joint Grazing Committee of the two national associations, cat-tle and sheep. In *Harper's* for March 1951 I described their efforts to write a bill which would get as much as seemed possible of what they wanted. They tinkered with it for another year before it satisfied them; then early in 1952 they unveiled the result. It is called "Proposal for an Act to provide for the orderly use, improvement, and development of the federal lands. . . ." and two more lines of nice-looking type. The plank in the Republican platform embodies this Proposal.

As we examine the plank, there are a couple of things to bear in mind. One of them is this: though the plank has the Soil Conservation Ser-vice in the corner of one eye, it is aimed at the Forest Service, which the Desmond gang has never been able to control, and refers solely to the regulation and administration of grazing ranges in the national forests. The other is this: the people for whose benefit it was written are only a small part of the Western stockgrowing interest. Even if they could speak for everybody who grazes stock in the national forests, they would be representing only some 10 per cent of the Western cattle business and about 30 per cent of the Western sheep business—all told only a minute percentage of the national business. But actually they do not speak for anywhere near so large a part of the Western interest. A very large number of stockmen who hold grazing permits in the national forests repudiate their objectives. The Grazing Committee and its

234 THE WESTERN LAND GRAB, 1950S

proposal represent a handful of big operators. Remember too that grazing is only a subsidiary use of the national forests, which exist primarily for watershed protection and the production of timber.

So let's construe. The pledge to "eliminate bureaucratic practices" is a pledge to take administration of the grazing ranges away from the Forest Service and hand it over to the holders of grazing permits. As things stand now, the Service determines what the proper number of stock for a given range is; if a range is being damaged by overgrazing or if some higher use is endangered it reduces the number of stock. To end this heinous solicitude for the public interest is the first objective of the sentence I have quoted, but it has other objectives too. It undertakes to give permit-holders power to determine *how* a range shall be used, to exclude other users who might curtail the stockmen's freedom of action, and to administer ranges without regard to the enormously more important interests of water production and watershed protection. It would empower the grazers themselves to set the grazing fees, which is letting the tenant decide how much rent he shall pay, and to determine the dates and duration of the grazing season, which is a license to impair and even destroy the ranges. It would prohibit the Forest Service, the agent of the public who owns the ranges, from making any changes in use or administration, from adopting any new methods or regulations, and from taking any other administrative action unless the permit-holders should consent. This is all wonderful stuff if you can get away with it, and the Desmond gang has been trying for years and years.

Another approach is contained in "we favor legislation to define the rights and privileges of grazers." (Disregard "other co-operators and users"—it doesn't mean a thing.) This is intended to charge Congress, in the belief that the Western bloc will be able to control it, with the direct administration of the public lands—to formulate grazing regulations by Act of Congress. It is contrary to all governmental practice and violates every principle of public administration. Congress creates an executive bureau to the end that trained specialists may do the administering. The Senate of the United States cannot determine how many sheep should graze along Nine Mile Creek—but if it starts debating the problem the owner of the sheep may do exactly as he pleases. Incidentally, no grazer has any "right" whatever in the national forests except the limited and entirely contingent rights stipulated by his grazing permit, which are permissive and are subject to modification or cancellation in the public interest. To get a legally vested right in the public lands has always been an ambition of the Desmond gang.

"The protection of independent judicial review" is another gimmick, related to another primary objective of these buccaneers. In no department of the government are the decisions of administrators of public property subject to review by the courts. Paralysis would result if they were, and that is the end in view here. Holders of grazing permits may now appeal any administrative decision of the Forest Service through the whole official structure up to the Chief Forester, beyond him to a special board of review, and on to the Secretary of Agriculture. The gimmick is intended to give them a chance to delay action further by tying it up in the courts for years, with luck forever. What action? A reduction in the number of stock grazed on a range in order to rehabilitate it, for instance, or a change in the terms on which a grazing permit is held, a change made on behalf of higher land use or of the public interest. To hell with the public interest; the boys want to run their stock as they may see fit to.

The last phrase, "corrupt or monopolistic exploitation and bureaucratic favoritism" may look like mere gobbledygook, without meaning. But it has an important meaning. The subsidy paid to holders of grazing permits in the form of low fees and service rendered greatly increases the value of their home ranches. (Sometimes up to $400 per cow the permit authorizes.) They can sell their base property for much more than they otherwise could merely because the Forest Service habitually transfers the permit to the person who buys the base property. The Desmond gang want an Act of Congress which will provide that the Forest Service cannot let anyone except the present permit-holders use a range without their consent. Such an Act would give legal recognition to the additional but now contingent capital value which a permit creates for them at public expense. It would give them a monopoly on grazing in the forests. No newcomer in the stock business could use forest ranges — only the heirs and assigns of the present permit-holders.

The public-lands plank can now be rewritten in plain English. "We pledge the Republican party to strip the Forest Service of its power to regulate and administer its grazing ranges, and to transfer that power to the present holders of grazing permits. We favor legislation which will put grazing, a subsidiary use of national forests and in dollars the least important one, in a position superior and adverse to other uses such as lumbering, mining, irrigation, municipal and industrial water supply, watershed protection, hunting, fishing, camping, all other kinds of recreation, and the public interest in general. We demand that there be no protection of ranges or watersheds by reducing the number of stock now permitted to graze them or by any change we do not like in the terms on which grazing permits are held. We also demand an Act of Congress that will give the present holders of grazing permits a legally vested hold on the national forests, will enable them to keep other stockmen out of the forests, will authorize them to set grazing fees as they may see fit, and will empower them to formulate and enforce their own regulations without regard to the public interest."

You must see the "we" of this plank as some fraction, indeterminable but less than half, of about 17,000 stockmen who now hold grazing permits in the forests. There are twice as many logging permits and the business they represent is many times greater. Hundreds of thousands of farmers depend on the forest watersheds for irrigation. All the municipalities of the mountain West depend on them for domestic and industrial water. Many millions of people use the forests for recreation. The plank makes a minority of stockmen a highly privileged class and puts them in a position superior to other users of the forests and to the American people who own the forests and pay the taxes. It stinks. But also it commits the Republican party to action.

How about it? How about it, General Eisenhower and the people who are thinking of voting for him?

Conservation:
Down and on the Way Out

(*Harper's Magazine*, August 1954)

Through many little measures—most of them scantily reported in the press—the Eisenhower Administration is reversing the nation's seventy-year-old policy for protecting our natural resources. Here, for the first time, is a complete picture of the devious campaign against America's forests, water power, parks, public lands, and soil conservation program.

An aphorism of the Chinese philosopher Mencius declares that the problem of government presents no difficulties: it is only necessary to avoid offending the influential families. In January 1953 the Business Administration in Washington took off from a related premise: that it was only necessary to get along with the trade associations.

This article deals with public power and the public lands, other natural resources, and the national conservation policies which have been developing for three-quarters of a century. In dealing with them the Administration had to convert into concrete measures the generalizations of the Republican platform and campaign promises. It had no problem when it took office. It was promptly handed one specific program, which the electric power companies had worked out in anticipation of a Republican victory in 1948. It has improvised several

others, playing by ear. On several problems, it apparently is not concerned with programs; it has simply drifted downward.

Perhaps I can formulate the campaign generalities as working principles. In fields where private enterprise could operate at a profit, the
Administration would try to reduce government operations. In fields
where private enterprise could not make profits, it would maintain government operation up to the minimum political necessity. In both areas
it would try to provide "a greater measure of local participation and
control," greater co-operation between federal and local governments,
and "a friendly partnership" with private business. It would try to "de-
centralize" federal administration, and it would—in an even more
opaque phrase—"operate at the grass roots."

There was an inherent weakness in these working principles. They
would throw the gates wide open to the boys in the back room unless
the Administration could get in first with programs of its own. It did
not and the boys—the trade associations, the lobbies, the special interest groups—rushed in with a loud whoop. During the campaign
Mr. Eisenhower once remarked that he would not interpret his election as a mandate to preside over the liquidation of the publicly owned
natural resources of the Unite States. Others *have* so interpreted it,
however; a considerable liquidation has been effected already and
much more is in the works. Eighteen months have made clear that the
executive departments and the independent agencies will go much farther than Congress in alienating public property—but not (except perhaps in the Department of the Interior) as far as the boys have in mind.

They pin their hopes to the new Hoover Commission. The first one
worked out intelligent plans for reorganizing the executive departments in the interests of efficiency and economy; but the second one is
clearly intended to slay Mr. Hoover's white whale at last. It is to erase
twenty years of infamy, root out all remnants of the New Deal, and
turn the clock back to 1928. There are those who regard 1928 as practically a pinko compromise: the clock should be turned back somewhere
beyond Theodore Roosevelt.

FIAT BY WASHINGTON

In the Departments of Agriculture and the Interior the business men
whom the Administration summoned to government promptly dis-

played the political ineptness visible in other departments. One reason may have been the sources of information which it was natural for them to rely on. A Congressman who wants a quick check on what the folks back home are thinking is apt to telephone to a local editor or political figure, or the head of some local labor or farm organization. From the top offices of Agriculture and Interior, however, the phone calls went instead to a chamber of commerce or to the Washington office of a trade association. The information available there being of a radically different kind, there followed such miscues as Secretary McKay's nomination to be Director of the Bureau of Mines of an open and recorded enemy of the services he would have to direct.

Top officials were also unable to recognize public opinion as a political force. Congressmen saw a clear portent in the widespread opposition to the Tidelands Bill—and in the public outrage when the Assistant Secretary of Commerce tried to discharge the Direct of the Bureau of Standards for affirming that the addition of a laxative to a storage battery would not improve it. But to the Business Men in Office these were unrelated and meaningless phenomena, just one of those things. The Department of Agriculture revealed this state of mind in its handling of the reorganization of the Soil Conservation Service. There could be no more local an organization than a Soil Conservation District; more than 2,500 of them cover the country and they are literally of the grass roots. But they were not consulted about the reorganization of SCS and indeed could not find out what was going on till it was completed. In Administration semantics, "local participation and control" had become "fiat by Washington." The districts were enraged; they still are.

This reorganization, an aggrandisement of the land-grant colleges and the Extension Service at the sacrifice of conservation values, was typical of the new order in several ways. SCS had originally been organized on the basis of state units but had evolved a much more effective organization in a series of regions, each with its own headquarters, specialists, and technicians. The reorganization plan proposed to dissolve the regions and substitute state units for them. The heart of SCS assistance to farmers was its six technical services; four of these were to be abandoned and the specialists of the other two were to be distributed among the land-grant colleges (so far as the colleges had jobs for them) and the Washington headquarters. For the immensely successful program of SCS, forty-eight fractional and necessarily un-harmonized programs were to be substituted; and these were to be ad-ministered from Washington. Decentralization had worked out in the semantics as greater centralization. Incentive to local conservation practices was to be provided by decreasing appropriations. And with technical service reduced, much research was to be abandoned.

But opposition to Tidelands and the firing of Dr. Astin had *not* been just one of those things, and nation-wide opposition to the new scheme forced the Department to reverse itself in midair. A new sys-tem of regional offices, under a different name and with headquarters in different cities, was extemporized. (In the semantics, A ceases to be A when you rename it B.) The technical services were retained, though in a more cumbersome and more expensive form.

As I write, SCS is half flux and half chaos. The technical teams have been broken up. Their invaluable pool of common experience at working to-gether has been dissipated. This drastic impairment of professional skills is typical of the administration of public resource in the new order. So are the increased expense, delay, red tape, and inefficiency. So is the de-struction of morale in a career service. Promising young men have left SCS in droves; promising young men who might have sought a career there are notably failing to join it. An Administration fetish whose name is Management-Practice Improvement has had its paper tribute, but a strait-jacket of mediocrity has been forced on public administra-tion. And a damaging blow has been struck at the conservation of American cropland and rangeland.

The Department of Agriculture, however, appears to have taken instruction from the public reaction. Evidently it has abandoned some reactionary changes which it had in mind a year ago and has nar-rowed the scope of some others. Not so the Department of the Inte-rior. The boys have practically taken it over; the predicted giveaways are in progress. There is a cynicism in Interior which reminds ob-servers of the aromatic days of the General Land Office. Yet some things that look like cynicism may be mere ineptness. Thus Secretary McKay at a moment when all the conservation organizations in the country—national, nonpartisan, and representing hundreds of thou-sands of votes—were denouncing his recommendation of Echo Park

Dam. Seeking for *le mot juste* to characterize conservationists, he came up with "punks."

The top officials of SCS have been put on Schedule C; so have those of all other conservation bureaus in Agriculture except (as yet, perhaps) the Forest Service, and all those in Interior except the Geological Survey. Schedule C is a classification withdrawn from Civil Service protection which permits discharge at the will of the Secretary, without regard to merit. It has a twofold purpose: (1) to provide jobs; (2) to substitute a pliable sycophancy for professional judgment in the making of policy. Promotion according to merit is abandoned for the spoils system, and career services become political footballs. The effect on the conservation agencies has been disastrous; it had not hitherto been supposed, and it cannot be supposed now, that the publicly owned resources could be administered on any basis except a purely professional one. These bureaus first introduced into the American government the concept of a professionally expert civil service. Staff them with spoilsmen, and the public resources must begin leaking away.

The Administrator of the Rural Electrification Administration is appointed to serve ten years. It was therefore a tipoff when the White House requested the resignation of Mr. Claude Wickard two and a half years before the end of his statutory term. Rural electrification and federal power can be treated together here, and several facts which are tirelessly misrepresented must be noted. The electric power generated at public installations runs between 13 and 16 per cent of the national total, never more. In spite of nationwide propaganda by the utilities (paid for out of tax money and rate-increases), unalterable natural circumstances make it certain that the percentage will decrease as time goes on. Furthermore, the consumer co-operatives which REA serves are strictly private enterprise, locally owned by their members and locally managed. They pay interest on the loans which REA makes them; they pay off the loans; they pay local taxes. They are "socialistic" only in the new semantics: in that they are not owned by the utility companies and they sell power to consumers so cheaply that their rates serve as a yardstick by which the rates of the utilities—a natural monopoly—can be regulated. Finally, most of the power they sell is bought from the utilities.

They constitute an area of private enterprise which the utilities had refused to pioneer or develop. In 1935 when REA was established, about 11 per cent of the farms in the United States had central-station power; in 1952 about 90 per cent had it. This constitutes an agricultural revolution even greater than that effected by SCS; it has transformed agricultural production, farm labor, and rural living. REA and the co-ops have greatly increased the business done by the utilities and very greatly increased that done by manufacturers of electrical equipment and appliances.

A multiple squeeze has been put on co-ops and REA. The Administration's first budget request drastically cut REA funds. Its power-generation program, and therefore its bargaining power with the utilities, would have been destroyed. Its ability to accommodate new co-ops and the ability of the co-ops to serve new customers would have been drastically reduced. Congress refused to go so far and saved much of the program by increasing the appropriation far above the request. But Congress did not vote an increase over the Budget's allotment for technical service. Thus the theme of SCS is repeated, for the abandonment or even any serious reduction of REA's technical service to the co-ops would be a serious blow, to some of them a fatal blow. Small co-ops, unable to afford such a technical staff as a utility company maintains, have been able to get their problems solved cheaply by REA. Moreover, the Power Use Section of REA was cut down, and the auditing services were abolished, thus increasing the financial hazards of the co-ops. A related but unsuccessful move was the attempt by Congressman Kit Clardy of Michigan—an old and dear friend of utility companies—to double the rate of interest which REA charges on loans to the co-ops.

Meanwhile what amounts to a rewriting of the Federal Power Act, supplementary acts, and even the Reclamation Act has been achieved by administrative action. The utilities would be glad to have the government build the large and expensive control dams—because they make private downstream dams efficient—provided they could buy the power generated at them on their own terms and could control its distribution. But they have always rebelled against the "preference clause."

This clause—which in essence goes back to the earliest conception of public power in Theodore Roosevelt's first Administration—is a provision that public bodies and co-operatives shall have first call on the power generated at federal dams. ("Public bodies" means primarily municipally owned systems and such organizations as the power districts of Oregon and Washington.) The ordinary growth of such systems was provided for by selling the rest of the power to utilities on short-term contracts only. By abandoning this practice, the Administration is in effect discarding the preference clause.

In the Northwest, utility contracts, previously short-term, now run twenty years. This limits the growth of co-ops, denies them new customers, and rations the power used by their present customers. A similar change in the Missouri Valley has been held up till after the November election. The co-ops have been faced with an impossible choice. Either they must forfeit their preference privilege, thus arresting their own growth, or they must contract for power far in advance of their needs and so pay a ruinous bonus for power which they could not use and which would have to be resold to the utilities at dump prices.

The utilities have fought the construction of steam-generating plants by REA to firm the power produced at government hydroelectric plants, a frequently necessary measure because of seasonal fluctuations in stream flow. And the low rates charged by the co-ops have always harrowed them, for the differential is all too visible. There would be no reason for co-ops if they could not pass on to their members the savings they effect, and Assistant Secretary of the Interior Aandahl announced the answer. Federal power rates, he said, would be raised to the point where there would be no incentive to continue REA or establish co-operatives. Here is one form of private business with which the Administration will not enter into a friendly partnership— and, as Senator Murray remarked, here is a negative yardstick for the power industry.

As for the generation of power, the Director of the Budget announced that there would be no "new starts"—no additional federal power projects—till arrangements had been made with local (which here means large-scale and absentee) interests to install the generating facilities.

He thus proclaimed publicly a policy which some members of the Administration were simultaneously denying. It is significant that of the twenty-three new starts so far made by the Corps of Engineers, none are multiple-purpose and none include power. And it seems likely that the Engineers will be favored over the Bureau of Reclamation in such new projects as are authorized. They are far friendlier to the utilities, they can legally assess against the taxpayers a larger percentage of the costs, and they are able to circumvent painful provisions of the Reclamation and Power Acts.

The program drawn up by the utilities in 1948 has not been carried out in full. But the process of strangulation that has been applied to REA should kill it in another two years. The co-ops will be withdrawn from competing with the utilities and furnishing data for the regulation of their rates. It would take considerably more than two years to get a wall round federal generation of power.

Secretary McKay's abandonment to the Idaho Power Company of the Hell's Canyon site—the greatest remaining one in the country—was geared to this policy. In the current semantics a consumer co-operative, owned and operated by farmers unable to get electricity except by their own efforts, would not be local enterprise; but Idaho Power is.

Idaho Power is a Maine corporation. About 7 per cent of its stockholders live in the mountain West; of its thirty largest stockholders all, except Harvard University and the Commonwealth Fund, are insurance companies or investment trusts; all but two are east of the Mississippi and those two are insurance companies. The corporation could satisfy its future needs more cheaply by building steam plants, but the idea is to keep federal power out of central and southern Idaho. The cost of the three small dams it currently proposes to build in Hell's Canyon will be taken care of by a rate increase—there being no public systems to provide a yardstick—and by the use for permanently profitable construction of the tax-amortization privilege which was intended to protect defense industries from losing money on temporary plant expansion. The Secretary also withdrew government opposition to the Pacific Gas & Electric Company's proposed developments on the North Fork of King's River—developments made possible by existing facilities built at public expense.

But much as Eastern-owned Western utilities respect the spirit of private initiative, the West needs dams and wants payrolls. The relinquishment of federal reserved sites and the no-new-starts policy caused uneasiness, and there was November to think of. So the Upper Colorado Storage Project was taken out of mothballs and nearly a billion dollars' worth of construction was recommended. (It will cost about twice that; for obvious reasons, Bureau of Reclamation estimates are poetic conventions.) Its political feasibility is obvious but its economic and social justification is open to the most serious doubt. Worse still, the plans for it are part fantasy and have been changed so often and so capriciously that no one knows to what extent its engineering is sound. But it satisfies the requirements. No corporation would ever want to build dams on this stretch of the Colorado, so there is no competition; but the promise of the Budget Director would attract corporate investment in the generating facilities, since the public would be paying all other costs.

The recommendation of this project breaches the basic national parks policy: one of the dams it includes, Echo Park, is to be built in Dinosaur National Monument. The dam will destroy the beauty of spectacular canyons of the Yampa and Green Rivers. There was a peak of cynicism in Mr. McKay's promise to spend $21 million of Bureau of Reclamation funds to build the roads now denied the Monument and to construct "recreational" facilities at the fluctuating, unsightly reservoir which the dam will create. This sum is equal to four-fifths of the drastically-cut 1955 appropriation for the entire National Park Service.

The progressive impairment of the parks by budgetary blood-letting is a national disgrace—but it is a smaller evil than Mr. McKay's approval of Echo Park Dam. Opening the parks to exploitation by the Bureau of Reclamation—which in the semantics is "co-operation between federal and state governments"—makes only a matter of time their exploitation by any corporations which may want their water, water power, timber, minerals, or grass, and which have sufficient capital to awe a business man in office.

Many trial balloons about TVA have been sent up. The refusal to reappoint Mr. Gordon Clapp as its Director made clear that career-service administration is not desired. His successor will need only a single qualification: a distaste for socialistically increasing private business in the Tennessee Valley by providing cheap power. Several other trial balloons from Interior are significant, such as suggestions that the tremendous Central Valley Project might be sold to the State of California. At the right price it would make a happy deal: the big corporate farms would get the water denied them by the 160-acre limitation they have been fighting since 1902 and PG&E would get the power facilities. This clue is underscored by a recent announcement that the utility companies of the Northwest are forming a syndicate capable of taking over all the federal dams and power plants on the Columbia River, the projects that brought industry and boom times to the Northwest.

If the Central Valley and the Columbia Basin projects should be handed over to utility corporations, how will flood control, erosion control, and the other conservation functions of federal projects be carried on? The utilities could not possibly assume them. Indeed a corporation has no proper concern with them, and no state has ever done an even passable job at any of them. Nevertheless, the clues suggest that the ground work is being laid for the property evaluators, rate specialists, and constitutional lawyers of the new Hoover Commission to propose that all federal reclamation and power projects be sold.

THE COWBOYS RIDE AGAIN

Both the platform and the campaign had promised to take care of the small but influential group of Western stockmen who ever since 1946 have been trying to gut the Forest Service and get hold of the grazing ranges in the national forests. A bill embodying as much of the malodorous "Stockmen's Proposal for an Act" as it seemed cagey to put in one package was sponsored (behind the scenes) by Senator Barrett of Wyoming—who as a Congressman had spearheaded the attempted landgrab of 1946–47. He has great parliamentary and backstage skill; but his sole victory with this bill was his success in keeping the Secretary of Agriculture's adverse report on it from reaching the House Subcommittee on Public Lands.

At the public hearing Western spokesmen—water users, sportsmen, wildlife specialists, hydrologists, city engineers, individual stockmen, small stock associations—ripped the bill to shreds. The Denver *Post* attacked it repeatedly; so did such other prominent papers as the Salt Lake *Tribune,* the Portland *Oregonian,* and the San Francisco *Chronicle.* More striking was the opposition of many small newspapers, even in

Wyoming, which had always before supported the plans of the stockmen's lobby. Whereas the attempted landgrab of six years before had to be stopped by the East, this time the West itself prevented a shameful raid on the public resources. Senator Barrett—seeing that the bill would be defeated if it came to a vote—maneuvered to keep it in committee and to prevent publication of the testimony at the hearings.

But something had to be done for the stockmen and so the Hope-Thye-Aiken Bill was made an Administration measure. Bad to begin with, it was rendered truly vicious by amendment; it has been passed by the Senate but as I write has not yet been taken up by the House. That such sound conservationists as Senator Aiken and Congressman Hope have been lined up behind so reprehensible a measure shows the formidable pressure that the U.S. Chamber of Commerce and other allies of the stockmen's lobby have succeeded in bringing to bear. Long since, Senator Aiken should have been attacking his own bill.

The bill would achieve three major objectives of the landgrabbers. It would give present holders of grazing permits in the national forests two different kinds of property rights in those forests, thus impairing the public title and in part alienating public property. It would enable the present permit-holders to sell the permits at will and without reference to the Forest Service, closing the ranges to newcomers and making monopolization of them certain. It would permit them to construct permanent improvements on the public ranges, further alienating public property and enabling the permit-holders to tie up the public lands indefinitely with lawsuits. Finally, it would cripple the regulatory power of the Forest Service by permitting appeal to the courts on various kinds of purely administrative decisions. It is a raid on the public land system and its passage would seriously undermine our conservation policy.

The House of Representatives stopped something even worse, a bill by Ellsworth of Oregon long a Congressional spokesman for big lumber interests. It provided that when the government acquired privately owned timberland, as for the reservoir of a dam, which a timber operator had under sustained yield (that is, cutting only in step with replacement by natural growth), the operator would have the option of being paid in cash or by the transfer to him of publicly owned timberland of equivalent value. This meant the national forests or the far smaller forests administered by the Bureau of Land Management—and in committee it was extended to include the forests in the national parks. Proof of operation under sustained yield was not stipulated and there was no guarantee that it would be used on the land to be acquired. The government bureau which must provide the timberland was given no control over its selection, and no power to require any kind of protection or conservation.

Barefaced as these provisions were, however, they were unimportant compared to the central fact: ostensibly a measure of relief for suffering corporations, the bill provided for the direct transfer of portions of the permanently reserved public lands to private ownership. Enemies of the public lands system have been trying to achieve precisely that fundamental step ever since the first reserves were made in Benjamin Harrison's time. The Hope-Thye-Aiken Bill would open fissures in the foundation of our national conservation policy—but the Ellsworth Bill would have shattered it.

The Secretary of Agriculture drew up an adverse report and this time it reached the committee. Normally this is enough to stop a bill. He was, however, prevailed on to withdraw it. No notice of the public hearing was given except the routine listing in the Gazette; conservation organizations and interested Congressmen did not know that it was to be held. It was attended only by representatives of the Department of the Interior, who had been instructed to think highly of the bill (one who wasn't thinking highly enough on the witness stand was called away by telephone), and of the Department of Agriculture, who had obviously been instructed not to think ill of it but to try to get it softened nevertheless. The committee reported it out and by a tricky lateral pass in the Rules Committee Mr. Ellsworth cleared the way for an attempt to slip it over on the House in the closing days of the session. Chance discovery at the last moment, however, scared him into holding it over till the next session.

By then the bill was in the open and it was murdered. The quarterbacking on the floor of the House was by Congressman Metcalf of Montana, who was making a distinguished record in his first term. His Democratic teammates were Madden of Indiana, Price of Illinois, and

Brooks of Texas, with McCarthy of Minnesota, Magnuson of Washington, and Hays of Ohio assisting at critical junctures. A striking development, however, was the co-operation of four Pennsylvania Republicans who were well acquainted with the issues at stake—Messrs. Gavin, Saylor, Fulton, and Mumma. Mr. Gavin's role in the debate was especially informed and expert. This extemporized coalition drew the bill's teeth with amendments and then, when the strength of the opposition became manifest, Mr. Metcalf moved to recommit it. His motion carried on a roll-call vote of 226 yeas and 161 nays—a brilliant victory for the freshman Congressman, who is not even a member of the relevant committee.

Perhaps a few other Republican Congressmen, who were active in opposition to the grazing bill, can be added to what looks like a conservation bloc. If the Republican party retains control of the House in November, this bloc will be important. For it is clear that if any of our historic conservation policy is to be saved, it must be saved in the House. Senator Langer fitfully opposed some anti-conservation measures but no other Republican Senator did. Senator Aiken, who devised the strategy for many earlier victories over anti-conservation forces, has now put his great prestige at the service of the attack on the Forest Service. The Independent party, Senator Morse, has been magnificent, making an all-out fight against every anti-conservation move.

"REORGANIZATION" WITH BURGLAR'S TOOLS

The Forest Service may also serve to illustrate dangers latent in other Administration fetishes—reorganization, consolidation, and a cant phrase from schools of business administration, "management-practice improvement." If consolidation and reorganization are the first recourse of a management engineer, they can serve more devious ends and become the last one of a lobby or a landgrabber.

The Forest Service has always been decentralized. It began with a regional organization, to prevent the delays and rigidities that half-paralyzed the General Land Office. There are now ten regions, each with headquarters and specialist staffs. Differences in terrain, climate, forestation, methods of lumber operations, and other complex variables make this the only kind of organization that could conceivably be efficient. To consolidate the regions, reducing them to four or even two, as has been proposed, would greatly increase expense and greatly reduce efficiency. It would increase travel, paper work, and red tape. It would slow up administration and all field operations. It would make the specialist and scientific activities of the Service more cumbersome and expensive. *In all these ways it would add to the costs of the private businesses that use the forests.* But the notion is attractive to the managerial mind. You consolidate the Omaha and Denver offices of Continental Gadgets; why not, then, consolidate Nebraska and Colorado?

There is a more sinister aspect. Weakening professional and administrative efficiency by such a consolidation of the regions would favor both the special-interest groups which want to exploit the national forests and those which want all federal regulation everywhere undermined. Also it would greatly reduce such ability as the Service now has to resist the attacks of its enemies. That is one of the ends in view.

All these hazards would be increased by the unbelievably idiotic plan, which has also been proposed, of abolishing the regional setup and achieving "local control" by grouping the national forests—which disregard state lines—in state units. Neither a forest stand nor the watershed of a river will stop short at a state boundary on Executive Order. But the thirty-eight miniature Forest Services thus created—in ten states there are no national forests—would be easy prey for the local special-interest groups. The Administration fetish which dreams of reorganizing federal conservation activities on a state-wide rather than a regional basis is a victory for the propaganda which represents issues as a conflict between local interests and Washington—when in fact they are conflicts between one local interest and all the others; that is, between a special interest and the public interest. In every aspect of conservation this kind of "local control" must inevitably mean local vulnerability, local manipulation, and local intimidation.

All research in the Department of Agriculture except that of the Forest Service has been grouped under one bureau. In some respects the results have been of no particular importance, in some others they have reduced expense and increased efficiency. But also in some instances they have reduced efficiency and increased expense. It seems likely that the eye of the management-improver is on Forest Service research, and that his table of organization calls for transferring it to the central bureau. To do so would be a truly stupendous blunder. Forest Service research created scientific forestry in the United States and is now the foremost in the world. It is so organically related to the field activities and daily jobs of the Forest Service that it could be dissected out only at the cost of permanent damage. The damage done would increase geometrically in the future.

And one wonders. The Forest Service, always the cornerstone of our national conservation policy, is the most vigorous of the conservation bureaus. That is precisely what is wrong with it in the eyes of the landgrabbers, the cowboys, the U.S. Chamber of Commerce, and its other organized enemies. It is three-fold: it consists of the national forests, its agencies which assist and supervise and co-operate with state forestry and private forestry, and its research programs and experiment stations. The effort by the Bureau of the Budget to abolish two of its co-operative programs suggests an intention eventually to amputate one full third of the Service. Removing its research to another bureau would also lop off a third. Reduced by two-thirds, it would be weak, ineffective, easily preyed upon, immensely less valuable to the American future. Is that the end in view? At any rate, in their most arrogant moments the landgrabbers never dreamed up so promising a way to make it impotent.

ARRIVAL OF THE BUZZARDS

In a year and a half the business men in office have reversed the conservation policy by which the United States has been working for more than seventy years to substitute wise use of its natural resources in place of reckless destruction for the profit of special corporate interests. They have reversed most of the policy, weakened all of it, opened the way to complete destruction. Every move in regard to conservation that the Administration has made has been against the public interest—which is to say against the future—and in favor of some special private interest. Most notably, too, every one has been in favor of some big special interest and against the local small ones. The friendly partnership with business has turned out to mean only some kinds of businesses, the bigger the better.

More important still is the appointment of officials friendly to the enemies of the public interest, for this is preparation for the future.

Judicious selection of a Director could doom TVA, for instance, and no doubt will. The utilities plan to "get the government out of the power business altogether," with all that that implies in destruction of resources and exploitation of consumers. Many other corporate plans look to getting hold of publicly owned resources and converting them to dividends. Under Secretary of the Interior Tudor has announced that his legal staff is rewriting contracts for the water from federal dams in such a way that the 160-acre limitation can be "by-passed"—which means that the government will connive at breaking the fundamental Reclamation laws. Assistant Secretary Lewis has said that he looks forward to the time when there need be no federal forestry. Their chief, Secretary McKay, has repeatedly said that he favors the disposal to private hands of various classes of public lands.

We called it corruption in Harding's time. It is not corruption when it is Administration policy. But it does show an intent, or perhaps only a willingness, to turn the clock back beyond Hoover, beyond the first Roosevelt, to the Old Stone Age of Republican domination by those to whom the infinite wisdom of Providence had entrusted the property interests of the country. Meanwhile the future of the United States is caught between the inexorable millstones. Population pressure steadily increases. The rivers fill with silt, the water table drops, the rains run off as floods. In the West, booms end because there is neither enough water nor enough electricity. The West too has had four years of drought, parts of it five years. Two dustbowls have formed: "The best place to get a Colorado farm is eastern Kansas." And the best place to get anything else you may want is the Department of the Interior.

Indirect damage such as the sacrifice of professionalism in the public service is manifest. But consider something else. If, for instance, the Central Valley Project should be sold to California, doubtless Mr. Hoover's evaluators could work out a price. (California utilities and the Department of the Interior co-operating.) What would be entirely beyond computation is the loss to the public in past investment, future waste, and future expense. Similarly with every other aspect of conservation—erosion control, flood control, watershed management, forestry, range improvement. Whatever is lost or weakened now will mean pyramiding loss in the future.

For it is the nature of the problems of land and water that damage done to either is cumulative. And it is also their nature, as the entire American experience has shown, that they can be grappled with effectively only by federal action.

Soil conservation districts, REA co-operatives, conservation organizations, browned-out areas of power consumers, towns and counties apprehensive about dust and drought—here are a lot of voters. One obvious giveaway is the presentation to the Democratic party of a shining issue for 1954 and 1956. And if Schedule C proved to be a fine means for a quick cleanup in top administrative offices, it will remain one after the elections.

In the early fall of 1953 Washington birdwalkers reported a phenomenon which their amiable hobby could not explain. The number of turkey buzzards resident in and near the city had increased remarkably. The buzzard population continued to grow through the winter and the following spring. By now it has created a sizable problem at feeding time at the zoo.

One-Way Partnership Derailed

(*Harper's Magazine*, January 1955)

Toward the end of the campaign a ranking Administration speaker, referring to some gloomy indications out West, said that if things went the way they seemed to be going the Republican party might "have to rethink the power and resources policy." The verb is from the advertising-agency jargon that the Administration has learned to speak so fluently but it is not likely to mean much. Things went the way indicated but rethinking the power and resources policy won't get farther than some new commercials.

Mr. Richard L. Neuberger's defeat of Senator Cordon has drawn attention away from other signs that point in the same direction. In spite of the Democratic sweep in Pennsylvania, the four Republican Congressmen who broke with the Administration's public lands policy were all re-elected. Congressman Leon H. Gavin was supposed to be in trouble because of severe unemployment in the Twenty-Third District, but his constituents remembered his decisive role in the defeat of the Administration's two grazing bills and its timberlands-exchange bill. The proximity of the Allegheny National Forest had educated them in the issues and they sent Mr. Gavin back to help fight off the next raids.

The Twenty-Second District proved to be easy for Mr. John P. Saylor, who had led the fight in the House on Echo Park Dam.

Mr. Saylor will be needed, for the Administration is not going to re-think Echo Park Dam. As I explained in the August *Harper's,* it can enthusiastically support federal dams on the Colorado River, for no utility company will ever want to build there. The Upper Colorado Storage Project would now be on the books if it had dissuaded Utah and Colorado from demanding that the Project continue to include this dam at the site originally selected, which is in Dinosaur National Monument. Conservation forces had beaten it once before and there is no doubt that the purpose it is intended to serve can be served just as well, if not better, by any of several alternatives outside the Monument. But the two states and the Bureau of Reclamation insisted on the original plans straight across the board, the President backed them up with a favorable statement, and the whole Project lost out.

But during the campaign the President took a refresher course in hydrology, engineering, and national-parks policy. During his swing through the West, that is, his plane made a detour that took him over Dinosaur Monument, with two representatives of the Bureau of Reclamation at his side. From a mile up it was obvious that the Monument was not worth preserving and that Echo Park was the only satisfactory site for the dam. As a result of this briefing, we are told, the President will send a special message to Congress recommending Echo Park when a new bill to authorize the Upper Colorado Project is introduced. The message will not get the dam authorized. Echo Park Dam will be beaten again and the whole Project will be held up for two more years. That may be time enough for the forces brilliantly represented by Mr. Raymond Moley to stop it for good.

In Idaho Mrs. Gracie Pfost was re-elected; her campaign focused on a single issue, a federal dam in Hell's Canyon. Congressman Lee Met-calf of Montana, the most effective opponent of the Administration re-sources policy in the last House, won hands down. Congressman Wes-ley D'Ewart, who had quarterbacked for the Administration in the same House, was defeated for the Senate. This was a vicious and foul cam-paign, full of slanders against Senator Murray by Madison Avenue's most expert copy-writers, but it got nowhere. Mr. D'Ewart was defeated on his demerits: on his energetic service to the power and resources policy that the Administration is now supposed to be rethinking.

Conservation won further victories with the return of Mr. O'Mahoney to the Senate and the re-election of Senator Anderson. We can take little comfort from the fact that Congressman Engle of California now becomes Chairman of the House Committee on Interior and Insular Affairs and, though Oregon elected a Democratic Congresswoman as an advocate of public power, Congressman Ellsworth, who spends his time assisting attacks on the public lands, survived the campaign. Mr. Ellsworth, however, will occupy the same hot spot as Secretary McKay, who—with Senator Morse on one side of him and Mr. Neuberger on the other—now becomes the most uncomfortable member of the Administration. A very tall pine indeed toppled when Senator Cordon was defeated. Mr. McKay, the giveaway emcee, is understood to have been his appointee and has certainly been his front man. The progressive curtailment of the public-power program has been carried on under his direction: in his quiet backstairs way he has led or helped most of the other giveaways; and no one of his skill at the job is left in either house of Congress. Senator Barrett, the rodeo star from Wyoming, is not first-team material and besides specializes in representing the cowboy lobby and attacking the Forest Service. His score so far is no hits, no runs, and a fistful of errors.

The meaning of Mr. Neuberger's victory is unmistakable and it is national. Oregon, which is as incorrigibly Republican as Vermont, had had enough of the principal Congressional architect of the Administration's resources policy. He had spent two years utilizing the golden opportunity which the Republican victory of 1952 provided to destroy our historic and once bipartisan policy of federal conservation; Mr. Neuberger stood squarely on that historic policy. Senator Cordon's managers had at their disposal as much money as they might need. Billboards advertising his achievements in burnished B.B.D.&O. slogans were on every road into and out of every town in Oregon. Radio and television programs practically used up the propaganda that had been stored in utility company safes. At one time seven Republican Senators, all irreproachably reactionary, were in the state campaigning for him. And as a climactic assist the President went to McNary Dam, where as a local wisecrack said at least the fifth generator was Republican, and delivered a funeral oration over public power.

Prematurely. The President's speech was most helpful to Mr. Neuberger. It was an exercise in creative imagination which, as Governor Stevenson promptly said, set up a straw man and knocked it flat. The President discovered a wholly non-existent intention by persons not named (but obviously including the voters of the Northwest) to create a federal power monopoly, which happens to be not only undesired by anyone but impossible as well. He described several other bugs and hobgoblins and made a number of severe statements about them that were simply not so, that the Northwest knew were not so. It was a nonsensical speech at an injudiciously chosen site. All the audience had to do was to take a look at the dam the President was dedicating. It did so and Oregon voted Mr. Neuberger in.

The defeat of Senator Cordon and Congressman D'Ewart, the re-election of Senator Anderson, Mrs. Pfost, Mr. Metcalf, and the Pennsylvania conservationists, the election of Mr. O'Mahoney, the House seat picked up in Oregon—they make as complete a repudiation of the Administration resources policy as could be achieved at a mid-term election. As I write, it is not entirely sure that the Democrats will organize the Senate but the House is theirs and, with the help of the Pennsylvania Republicans, they should be able to stop the giveaways. So far, that is, as Congress can stop a process so much of which can be continued by administrative ruling in the Executive departments and agencies. We may reasonably expect that the forays against the national forests by the cowboys and the trade associations of the lumber manufacturers will be stopped even colder than they have been up to now, that the Bureau of Reclamation will be kept out of Dinosaur Monument, and that a half-dozen other current or planned raids on various national parks will get nowhere. The loan and operating funds of REA will be increased but we can only speculate about the other nooses that the Administration has knotted round its neck, the contracts that limit the sale of federal power to rural co-operatives and the process of forcing them to raise their rates.

So far the Administration has been able to conduct the assault on REA and the public-power program without much reference to Congress. It is always possible to pass another semantic miracle and renegotiate the already renegotiated contracts, or possibly Congress can void them. Indeed the Administration might call on semantics to make clear that it is much more in favor of public power than has been suspected. Even before the election, though with the election in view, trumpets were blown for Libby Dam on the Kutenai River. It was a safe and in-expensive fanfare, for the dam cannot be built now and maybe it never can be built. The future of REA depends in part too on the investiga-tion of the Dixon-Yates affair that Congress is certain to make. So does the immediate future of TVA, though the effort to begin its strangula-tion has been at least temporarily interrupted. The Dixon-Yates inves-tigation is certain to produce fireworks. It will go into the workings of the Holding Companies Act and it may very well embarrass the Secu-rities and Exchange Commission. We are going to hear a lot of in-genious semantics.

Of course, we may get in the end nothing but some more slogans, a mass-medium campaign in "consumer education" as silly as the Presi-dent's speech at McNary Dam. And there is another possibility: the boys may decide that they are on the way out, that they won't be around after 1956, and so had better get rid of as many public assets as they can in the remaining two years. The new Hoover Commission is about ready to recommend the abolition of the Twentieth Century by procla-mation, the sale not only of the federal dams but of the reclamation projects, the national forests, and all other federal holdings except, pos-sibly, the national parks.

So much the better; the recommendation will get things in the open where everyone can see them. It won't get to first base in the 84th Congress, or in any later one, but the trade associations and the utility companies will have to stop working both sides of the street. This is their Commission and they will have to line up beside it.

Conservation proved to be a winning issue for the Democrats. It will be even more important in 1956 and the Democratic party had better spend the next two years working out a co-ordinated program. In the campaign just finished the defense of the public lands, public power, and the related values was extemporized and essentially a rebuttal. No doubt it had to be, for the Administration attack had been piecemeal and in part by stealth. But we know now both where the Administration stands and where the voters stand. It is possible to abandon the defensive policy of merely holding the line and to plan positively.

In some areas of conservation, thinking has long been static; it badly needs revision and invigoration. As a single example, reclamation. The most urgent reality in the West is the need of metropolitan and industrial complexes for water. We are now put to the expensive subterfuge of assuring such water supplies as a secondary result of spending five hundred dollars an acre to make two-dollar land worth forty dollars. This concept, which was sound and much less expensive in 1902, needs modernization. Also, I for one can tranquilly contemplate abandoning, in some specific areas and under intelligent safeguards, the concept of multiple use. National forests near Los Angeles, Denver, and Salt Lake City are now used by several million people a year; once remote and difficult of access, they are now practically in the suburbs. The basic necessity will always be to protect the watersheds; but it seems clear that, this being assured, sizable areas must be devoted to the purposes unsatisfactorily called "recreation" and that other uses, grazing and timber-cutting among them, must be restricted or prohibited in those areas.

Again, there should be a strenuous counter-attack on the foolish allegation that REA, TVA, and the public-power program are "socialistic." These are no more socialistic than the Post Office Department or a church supper. On the strictest theory of classic capitalism they are capitalistic instruments, far more so than the private collectivism of the holding companies, as conveniently illustrated by Dixon-Yates. Finally, if it is desirable to have the federal government generate 15 per cent of our electric power, instead of the 10 per cent it now generates, or to have what the Chamber of Commerce calls "a land-hungry bureaucracy" buy up another million acres of cut-over and eroding timberland in the East and South, there is no reason to be defensive. Add such measures to the program and start fighting for them.

The principles behind these remarks apply, I believe, to the entire Democratic preparation for the campaign of 1956. National campaigns by a major party cannot be fitted together as perfectly as a watch, but they need not be as spasmodic and unco-ordinated as those of 1952 and

1954. Governor Stevenson, for instance, emerged from the recent one with notably increased stature, influence, and power but he was used haphazardly. He was a lead-off man and both a cleanup hitter and a pinch-hitter as well, and though he was effective in all three roles it was an inefficient use of talent. The idea seems to have been to have him speak as often and in as many places as possible, without regard to the cumulative effect that might have been secured by programming his campaign. It would have been much better to provide a planned structure, so that his speeches could have constantly gathered momentum and ended in a climax that would have unified the whole Democratic campaign. It would also have been sagacious to provide him with a larger staff.

The election established that there is a Democratic drift but clearly it is not one that can be increased or even maintained without strenuous labor. The Democratic party is now on the hot spot. As the opposition it could be opportunistic and *ad hoc;* as a party which is in control of Congress under a Republican Executive, it has got to have a coherent, planned program. And as with the resources problem, the program has got to be more than one of holding the line and re-establishing it where the trade associations have broken through. Simply standing on the achievements from 1932 to 1952 could be as disastrous as looking back to 1896 has proved to be for the Republicans this year. The program has got to be progressive, and progressive not only in agreeable generalizations but in concrete measures to which the party will commit itself.

This year and in the 1952 campaign as well there was too much extemporization and too little co-ordination. There has been too much undirected amateur effort. There has been too little co-operation among the state organizations and too little teamwork between Congressional leaders and such leaders who do not hold office, as Governor Stevenson and, before the election, Mr. Harriman. Almost no use has been made of the remarkable capacities manifested in 1952 by the people who temporarily organized themselves as the Volunteers for Stevenson. They are a reservoir of very willing, very useful, and often very talented people positively crying aloud to be used. The organization was properly dissolved after the 1952 election; but something could have been done to incorporate its members in the regular organizations, which uttered some perfunctory and usually unfelt expressions of good will and dropped the matter. But the professional organizations need more renewal than they have had and the best source of renewal is this unused group, which contains most of the independents who voted Democratic in 1952 and a great majority of the eggheads. The eggheads are indispensable to the Democratic party; let's face it, they will provide most of the outline, at least, of the program that is going to be developed, as in fact they have always done. A scarcity of eggheads is one of the signal weaknesses of the Republicans.

The need for co-ordination of the various elements of Democratic strength is highlighted by the capture of seven state legislatures and eight governorships. They are as important for 1956 as control of Congress, very likely more important. The party needs a mechanism for assuring continuous liaison among its various power sources. Each house of Congress has a committee that is supposed to do that job incidentally to many others. The National Committee is in the same situation; its paramount duties leave it too little time. A new body is called for, designed for this sole purpose. I do not pretend to say how large it should be or who should compose it, but it ought to contain Senators and Congressmen, Governors, representatives of the National Committee and of the state organizations, and representatives of the Volunteers for Stevenson, who were amateurs in 1952 but do not all have to retain their amateur status in the 1956 campaign. It should be organized right now and get about its arduous job.

Providing a coherent, specific, progressive program is a job for all elements of the party, but such a board as I suggest could give it the maximum cumulative effect through the next two years. The board should not, however, be called a general staff or a team; in the established semantics those terms have come to mean advertising copy and the Democratic party has no need for it.

A Bibliography of DeVoto's West

I. Books on the West by Bernard DeVoto

   A. Nonfiction

      The Year of Decision: 1846. Boston: Little, Brown, 1943.
      Across the Wide Missouri. Boston: Houghton Mifflin, 1947.
      The Course of Empire. Boston: Houghton Mifflin, 1952.
      Editor, *The Journals of Lewis and Clark.* Boston: Houghton
        Mifflin, 1953.

   B. Fiction

      The Crooked Mile. New York: Minton Balch, 1924.
      The Chariot of Fire. New York: Macmillan, 1926.
      The House of Sun-Goes-Down. New York: Macmillan, 1928.
      Mountain Time. Boston: Little, Brown, 1947.

II. Articles on the West by Bernard DeVoto

      "Utah." *American Mercury* 7 (March 1926): 317–23.
      "The Mountain Men." *American Mercury* 9 (December 1926):
        472–79.
      "Footnote on the West." *Harper's Magazine* 155 (November 1927):
        713–22.
      "The Centennial of Mormonism." *American Mercury* 19 (January
        1930): 1–13.
      "The Real Frontier." *Harper's Magazine* 163 (June 1930): 60–71.
      "Jonathan Dyer, Frontiersman." *Harper's Magazine* 167 (Septem-
        ber 1933): 491–501.
      "The West: A Plundered Province." *Harper's Magazine* 169 (Au-
        gust 1934): 355–64.
      "Fossil Remnants of the Frontier: Notes on a Utah Boyhood."
        Harper's Magazine 170 (April 1935): 590–600.
      "Letters from Sante Fe." *Harper's Magazine* 181 (August 1940):
        333–36.

"Main Street Twenty Years After." *Harper's Magazine* 181 (November 1940): 580–87.

"The Lewis and Clark Expedition." *Harper's Magazine* 190 (March 1945): 311–14.

"A Revaluation." *Rocky Mountain Review* 10 (Autumn 1945): 7–11.

"George Catlin and Bill Cody." *Harper's Magazine* 192 (May 1946): 462–65.

"Western Trip, Impressions and Experiences." *Harper's Magazine* 193 (August 1946): 126–29.

"Western Trip, Impressions and Experiences." *Harper's Magazine* 193 (September 1946): 229–32.

"Western Trip, Impressions and Experiences." *Harper's Magazine* 193 (October 1946): 313–16.

"Western Trip, Impressions and Experiences." *Harper's Magazine* 193 (November 1946): 430–33.

"The Anxious West." *Harper's Magazine* 193 (December 1946): 481–91.

"The West." *Harper's Magazine* 194 (January 1947): 45–48.

"The West Against Itself." *Harper's Magazine* 194 (January 1947): 1–13.

"The National Parks." *Fortune* 35 (June 1947): 120–35.

"The Western Land Grab." *Harper's Magazine* 140 (June 1947): 543–46.

"U.S. Forest Service and the Western Land Grab." *Harper's Magazine* 196 (January 1948): 28–31.

"Gifford Pinchot's *Breaking New Ground*." *Harper's Magazine* 196 (May 1948): 441–44.

"Statesmen on the Lam." *Harper's Magazine* 197 (July 1948): 108–12.

"Sacred Cows and Public Lands." *Harper's Magazine* 197 (July 1948): 44–55.

"The Desert Threat." *University of Colorado Bulletin* 48 (July 1948): 3–4, 6–10.

"Conservation and the Coming Crisis." *New York Herald Tribune,* October 11, 1948.

"What Land Policy for America?" *New York Herald Tribune,* October 18, 1948.

"For Public Control of Public Lands." *The Land* (Winter 1948–49): 593–94.

"Water Runs Downhill." *Woman's Day,* January 1949, 41–43+.

"National Park Service." *Harper's Magazine* 198 (March 1949): 64–67.

"Restoration in the Wasatch." *American Scholar* 18 (October 1949): 425–32.

"South Pass by Air." *Harper's Magazine* 201 (July 1950): 22–55.

"Shall We Let Them Ruin Our National Parks?" *Saturday Evening Post,* July 22, 1950, 17–19+.

"Our Hundred Year Plan." *Harper's Magazine* 201 (August 1950): 60–64.

"Two-Gun Desmond Is Back." *Harper's Magazine* 202 (March 1951): 48–51.

"The Smoke Jumpers." *Harper's Magazine* 203 (November 1951): 54–61.

"These Lands Are Yours." *Woman's Day,* February 1952, 61–68+.

"Flood in the Desert." *Harper's Magazine* 205 (August 1952): 58–61.

"An Old Steal Refurbished." *Harper's Magazine* 205 (October 1952): 65–68.

"The High Country." *Woman's Day,* December 1952, 60–61+.

"Billion Dollar Jackpot." *Harper's Magazine* 206 (February 1953): 53–56.

"Celebrating 150 Years of the Louisiana Purchase." *Collier's,* March 21, 1953, 44–50+.

"The Sturdy Corporate Homesteader." *Harper's Magazine* 206 (May 1953): 57–60.

"Heading for the Last Roundup." *Harper's Magazine* 207 (July 1953): 49–52.

"Let's Close the National Parks." *Harper's Magazine* 207 (October 1953): 49–52.

"Notes on Western Travel." *Harper's Magazine* 207 (November 1953): 45–48.

"Our Great West, Boom or Bust?" *Collier's,* December 25, 1953, 46–50+.

"Traveling the Louisiana Purchase." *Ford Times* 45 (December 1953): 2–8.

"Parks and Pictures." *Harper's Magazine* 208 (February 1954): 12+.

"Intramural Giveaway." *Harper's Magazine* 208 (March 1954): 10–11+.

"Wild West." *Holiday* 16 (July 1954): 34–43+.

"Conservation: Down and on the Way Out." *Harper's Magazine* 209 (August 1954): 66–74.

"And Fractions Drive Me Mad." *Harper's Magazine* 209 (September 1954): 10–11+.
"In the Horse Latitudes." *Harper's Magazine* 209 (November 1954): 8–9+.
"One-Way Partnership Derailed." *Harper's Magazine* 210 (January 1955): 12–15+.
"Current Comic Strips." *Harper's Magazine* 210 (May 1955): 8–9+.
"Good Place to Grow In." *Lincoln-Mercury Times* 8 (March-April 1956): 1–3.
"Uncle Sam's Campgrounds." *Ford Times* 48 (June 1956): 2–10.
"Let Me Tell You about the Wasatch." *Lincoln-Mercury Times* 7 (July-August 1956): 12–15.
"Your National Forest." *Holiday* 20 (August 1956): 93+.

III. Chapters, Introductions, and Forewords

"Ogden: The Underwriters of Salvation." In *The Taming of the Frontier,* edited by Duncan Aikman, 25–60. New York: Minton, Balch, 1925.
Preface and introduction to *The Life and Adventures of James P. Beckwourth,* edited by T. D. Bonner. New York: Alfred A. Knopf, 1931.
"Joseph Smith" and "Brigham Young." In *Dictionary of American Biography,* under the auspices of American Council of Learned Societies. New York: Charles Scribner's Sons, 1928–35.
Foreword to *A Treasury of Western Folklore,* edited by B. A. Botkin New York: Crown, 1951.
Introduction to *Beyond the Hundredth Meridian: John Wesley Powell and the Second Opening of the West,* by Wallace Stegner. Boston: Houghton Mifflin, 1954.
Introduction to *Timber in Your Life,* by Arthur H. Carhart. Philadelphia: J. B. Lippincott, 1955.

IV. Letters

Stegner, Wallace, ed. *The Letters of Bernard DeVoto.* Garden City, NY: Doubleday, 1975.

V. About Bernard DeVoto

Four Portraits and One Subject: Bernard DeVoto. Boston: Houghton Mifflin, 1963.
Sawey, Orlan. *Bernard DeVoto.* New York: Twayne, 1969.

Stegner, Wallace. "The West Emphatic: Bernard DeVoto." In *The Sound of Mountain Water,* 250–75. Garden City, NY: Doubleday, 1969; reprint, Lincoln: University of Nebraska Press, 1985.

———. *The Uneasy Chair: A Biography of Bernard DeVoto.* Garden City, NY: Doubleday, 1974; reprint, Salt Lake City, UT: Gibbs Smith Publisher, 1988.

Index